Comparative Perspectives on Early School Leaving in the European Union

Comparative Perspectives on Early School Leaving in the European Union provides an analysis of early school leaving (ESL) in nine European Union countries, with a particular focus on young people who were previously enrolled in educational institutions inside and outside mainstream secondary education. The comparative approach employed by this volume adds to the existing body of knowledge on ESL and develops an understanding of how young people navigate through different educational systems.

Contributors acknowledge the importance of reconstructing educational trajectories from the perspective of the individuals involved and, as a result, the book includes data collected during in-depth interviews, surveys, and insights from educational professionals, policymakers and representatives from civil society organisations. Adopting a classic tripartite approach, which acknowledges the complex nature of ESL, the book addresses individual, institutional and systemic factors. It identifies and analyses the prevention, intervention and compensation measures that can succeed in supporting young people's attainment, and demonstrates how these can be used to reduce ESL.

This unique book will be highly relevant for academics, researchers and postgraduate students, as well as educational practitioners. Drawing on the insights provided by the authors, the book formulates policy recommendations that should also be of interest for policymakers in European countries and beyond.

Lore Van Praag, PhD Ghent University, is research coordinator at the Centre for Migration and Intercultural Studies, University of Antwerp, and project manager of the RESL.eu project. Her research interests focus on inequalities in education, tracking practices, ethnic minorities, early school leavers and humour.

Ward Nouwen is a sociologist of education and a PhD researcher at the Centre for Migration and Intercultural Studies of the University of Antwerp. His main research topics are school segregation, educational tracking, early school leaving and work-based learning.

Rut Van Caudenberg is a joint PhD candidate at the Centre for Migration and Intercultural Studies, University of Antwerp (Belgium) and the Department of Social and Cultural Anthropology, Universitat Autònoma de Barcelona (Spain). Her research focuses on urban youths' lived experiences of schooling and education in Flanders and Catalonia.

Noel Clycq, PhD University of Antwerp, is a visiting professor and holds the chair in 'European values: discourses and prospects' at the Faculty of Arts and is a member of the Centre for Migration and Intercultural Studies (CeMIS), both at the University of Antwerp. His main research interests are socialisation and identification processes in educational and family settings, with a focus on migration, diversity and Europe.

Christiane Timmerman, PhD Catholic University of Leuven, is the head of the Centre for Migration and Intercultural Studies, University of Antwerp. She has published on migration, ethnic minorities and education. She has coordinated various international projects, such as the RESL.eu project and the EUMAGINE project.

Routledge Research in International and Comparative Education

This is a series that offers a global platform to engage scholars in continuous academic debate on key challenges and the latest thinking on issues in the fast-growing field of International and Comparative Education.

Books in the series include:

Globalization and Japanese "Exceptionalism" in Education
Insider's Views into a Changing System
Edited by Ryoko Tsuneyoshi

Canadian Teacher Education
A Curriculum History
Edited by Theodore Michael Christou

The Shifting Global World of Youth and Education
Edited by Mabel Ann Brown

The Making of Indigeneity, Curriculum History, and the Limits of Diversity
Ligia L. López López

Civil Society Organizations in Latin American Education
Case Studies and Perspectives on Advocacy
Regina Cortina and Constanza Lafuente

Navigating the Common Good in Teacher Education Policy
Critical and International Perspectives
Edited by Nikola Hobbel and Barbara L. Bales

Comparative Perspectives on Early School Leaving in the European Union
Edited by Lore Van Praag, Ward Nouwen, Rut Van Caudenberg, Noel Clycq and Christiane Timmerman

For more information about the series, please visit www.routledge.com.

Comparative Perspectives on Early School Leaving in the European Union

Edited by Lore Van Praag,
Ward Nouwen, Rut Van Caudenberg,
Noel Clycq and
Christiane Timmerman

LONDON AND NEW YORK

First published 2018
by Routledge
2 Park Square, Milton Park, Abingdon, Oxon OX14 4RN

and by Routledge
711 Third Avenue, New York, NY 10017

Routledge is an imprint of the Taylor & Francis Group, an informa business

© 2018 selection and editorial matter, Lore Van Praag, Ward Nouwen, Rut Van Caudenberg, Noel Clycq and Christiane Timmerman; individual chapters, the contributors

The right of the editors to be identified as the authors of the editorial material, and of the authors for their individual chapters, has been asserted in accordance with sections 77 and 78 of the Copyright, Designs and Patents Act 1988.

All rights reserved. No part of this book may be reprinted or reproduced or utilised in any form or by any electronic, mechanical, or other means, now known or hereafter invented, including photocopying and recording, or in any information storage or retrieval system, without permission in writing from the publishers.

Trademark notice: Product or corporate names may be trademarks or registered trademarks, and are used only for identification and explanation without intent to infringe.

British Library Cataloguing-in-Publication Data
A catalogue record for this book is available from the British Library

Library of Congress Cataloging-in-Publication Data
A catalog record for this book has been requested

ISBN: 978-1-138-04807-2 (hbk)
ISBN: 978-1-315-17040-4 (ebk)

Typeset in Bembo
by Apex CoVantage, LLC

Contents

List of figures	viii
List of tables	ix
Acknowledgements	x
List of contributors	xi

Introduction: theoretical and conceptual framework of the RESL.eu project — 1
LORE VAN PRAAG, WARD NOUWEN, RUT VAN CAUDENBERG,
NOEL CLYCQ AND CHRISTIANE TIMMERMAN

PART I
State of the art and impact of early school leaving across European countries — 15

1 **Disengaged students: insights from the RESL.eu international survey** — 17
ALESSIO D'ANGELO AND NEIL KAYE

2 **Pathways to early school leaving in Hungary: ethnicised inequalities in education and the case of Roma youth** — 33
ÁGNES KENDE AND JÚLIA SZALAI

3 **Shaping the policies towards early school leaving in Portugal, Sweden and Poland** — 47
HELENA C. ARAÚJO, EUNICE MACEDO, ALIREZA BEHTOUI, HANNA
TOMASZEWSKA-PĘKAŁA, PAULINA MARCHLIK, ANNA WRONA
AND CRISTINA ROCHA

4 **The individual and economic costs of early school leaving** — 61
MARIE GITSCHTHALER AND ERNA NAIRZ-WIRTH

vi *Contents*

PART II
Youngsters' perspectives on early school leaving and schooling

75

5 **A narrative approach exploring youngsters' experiences of schooling and leaving school early in Flanders (Belgium): the stories of Simon and Karim**

77

RUT VAN CAUDENBERG, NOEL CLYCQ AND CHRISTIANE TIMMERMAN

6 **Struggling against the waves or taking another course: school disengagement in the educational trajectories of early school leavers from Warsaw**

90

PAULINA MARCHLIK, ANNA WRONA AND HANNA TOMASZEWSKA-PĘKAŁA

7 **The social relations and educational expectations of young people in marginalised areas: evidence from Sweden**

102

ALIREZA BEHTOUI, MARIE BJÖRKLÖF AND ISABELLA STRÖMBERG

8 **What's school got to do with it? Comparing educational aspirations of Dutch and English ethnic white girls from lower socioeconomic backgrounds**

117

TALITHA STAM AND MAURICE CRUL

PART III
Educational trajectories of youth (at risk of) leaving school early

133

9 **Switching practices in vocational education: a comparative case study in Flanders (Belgium) and the Netherlands**

135

LORE VAN PRAAG, ELIF KESKINER, RUT VAN CAUDENBERG, WARD NOUWEN, TALITHA STAM, NOEL CLYCQ, MARIANA OROZCO, CHRISTIANE TIMMERMAN AND MAURICE CRUL

10 **Educational trajectories of early school leavers in Portugal: processes and conditions of (in)equality**

149

SOFIA A. SANTOS, EUNICE MACEDO AND HELENA C. ARAÚJO

Contents vii

11 **Neglected aspirations: academic trajectories and the risk of early school leaving amongst immigrant and Roma youth in Spain** 164

SILVIA CARRASCO, LAIA NARCISO AND MARTA BERTRAN-TARRÉS

PART IV
Strategies to deal with early school leaving 183

12 **No bridges to re-engagement? Exploring compensatory measures for early school leavers in Catalonia (Spain) from a qualitative approach** 185

SILVIA CARRASCO, ISIDORO RUIZ-HARO AND BÁLINT-ÁBEL BEREMÉNYI

13 **Alternative learning arenas in Portugal: hope for young adults?** 199

EUNICE MACEDO, SOFIA A. SANTOS AND ALEXANDRA OLIVEIRA DOROFTEI

14 **The opportunities and challenges of apprenticeships in England: alternative learning arenas or sites of exploitation?** 215

LOUISE RYAN AND MAGDOLNA LŐRINC

Conclusion: lessons learned from the RESL.eu project: main findings and policy advice 230

ELIF KESKINER AND MAURICE CRUL

Index 246

Figures

0.1	Conceptual model	4
14.1	Employment rates by highest level of qualification, ages 25 to 34; England and Wales, 2011	216

Tables

0.1	Overview of recruited respondents of the qualitative data collection in the seven main partner countries	8
1.1	Demographic characteristics of survey respondents	21
1.2	Descriptive statistics for school engagement scale	22
1.3	Multiple linear regression on school engagement	24
1.4	Multiple regression analysis on school engagement by country of survey, standardised coefficients	26
4.1	Overview of the private, social and fiscal costs of early school leaving	63
7.1	Determinants of educational expectation, ordinary least squares (OLS) regression, partial (and standardised) coefficients	108
8.1	Differences in school characteristics and tracking differences between two target schools in England and the Netherlands	120
9.1	Background and educational features of the selected youngsters	139
10.1	Characteristics and trajectories of early school leavers	152
11.1	Brief description of cases	167
11.2	Students' ordinary and possibly specific trajectories in Spain	173
11.3	Trajectories of immigrant and minority case-study youngsters	175
13.1	The research settings: features and educational offerings	202
13.2	Sociodemographic features of participants in focus group discussions	203
14.1	Apprenticeship starts in England by sector subject in 2015/16	219

Acknowledgements

The authors and editors acknowledge financial support from the European Union's Seventh Framework programme under Grant Agreement number SSH-CT-2011–320223 (Acronym: RESL.eu).

Contributors

In order of appearance in the book:

Lore Van Praag, PhD Ghent University, is research coordinator at the Centre for Migration and Intercultural Studies (CeMIS), University of Antwerp, and project manager of the RESL.eu project. Her research interests focus on inequalities in education, tracking practices, ethnic minorities, early school leavers and humour.

Ward Nouwen is a sociologist of education and a PhD researcher at the Centre for Migration and Intercultural Studies of the University of Antwerp. His main research topics are school segregation, educational tracking, early school leaving and work-based learning.

Rut Van Caudenberg is a joint PhD candidate at the Centre for Migration and Intercultural Studies, University of Antwerp (Belgium), and the Department of Social and Cultural Anthropology, Universitat Autònoma de Barcelona (Spain). Her research focuses on urban youths' lived experiences of schooling and education in Flanders and Catalonia.

Noel Clycq, PhD University of Antwerp, is a visiting professor and holds the chair in 'European values: discourses and prospects' at the Faculty of Arts and is a member of the Centre for Migration and Intercultural Studies (CeMIS), both at the University of Antwerp. His main research interests are socialisation and identification processes in educational and family settings, with a focus on migration, diversity and Europe.

Christiane Timmerman, PhD Catholic University of Leuven, is the head of the Centre for Migration and Intercultural Studies, University of Antwerp. She has published on migration, ethnic minorities and education. She has coordinated various international projects, such as the RESL.eu project and the EUMAGINE project.

Alessio D'Angelo, PhD, is co-director of the Social Policy Research Centre (SPRC) and a senior lecturer in social sciences at Middlesex University, London. He works on migration, ethnicity, inequalities and public services, most recently focusing on education, and has a particular expertise in mixed-methods research.

xii *Contributors*

Neil Kaye is a PhD candidate and a doctoral research assistant in the Department of Criminology and Sociology at Middlesex University in London. He is writing his thesis on the role of teacher support in promoting resilience amongst at-risk young people.

Ágnes Kende is a research associate at the Centre for Policy Studies, Central European University, Budapest, and a PhD candidate at ELTE University, Budapest. Her PhD thesis discusses the role of educational inequalities in the school failures of Roma students.

Júlia Szalai is professor emeritus of sociology of the Hungarian Academy of Sciences and senior research fellow at the Center for Policy Studies of the Central European University, Budapest. She has published widely on poverty and social exclusion, the outcaste state of Roma in Central and Eastern Europe, and the constraints of the development of the post-socialist welfare states in a comparative perspective.

Helena C. Araújo is a full professor in the Department of Education, University of Porto (Portugal), Faculty of Psychology and Education Sciences. She is the director of the Centre for Research and Intervention in Education (CIIE/FPCEUP). She supervises several doctoral candidates in education. She has been the project leader of financed projects. Her research interests and publications include education as a social right, school disengagement, young people's biographies and pathways, and women's participation in higher education.

Eunice Macedo is an assistant professor at the Faculty of Psychology and Educational Sciences of Porto University (FPCE.UP), and a researcher at the Centre for Research and Intervention in Education (CIIE) for several international projects. An author of several works, her research on education, citizenship and gender supports her intervention with communities, in search of ways of education with happiness and personal fulfilment.

Alireza Behtoui is professor of sociology at Stockholm and Södertörn University, Sweden. His research is primarily focused on the impact of social capital on the stratification process in fields such as education, transition from school to work and the labour market, with a focus on socioeconomic backgrounds, gender and immigrant backgrounds.

Hanna Tomaszewska-Pękała, PhD, Social Pedagogy, is an assistant professor (adjunct) at the Faculty of Education at the University of Warsaw (Department of Education Policy and Social Research on Education). Her research interests include the role of new media in social relationships of children, youth and families; assessment of social and educational situations of children from migrant families; and early leaving from education and training.

Paulina Marchlik obtained a master's degree in linguistics and is a research assistant and PhD student at the Faculty of Education at the University of

Warsaw (Department of Education Policy and Social Research on Education). Her research interests include language teaching, education, teacher education, early leaving from education and training, and youth at risk of exclusion.

Anna Wrona holds a master's degree in sociology and is a research assistant for the project *Reducing Early School Leaving in Europe* (RESL.eu) at the Faculty of Education at the University of Warsaw. She is preparing a PhD dissertation at the Institute of Philosophy and Sociology Polish Academy of Sciences on the topic of contemporary urban to rural migration in Poland.

Cristina Rocha is an associate professor at the Faculty of Psychology and Educational Sciences of Porto University and a full researcher at the Centre for Research and Intervention in Education (CIIE). She has developed several projects and supervised students in the following fields: sociology of family and childhood, social policies and social protection contexts, and educational systems.

Marie Gitschthaler is a post-doctoral research and training associate at the Education Sciences Group at Vienna University of Economics and Business in Austria. In her dissertation she explored the experiences of social exclusion of early school leavers.

Erna Nairz-Wirth, PhD, is professor of education sciences and head of the Education Sciences Group at Vienna University of Economics and Business. Her research focuses on inequality in education, especially in the context of educational pathways, transitions, school dropout and dropout in higher education.

Marie Björklöf works as a research assistant at the Department of Social Anthropology at Stockholm University, Sweden.

Isabella Strömberg is a PhD candidate in social anthropology at Stockholm University, Sweden. Her research focuses on ninth-grade students' involvement in out-of-school activities and how these activities may affect the students' possibilities within the educational system.

Talitha Stam is a PhD researcher in the Department of Public Administration and Sociology at Erasmus University, Rotterdam. Her doctoral thesis is an ethnographic study on the aspirations of ethnic white working-class girls in secondary education in England and the Netherlands.

Maurice Crul is a professor at the Vrije Universiteit, Amsterdam, and Erasmus University, Rotterdam. He is the international chair of IMISCOE network, a network of excellence that includes 38 research institutes in the fields of migration and diversity in 18 European countries. In the past 20 years, he mostly worked on the topic of education and children of immigrants, first within the Dutch context and in the past ten years in a comparative European and transatlantic context.

xiv *Contributors*

Elif Keskiner is a post-doctoral researcher at Erasmus University, Rotterdam. Her research interests cover a wide range of subjects in sociology such as youth transitions, descendants of migrants, social mobility patterns and elite formation, social capital formation and development of various forms of capital amongst minority youth, transnationalism and educational inequality.

Mariana Orozco is a PhD student at the University of Antwerp in the Faculty of Social Sciences. Her research focuses on learning processes in (higher) education and at the workplace. She is currently investigating students' integrative learning in combined school-based and work-based technical vocational education.

Sofia A. Santos is a post-doctoral researcher at the University of Porto, Portugal, and a full member of the Centre for Research and Intervention in Education (CIIE). She has been a visiting scholar and research assistant in several projects within the sociology of education, gender, sexual and youth studies. She has published in these fields and participated with paper presentations in several national and international conferences.

Silvia Carrasco, PhD, is professor of social anthropology and founder of the Research Centre for Migration Studies – EMIGRA, Universitat Autònoma de Barcelona. She has worked extensively in the field of educational inequalities and education policies, especially focusing on school experiences and trajectories of the children of immigrants and minorities.

Laia Narciso, master in migration studies and applied anthropology, is an early career researcher at the Research Centre for Migration Studies – EMIGRA, Universitat Autònoma de Barcelona. She is completing a dissertation on transitions to adulthood, racialisation processes and school experience of the children of West African immigrants in Catalonia.

Marta Bertran-Tarrés, PhD, is a tenure-track lecturer in Systematic and Social Pedagogy and researcher at the Research Centre for Migration Studies – EMIGRA, Universitat Autònoma de Barcelona. Her research focuses on (dis)contintuities in socialisation in early childhood, family negotiations and gender amongst the children of immigrants.

Isidoro Ruiz-Haro, master in applied anthropology, is an early career researcher at the Research Centre for Migration Studies – EMIGRA, Universitat Autònoma de Barcelona. His research focuses on school-to-work transitions, vulnerable youth and inequalities in education, and he is writing a dissertation on early school leavers and active labour market policies for youth.

Bálint-Ábel Bereményi, PhD, is a social anthropologist and researcher at the Research Centre for Migration Studies – EMIGRA, Universitat Autònoma de Barcelona. His research interests focus on minorities, social exclusion and evaluation of public policies, as well as on youth, schooling and educational inequalities.

Alexandra Oliveira Doroftei is a PhD student in educational sciences at the Faculty of Psychology and Educational Sciences of the University of Porto, Portugal, and a member of the Centre for Research and Intervention in Education (CIIE). Her research interests are Initial Vocational Education and Training (IVET), apprenticeship courses, social justice and early leaving from education and training.

Louise Ryan, PhD, is professor of sociology and co-director of the Migration Research Group at the University of Sheffield. She has published extensively on migration, social networks and research methodology.

Magdolna Lőrinc is an early career researcher at the Social Policy Research Centre, Middlesex University, London. She is currently undertaking her doctoral studies, researching young people's aspirations and their career decision-making. Her research interests include youth transitions from education to employment, supplementary and post-compulsory education, youth policy and research methods.

Introduction

Theoretical and conceptual framework of the RESL.eu project

Lore Van Praag, Ward Nouwen, Rut Van Caudenberg,
Noel Clycq and Christiane Timmerman

In this interdisciplinary and comparative book, we bring together findings that stem from a five-year-long research project on early school leaving (ESL) in Europe. The EU-funded research project, *"Reducing Early School Leaving in Europe"* – RESL.eu (2013–2018), brought together researchers with a variety of disciplinary backgrounds – including but not limited to sociology, anthropology and educational sciences – from nine EU-member states: Austria, Belgium (Flanders), Hungary, the Netherlands, Poland, Portugal, Spain, Sweden and the UK. To identify 'early school leavers', we started from the definition that is used at the EU level and defines early school leavers as '*those young people who leave education and training with only lower secondary education or less, and who are no longer in education and training*'. This definition is measured by looking at '*the percentage of 18–24 year olds with only lower secondary education or less and no longer in education or training*' (Eurostat, 2012). Or put differently, we focused on youngsters who did not attain an upper secondary education degree (ISCED [International Standard Classification of Education] 3). Joined by concerns of policy makers, societal stakeholders and researchers about the relatively high rates of ESL across EU member states and – in many cases – the large disparities between ESL rates of different social groups within these societies, we studied this complex phenomenon from a multi-disciplinary and multi-level perspective. The rationale behind this book, as well as the RESL.eu project, is the premise that early school leaving in the EU is primarily a symptom of traditional educational systems' difficulties to adapt to changing societal dynamics resulting from shifting social and economic contexts. The RESL.eu project aimed to gain in-depth insights into the mechanisms and processes leading to a student's decision to leave school or training early, allowing us to uncover many relevant and interrelated indicators of structural/systemic, institutional and individual difficulties to adapt to and overcome these social transformations. Along with this focus on understanding processes of ESL more in-depth, the RESL.eu project also aimed to identify and analyse prevention, intervention and compensation measures inside and outside mainstream educational settings that aim to support youngsters in attaining an upper secondary education degree (ISCED 3). The combination of both focuses enabled us to identify

2   *Lore Van Praag et al.*

many important risk and protective factors on various levels and contexts that influence young people's educational trajectories.

Our collective efforts resulted in a vast amount of new empirical quantitative and qualitative data collected in all of the RESL.eu-participating countries, except for Austria and Hungary. Over the course of the years, all these data were analysed both at the country and cross-country level, and insights stemming from these analyses were discussed in numerous RESL.eu Country Reports, Project Papers, Publications and Policy Briefs, which can be consulted on the project website: www.resl-eu.org. In this book, the authors – all of whom participated in the RESL.eu project – draw on these data and elaborate further on these insights of the RESL.eu project by taking a specific, and sometimes comparative, focus. Some study the educational experiences of specific vulnerable groups such as (second-generation) immigrants, lower social classes or Roma populations, while others focus on measures within educational institutions, governmental ESL policies, or the impact of features of educational systems. The main and overarching focus of the book, however, is studying ESL as a wider social phenomenon that manifests itself in young people leaving education or training early. The study therefore primarily focuses on young people (15–24 years old) who were (previously) enrolled in a wide range of educational institutions in and outside mainstream secondary education, in order to provide more insights into the mechanisms and processes that lead to ESL, as well as into the decision of school leavers to enrol in alternative learning arenas.

Here in the Introduction, we briefly set out the theoretical and conceptual framework on which the RESL.eu project is based and to which all the chapters of this book relate. Then we give more information about the methods used to collect the data of the RESL.eu project (see also Clycq, Nouwen, Braspennings, et al., 2014), which should enable the reader to situate the data used for each chapter within the project. Subsequently, we provide an overview of the distinct chapters and how they relate to one another and how they are organised in the book.

A theoretical and conceptual framework to study the multi-levelled social phenomenon of early school leaving

Since the 1960s (e.g. The Coleman Report, 1966) and 1970s (Bourdieu & Passeron, 1977; Jencks, 1972), research has demonstrated that socioeconomic status (SES) remains the main predictor of differences in educational attainment indicators, such as grade retention or ESL. This is a sobering finding after half a century of research on educational inequalities and how to overcome them. However, notwithstanding this preponderance of SES, an intersectional approach to educational differences that takes into account demographic variables, such as gender, ethnicity and migration background, but also religious or cultural identity and language spoken at home, paints a more complex picture (Driessen, 2001; Yuval-Davis, 2010). At the same time, many scholars point to the necessity of not only an intersectional but also a multi-level and multi-disciplinary approach to study social phenomena. Explanations and profound understanding of these phenomena are found not solely on the micro level of the pupil and individual agency, but also on the meso level of social institutions (e.g. school, family, peers) and the macro level of the educational system, the labour market and broader society in general.

Taking this into account, the RESL.eu project has tried to complement existing, rational choice-oriented theories by acknowledging human beings as rational but simultaneously bounded in their agency as they interact with and within social and structural opportunities and constraints (see e.g. Crossley, 2001; Evans, 2007). Consequently, their lives are (in)formed by the relations of power inherent to the social locations they live in, the Bernsteinian 'sub-voices' (Bernstein, 1996; see Clycq, Nouwen, & Timmerman, 2014). At the same time, the project acknowledges the importance of reconstructing educational trajectories from the perspective of the individuals involved. This starts by allowing youngsters to express their voices, but also by focusing on the significant others involved, such as teachers or parents. Moreover, it is important to take into account the role of (hegemonic) ideological frameworks and social imaginaries concerning meritocracy and democratic education. Although often overlooked, these broadly shared narratives that become unquestioned representations of social reality (Hannerz, 1992) are important factors that need to be included for a deeper understanding of the dynamics of inequality. Hence, the conceptual model of the RESL.eu project, and of this book, considers the standpoints of the individuals involved as well as their embeddedness in various contexts and the influences of social institutions, imaginaries and structures. We therefore departed from a rather classic tripartite (or all-factors) approach, which addresses the individual (micro), institutional (meso – including family, school and community related factors) and systemic/structural (macro) levels (NESSE, 2010; Lamb, Markussen, Teese, Sandberg, & Polesel, 2011). Throughout the course of the RESL.eu project, the findings revealed that a traditional linear approach, in which ESL is considered an end point after a process of disengagement from school, does not often capture the complex and processual nature of the phenomenon. Indeed, many students who have experienced school disengagement and ESL can – through resiliency factors and mechanisms at the micro, meso and macro level – be re-engaged in education and training. Consequently, we approach school disengagement and ESL from a more processual point of view, in which youngsters who are considered 'at-risk' of ESL based on socio-demographic background characteristics and prior experiences of educational failure can fight against the odds when provided with the right support and opportunity structures.

As shown in Figure 0.1, this conceptual model illustrates how the RESL.eu project approaches the interplay between risk- and protective factors for ESL by focusing on the role of the institutional context such as school policies and practices and capital resources, enabling us to link the structural macro context with individual trajectories through a youngster's embeddedness in his/her school, alternative learning arena, family, peer group and/or community.

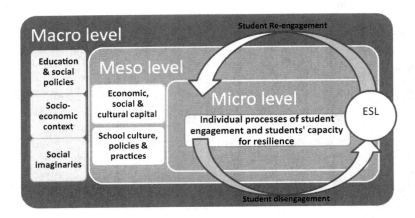

Figure 0.1 Conceptual model

As becomes clear in the next paragraphs, various methods for data collection were used throughout the project to delve deeper into some specific aspects of this model. While the different chapters, which focus on specific research questions, do not necessarily consider all aspects of this conceptual model, they can always be situated within it to try to capture how the distinct factors shown in this model seem to either contextualise or to interplay with the findings.

Methods

Given the complex nature of the phenomenon of early school leaving, the RESL.eu project relied on a mixed approach of quantitative and qualitative methods of data collection. The project was innovative in the sense that we were able to design the qualitative and quantitative research parts together and use the strengths of each method for the selection of the respondents and the interpretation of the data. The continuous cross-fertilization enabled the researchers to build upon each method's – quantitative and qualitative – findings. First, we discuss the rationale behind each method and the aim of this type of data collection, and subsequently, we provide more information about the actual data that was collected in this project and on which the chapters are based.

Quantitative data collection

Quantitative data were collected by means of two surveys that were designed specifically for the RESL.eu project: one longitudinal survey that was administered at two points in time and was directed at students in mainstream education who theoretically could be considered at-risk of ESL, and a second survey focusing on school staff. These surveys were administered in seven of the nine

RESL.eu partner countries: Sweden, United Kingdom, Belgium, the Netherlands, Spain, Portugal and Poland.

Overall, a total of 19,631 students took part in the first survey, with at least 2,000 respondents in each country (Kaye, D'Angelo, Ryan, & Lőrinc, 2015). The main objectives of this survey were:

1) to understand the socio-demographic profile of at-risk students;
2) to identify other – more alterable – risk and protective factors for students becoming early school leavers; and
3) to monitor and explore the early educational trajectories and perceptions of students at-risk of becoming early school leavers.

After an initial piloting phase in 2013, the survey was carried out in the academic year 2013/14 (more specifically spring 2014); and the follow-up survey was administered two years later in the academic year 2015/16 (more specifically spring 2016). The rationale behind this two-wave survey was to collect a wealth of information over a longer period and to reconstruct the trajectories of youngsters in order to identify patterns of risk amongst young people who became early school leavers and protective factors for those identified as 'at-risk' but still attaining an ISCED 3 level. Bearing this in mind, two cohorts of students were identified as the most relevant for our data collection: one cohort had two years of upper secondary education left at the time of the first wave, and the other was in its last months of finishing. Both cohorts were attending mainstream educational institutions in two particular research areas of each of the seven EU member states. This means that respondents were not selected based on age, but rather on the academic year in which they were enrolled.

The particular research areas were selected based upon high levels of youth unemployment and, in most cases, are urban areas characterised by schools with socially disadvantaged and/or ethnically diverse student populations. Within each of the research areas, distinct numbers of schools were selected, depending on the size of schools, in order to achieve the minimum sample size of 2,000 students per country for the first wave of the survey. Schools were selected based on their individual characteristics and profiles, with the aim of capturing the students who could theoretically be considered 'at-risk' of becoming early school leavers in subsequent years. The first questionnaire was administered within the schools via an online survey platform (Qualtrics) or (in some countries) making use of paper questionnaires that were later entered in the digital database. The follow-up questionnaire – two years later – was considerably shorter and administered via an online questionnaire. Besides this, much effort was put in contacting youngsters to participate in the second wave of the data collection through, for example, Whatsapp messages, telephone calls, contacting their schools and parents, etc., which had varying rates of success according to country-specific factors and ways of communication (see Kaye, D'Angelo, Ryan, & Lőrinc, 2017).

6 *Lore Van Praag et al.*

Building further on the theoretical and conceptual model of the project (see Clycq, Nouwen, & Timmerman, 2014), in the surveys,[1] key demographic variables, such as gender, age, ethnicity, country of birth, migrant status and family socioeconomic status were collected, as well as factual information about respondents' educational trajectories (e.g. attendance at pre-school, repetition of school year, level and track at which they were currently studying). Additionally, several psychometric scales were included in order to gauge participants' attitudes to education, their own academic self-concept, relationships and support from parents, peers and teachers and their behaviour, motivations and aspirations with respect to school (Kaye et al., 2015, 2017).

The second survey focused on the study of the views and opinions of school personnel. In the same educational institutions where we collected data about the students, we administered this second survey, which asked school staff and school administrators about their views of and experiences with ESL and policies aimed at reducing ESL. In total, responses of 1,977 school staff were collected in the seven EU member states. The main objective of the staff survey was to gain insights into schools' policies to reduce ESL. Furthermore, this survey also provided an opportunity to capture staff members' opinions on which factors are most associated with risk of ESL and their attitudes towards the effectiveness of interventions, strategies and policies aimed at reducing it. The first student survey took place during the earlier phases of the RESL.eu project and was important for the recruitment of respondents for the qualitative data collection. The second survey wave with youngsters allowed researchers to recruit potential early school leavers amongst the survey respondents from wave 1 that might otherwise have gone undetected.

Qualitative data collection

While quantitative data were collected in two urban areas in each country, the majority of the qualitative data collection was concentrated in one urban area, as this allowed us to carry out more in-depth research and to analyse more profoundly one particular educational context in each country. The major objectives of the qualitative field work were to study the trajectories of youngsters by (re)constructing their trajectories from their perspectives, and to focus on a theory-driven stakeholder evaluation of existing measures and policies to address ESL. Qualitative data were collected via focus group discussions and in-depth semi-structured interviews with local, national and European policymakers, representatives of a wide range of civil society organisations, educational professionals and youngsters in- and outside education. In an initial phase of the project, we sketched the prevailing policies and policy discourses on early school leaving in all nine countries by doing a systematic analysis of policy documents at various levels, and by conducting interviews and focus group discussions with key figures at all relevant policy levels (see Araújo, Magalhães, Rocha, & Macedo 2014).

In the second phase, space was given to the voices and perspectives of those actors who are often marginalised, mainly because of a lack of power, in the seven countries in which the surveys were administered. Youngsters in socially vulnerable circumstances in particular struggle with this, making them our main target group via whom we try to construct a broader understanding of the process of ESL. More in particular, we listened to three different categories of youngsters 'at risk of ESL': those who were still enrolled in mainstream secondary schools, those who left mainstream secondary education and enrolled in alternative learning arenas, and those who left secondary education without attaining an ISCED 3 qualification and were not involved in education or training. Overall, we aimed to interview at least 24 youngsters per country twice, with approximately 6 to 12 months in between each interview (for more information see Clycq, Nouwen, & Timmerman, 2014; Nouwen, Van Praag, Van Caudenberg, Clycq, & Timmerman, 2016; Van Caudenberg et al., 2017). The respondents at risk of ESL were carefully selected based on the educational programmes in which they were (previously) enrolled or their status of early school leaver. For students in mainstream education, only students with a 'risk' profile (constructed from school engagement, social capital, socio-demographic and educational background variables, administered in the survey) and who were enrolled in a school with a low level of aggregated perceived teacher support were selected (see Van Caudenberg et al., 2017).

Simultaneously, data were collected in the same educational institutions to carry out an evaluation of the initiatives and programmes taken by or set up in mainstream secondary schools and other organisations ('alternative learning arenas') to prevent or compensate for ESL, by means of an adapted theory-driven stakeholder evaluation (Hansen & Vedung, 2010). The programmes or institutions were selected because they aimed to provide youngsters considered at-risk of ESL or those who had previously been early school leavers, with an ISCED 3–level qualification. Educational institutions that aimed to provide all youngsters with an ISCED 3–level qualification were selected to assess the prevention, intervention and compensatory measures (NESSE, 2010; European Commission, 2013) that educational institutions undertake to tackle or compensate for ESL. Following this adapted theory-driven stakeholder evaluation, data collection involved focus group discussions and semi-structured interviews with the so-called *designers* of the initiatives or programmes (usually school principals or management staff), the *implementers* (teachers and other school staff) and the *target group* (the students). As a consequence, not only the voices of the youngsters were heard, but also those of teachers and other support and management staff.

To provide the reader with an overview of the type of respondents who were involved in the qualitative data collection in each of the seven main partner countries, Table 0.1 presents the interviews and focus group discussions that were carried out.

To ensure meeting the longitudinal ambition of the project, there was an oversampling of respondents during the initial sampling, because we expected that some youngsters would stop participating in our fieldwork, since it covered a period of two years. However, considering the specific focus of a more

8 *Lore Van Praag et al.*

Table 0.1 Overview of recruited respondents of the qualitative data collection in the seven main partner countries[2]

Longitudinal study of youngsters at risk of early school leaving		Evaluation of intervention, prevention and compensatory initiatives/programmes	
First interviews	Follow-up interviews	Intervention and prevention	Compensation
Eight interviews with youngsters in school	Eight interviews with youngsters in school	Four interviews with school principals	Eight interviews with staff members
Eight interviews with NE(E)T★ youngsters	Eight interviews with NE(E)T youngsters	Four focus group discussions with peers in interventions/ classmates	Four focus group discussions with peers
Eight interviews with youngsters enrolled in intervention and prevention measures	Eight interviews with youngsters enrolled in intervention and prevention measures	Four focus group discussions with school staff	Eight interviews with youngsters enrolled in these institutions
Eight interviews with youngsters enrolled in these compensatory institutions	Eight interviews with youngsters enrolled in these compensatory institutions	Combined with interviews with youngsters (see longitudinal study)	Combined with interviews with youngsters (see longitudinal study)
	Four focus group discussions with peers of NE(E)Ts		

★ NE(E)T: Not in Education, (Employment), or Training

qualitative approach to fieldwork, we deliberately opened up new ways of recruiting respondents – especially those enrolled in alternative learning arenas and those identified as actual early school leavers – whom we might not find based solely upon the first wave of the survey. To be able to compare the data across countries, topic guides with a common core of issues were used to support all the interviews and focus group discussions across the seven countries. For the longitudinal data collection these topic guides focused on the following themes: 1) aspirations and motivations; 2) educational trajectory; 3) connectedness to school and education; 4) school-related behaviour; 5) initiatives and programmes in regular secondary education and in alternative learning arenas; 6) study behaviours, plans, strategies, preparedness; 7) employment experience; 8) perceived challenges and resilience; 9) identity and 10) social (support) networks. For each of these themes, the data were collected in such a way that it was possible to set out the similarities and differences between (groups of) cases, based on, for example, age, ethnicity, social class, previous track, etc., and to describe the context-specific factors of these trajectories at meso and/or macro levels (e.g. related to teachers, discrimination, labour market characteristics) and to understand (reasons for) change over time. For the evaluation of prevention, intervention and compensatory measures/initiatives, the topic guides focused on eliciting information about, for example: Why is the measure designed? What is the target audience? Who are the implementers? What are the expected outcomes? What are the resources allocated? As mentioned, answers to these questions enable us to reconstruct the programme theory of the measures: that is, the designers' theoretical assumptions behind tackling ESL, as well as the different actors' (designers, implementers and target group) appreciation of the implementation and outcomes of the measures.

To summarise, qualitative data were collected to understand the policy discourses that contextualise ESL and to study in-depth the (educational) trajectories of three specific categories of students as well as to assess and evaluate measures developed in mainstream secondary schools and alternative learning arenas to tackle and compensate for ESL.

Structure of the book

We organised the different contributions, all based upon the RESL.eu project, into four main parts, and summarised them in a concluding section.

In the first part of the book 'State of the art and impact of early school leaving across European countries', we aim to sketch an overview of the overall situation of early school leaving in different countries and the costs (and benefits) associated with (tackling) early school leaving. In this part, comparisons are made not only of the ESL rates and the fiscal, social and individual costs of early school leaving, but also within and between distinct measures to reduce ESL, in order to gain a better understanding of the importance of the institutional context for early school leaving in Europe and its consequences for early school leavers and/or young people at risk of early school leaving. In Chapter 1, Alessio D'Angelo and Neil Kaye (Middlesex University, UK) develop profiles of young people based on the quantitative RESL.eu student dataset, to be used as a starting point to examine the commonalities and differences that exist within and between the seven national samples and to discuss the nature of early school leaving in a European context. Chapter 2, written by Ágnes Kende and Júlia Szalai (Central European University, Budapest), looks at the processes of how the respective indices and measures related to ESL are 'produced' in the field and how this could lead to the exclusion of particular groups. This chapter illustrates how such sociologies of method can 'forget' to incorporate specific target groups, such as parts of the young Roma adult population in Hungary. Chapter 3 gathers information on three countries, written by Helena C. Araújo, Eunice Macedo, Alireza Behtoui, Hanna Tomaszewska-Pękała Paulina Marchlik, Anna Wrona and Cristina Rocha (University of Porto, Stockholm University and University of Warsaw). In this contribution, three countries with very diverse positions in the EU in terms of ESL rates, namely Portugal, Sweden and Poland, will be compared with one another to study the political construction of ESL and the fight against ESL that is being developed in

10 *Lore Van Praag et al.*

each country. Finally, in Chapter 4, 'The individual and economic costs of early school leaving', Marie Gitschthaler and Erna Nairz-Wirth (Vienna University of Economics and Business) map out the state of research on the costs of early school leaving, and then offer an overview of cost-benefit analyses of American and European measures in order to understand the impact of measures in different stages of young people's educational careers.

The second part of this book, 'Youngsters' perspectives on early school leaving and schooling', focuses on youngsters' experiences, their understanding of what it is to be engaged in school (or not), and how they imagine their future. Given the complexity of the processes leading young people to decide to leave formal education, in Chapter 5, Rut Van Caudenberg, Noel Clycq and Christiane Timmerman (University of Antwerp) delve into the school narratives of two early school leavers in Flanders (Belgium), exploring how their schooling experiences unfold and are impacted by their social position in a socially and ethnically stratified educational system. Paulina Marchlik, Anna Wrona and Hanna Tomaszewska-Pękała (University of Warsaw) elaborate further on these experiences in Chapter 6 by examining the concept of '(dis)engagement'. Doing so, these authors aim to understand the importance of school engagement by examining the perceptions of young people's disengagement of students and staff in an 'increased risk' area in Warsaw. In line with the previous chapters, in Chapter 7, the determinants of the 'educational expectations' of young people in disadvantaged urban areas in three large cities in Sweden is studied by Alireza Behtoui, Marie Björklöf and Isabella Strömberg (Stockholm University). Finally, the transition between the first and second parts of this book is initiated with Chapter 8, written by Talitha Stam and Maurice Crul (Erasmus University, Rotterdam), which compares the Netherlands and the United Kingdom to understand how white female pupils from lower socioeconomic backgrounds develop educational and occupational aspirations in the school context. This final chapter in Part II connects students' perspectives on schooling with the actual educational trajectories they have followed.

In the third part of the book, 'Educational trajectories of youth (at risk of) leaving school early', the different contributions focus on the educational trajectories of youth (at risk of) leaving school early. In Chapter 9, written by Lore Van Praag, Elif Keskiner, Rut Van Caudenberg, Ward Nouwen, Talitha Stam, Noel Clycq, Mariana Orozco, Christiane Timmerman and Maurice Crul (University of Antwerp and Erasmus University Rotterdam), the educational trajectories of young people in two neighbouring and similar educational systems, namely Flanders (Belgium) and the Netherlands, are compared with one another to understand how differences in their educational systems affect vulnerable groups and how that influences young people's school careers. Subsequently, in the second contribution of this part of the book, Chapter 10, Sofia A. Santos, Eunice Macedo and Helena C. Araújo, pay special attention to the educational trajectories and processes of inequality of young adults who left school without attaining the compulsory education in Portugal. Finally, in Chapter 11, authored by Silvia Carrasco, Laia Narciso and Marta Bertran-Tarrés (Autonomous University of Barcelona), the academic trajectories of one particular group, namely of immigrant youth, are examined in depth in Catalonia (Spain).

While in the first three parts of the book we focus upon the current situation of young people's educational trajectories in different educational institutions and structures, in the fourth and final part of the book, 'Strategies to deal with early school leaving', we look for solutions and give an overview of strategies used to prevent and deal with early school leaving. In a first chapter (Chapter 12), written by Silvia Carrasco, Isidoro Ruiz-Haro and Bálint-Ábel Bereményi (Autonomous University of Barcelona), differences within one country are studied by focusing on the educational strategies to reduce ESL in a polarised school system in Catalonia. In the following contribution (Chapter 13), based upon data collected in Portugal, Eunice Macedo, Sofia A. Santos and Alexandra Oliveira Doroftei (University of Porto) study the pathways and subjectivities of early school leavers that reinvest in their education. In Chapter 14, the final contribution, Louise Ryan and Magdolna Lőrinc (Sheffield University and Middlesex University) offer more insights into the reasons why young people decide to enrol in apprenticeships and how they prepare young people for the labour market in two English boroughs.

Based on the insights that resulted from the project, Elif Keskiner and Maurice Crul in a concluding section formulate policy recommendations at the European level, at a country level and at the school level.

Notes

1 For more information about the research questionnaire, see Kaye et al., 2015, Kaye et al., 2016 and Kaye et al., 2017.
2 For more information, see Clycq, Nouwen, Braspennings, et al., 2014; Nouwen et al., 2015; Nouwen et al., 2016; Van Caudenberg et al., 2017.

References

Araújo, H. C., Magalhães, A., Rocha, C., & Macedo, E. (2014). *Policies on early school leaving in nine European countries: A comparative analysis*. RESL.eu Publication 1. Porto: Portugal. Retrieved from www.uantwerpen.be/en/projects/resl-eu/deliverables/resl-eu-publications/
Bernstein, B. (1996). *Pedagogy, symbolic control and identity: Theory, research, critique*. London: Taylor & Francis.
Bourdieu, P., & Passeron, J-C. (1977). *Reproduction in education, society, and culture*. Beverly Hills, CA: Sage.
Clycq, N., Nouwen, W., Braspennings, M., Timmerman, C., D'Angelo, A., & Kaye, N. (2014). *Methodological approach of the qualitative fieldwork, CeMIS – University of Antwerp*. Retrieved from www.uantwerpen.be/images/uantwerpen/container23160/files/WP4/RESL%20eu%20Project%20Paper%204%20-%20CeMIS%20%20UA%20-24%2011%20 2014%20-%20Final%20version.pdf

Clycq, N., Nouwen, W., & Timmerman, C. (2014). *Theoretical and methodological framework on early school leaving*. CeMIS – University of Antwerp. Retrieved from www.uantwerpen. be/images/uantwerpen/container23160/files/Project%20Paper%202%20-%20final%20 version%20-%2009%2005%202014.pdf

Coleman, J. S. (1966). *Equality of educational opportunity*. Washington, DC: U.S. Government Printing Office.

Crossley, N. (2001). The phenomenological habitus and its construction. *Theory and Society*, *30*(1), 81–120.

Driessen, G. (2001). Ethnicity, forms of capital, and educational achievement. *International Review of Education*, *47*, 513–537.

European Commission. (2013). Reducing early school leaving: Key messages and policy support. *Final report on the thematic working group on early school leaving*. Brussels: DG Education and Training.

Eurostat. (2012). *Europe in figures – Eurostat yearbook 2012*. Retrieved from http://bit.ly/ Eurostat_yearbook.

Evans, K. (2007). Concepts of bounded agency in education, work, and the personal lives of young adults. *International Journal of Psychology*, *42*(2), 85–93.

Hannerz, U. (1992). *Cultural complexity: Studies in the social organization of meaning*. New York: Columbia University Press.

Hansen, M. B., & Vedung, E. (2010). Theory-based stakeholder evaluation. *American Journal of Evaluation*, *31*(3), 295–313.

Jencks, C. (1972). *Inequality: A reassessment of the effects of family and schooling in America*. New York: Basic.

Kaye, N., D'Angelo, A., Ryan, L., & Lőrinc, M. (2015). *Students' survey (A1): Preliminary analysis*. Social Policy Research Centre, Middlesex University. Retrieved from www.uant werpen.be/images/uantwerpen/container23160/files/Project%20Paper%205_FinalVer sion_revised.pdf

Kaye, N., D'Angelo, A., Ryan, L., & Lőrinc, M. (2016). *Attitudes of school personnel to early school leaving*. Middlesex University. Retrieved from www.uantwerpen.be/images/uant werpen/container23160/files/Publication%202_revisedfinal.pdf

Kaye, N., D'Angelo, A., Ryan, L., & Lőrinc, M. (2017). *Early school leaving: Risk and protective factors findings from the RESL.eu international survey*. Social Policy Research Centre, Middlesex University. Retrieved from www.uantwerpen.be/en/projects/resl-eu/deliverables/ resl-eu-publications/

Lamb, S., Markussen, E., Teese, R., Sandberg, N., & Polesel, J. (Eds.) (2011). *School dropout and completion: International comparative studies in theory and policy*. Dordrecht-Heidelberg, London & New York: Springer.

NESSE. (2010). *Early school leaving, lessons from research for policy makers an independent expert report submitted to the European Commission*. Luxembourg: Publications Office of the European Union.

Nouwen, W., Clycq, N., Braspennings, M., & Timmerman, C. (2015). *Cross-case analyses of school – based prevention and intervention measures*. CeMIS, University of Antwerp. Retrieved from www.uantwerpen.be/images/uantwerpen/container23160/files/RESL%20eu%20 Project%20Paper%206%20-%20Final%20version.pdf

Nouwen, W., Van Praag, L., Van Caudenberg, R., Clycq, N., & Timmerman, C. (2016). *School-based prevention and intervention measures and alternative learning approaches to reduce early school leaving*. CeMIS, University of Antwerp. Retrieved from www.uantwerpen.be/ images/uantwerpen/container23160/files/RESL_Publicatie_A4_v5.pdf

Van Caudenberg, R., Van Praag, L., Nouwen W., Clycq, N., & Timmerman, C. (2017). *A longitudinal study of educational trajectories of youth at risk of early school leaving*. CeMIS, University of Antwerp: Retrieved from https://www.uantwerpen.be/images/uantwerpen/container23160/files/RESL%20eu%20Publication%205%20FINAL%202.pdf

Van Praag, L., Nouwen, W., Van Caudenberg, R., Clycq, N., & Timmerman, C. (2016). *Cross-case analysis of measures in alternative learning pathways*. CeMIS, University of Antwerp, Retrieved from www.uantwerpen.be/images/uantwerpen/container23160/files/RESL%20eu%20Project%20Paper%207%20FINAL%2026-09-2016.pdf

Yuval-Davis, N. (2010). Theorizing identity: Beyond the 'us' and 'them' dichotomy. *Patterns of Prejudice, 44*(3), 261–280.

Part I

State of the art and impact of early school leaving across European countries

1 Disengaged students

Insights from the RESL.eu international survey

Alessio D'Angelo and Neil Kaye

Introduction

It is widely recognised that positive educational outcomes have benefits both for individuals and more broadly for societal development and economic growth. Conversely, negative outcomes, such as poor attainment and early school leaving (ESL), can impact upon career prospects and psychological well-being and can lead to negative effects that persist well beyond the end of compulsory education. Identifying which students are most at risk of ESL is therefore of prime importance to schools, practitioners and policy makers. School engagement – the extent to which young people are involved, committed and motivated to learn and work towards their academic careers – provides a useful concept through which to assess the likelihood that young people will leave school early (Ferguson et al., 2005; Fredricks, Blumenfeld, & Paris, 2004; Rumberger, 2011). In fact, theories on dropout and ESL emphasise these outcomes are usually the end result of a gradual process of disengagement from school (Alexander, Entwisle, & Olson, 2001; Rumberger, 1987).

In this chapter, we present insights based on an analysis of data collected as part of the RESL.eu international survey. Conducted in seven European countries (Belgium, the Netherlands, Poland, Portugal, Spain, Sweden and the UK), this represents an important and innovative source of empirical data, providing detailed sociodemographic and attitudinal information from almost 20,000 young people. In particular, our data analysis shows the important role of self-perceptions and key personal relations in the individual pathways determining levels of school engagement, irrespective of the national contexts and school settings and beyond the predictive power of specific demographic and socioeconomic characteristics.

The next section discusses the concept of school engagement and how this can be operationalised and measured in empirical research. Next, we present the RESL.eu survey and outline the dimensions of school engagement and other key variables relating to the survey sample. Our findings section presents a statistical model of school engagement on the basis of the international dataset and highlights the main protective factors that can promote and increase school engagement for students. The chapter concludes with a discussion of the implications for these findings in relation to cross-national policy and practice.

Understanding school engagement

School engagement refers to students' level of involvement, commitment and effort in relation to their school careers. Chase, Warren, and Lerner (2015) describe the concept in terms of "the extent to which students participate in the academic and non-academic activities of school, feel connected to school and value the goals of education" (p. 58).

Much has been written on the antecedents, processes and outcomes associated with students' engagement at school within both North American and European contexts. Quin's (2017) review highlights that the study of student engagement has developed along two parallel paths: the first focusing on reducing disengagement and its associated 'problem' behaviours at school, targeting specific students; the second, centred on the promotion of a culture of engagement for all students, with a view to achieving more long-term developmental outcomes (p. 345).

Indeed, recent studies have emphasised the positive impact school engagement can have in an academic setting as a whole (Fredricks et al., 2004; Lawson & Lawson, 2013). High levels of engagement have been shown to be associated with positive youth development outcomes, most notably with academic success (Finn & Rock, 1997) and psychological well-being or adjustment (Li & Lerner, 2011).

Conversely, student disengagement can have negative effects on the individual level that persist across the whole life-course, including reduced employment opportunities and economic independence, poor health outcomes and even increased mortality. On the societal level, high levels of school disengagement can, in the long run, negatively impact economic and labour market efficiency, the sustainability of the welfare system and public health (Belfield & Levin, 2007; Klem & Connell, 2004; Woolf, Johnson, Phillips Jr, & Philipsen, 2007).

Measuring engagement

School engagement has typically been described as a multidimensional construct, encompassing several dimensions relating to students' attitudes, behaviours and motivations (Appleton, Christenson, & Furlong, 2008; Finn, 1989; Fredricks et al., 2004; Jimerson, Campos, & Greif, 2003). More recently, studies have defined school engagement as a three-dimensional construct, incorporating dimensions of behavioural, affective and cognitive engagement (Archambault, Janosz, Fallu, & Pagani, 2009; Carter, Reschly, Lovelace, Appleton, & Thompson, 2012; Wang, Willett, & Eccles, 2011). 'Behavioural engagement' elaborates on Finn's (1989) notion of 'participation' and includes student involvement in academic and extra-curricular activities. More broadly, it encompasses adherence to the school rules, high levels of school attendance and an absence of disruptive behaviours (Fredricks et al., 2004). 'Affective engagement', also referred to as *emotional engagement*, relates to feelings of institutional belonging and identification to one's school (Finn, 1989; Fredricks et al., 2004). The 'cognitive' dimension of engagement involves students' motivation and use of self-regulated learning strategies. Beyond assessing the level of effort students put into their work, cognitive engagement implies an "active, constructive process whereby learners set goals for their learning and then attempt to monitor, regulate, and control their cognition" (Pintrich & Zusho, 2002, p. 250). It is important to stress that this conceptualisation of school engagement, as a "multidimensional, developing, and malleable construct including students' behaviours, emotions and cognitions while studying" (Upadyaya & Salmela-Aro, 2013, p. 138), relates primarily to patterns rather than causes behind one's actions.

The operationalisation of school engagement through the RESL.eu questionnaire was informed by the literature and previous empirical research; a substantial number of questionnaire items were selected from previously validated studies on student trajectories and school engagement (Liu & Wang, 2005; McCoach, 2002; Martin & Marsh, 2006; Wang et al., 2011). Whilst detailed analysis was undertaken in relation to the sub-dimensions of school engagement (see Kaye, D'Angelo, Ryan, & Lőrinc, 2017), our focus in this chapter is to explore and understand how 'overall' levels of this multidimensional construct are influenced by a range of factors. This is of particular relevance for policy and practice, allowing us to identify key areas in which intervention can promote overall student engagement.

The role of contextual factors and background characteristics

Students' school engagement cannot be understood in a contextual vacuum. Research has shown that a number of structural – demographic, contextual or environmental – factors can also influence levels of school engagement. In particular, the intersection between class, gender and ethnicity is extremely complex and dynamic and has been the subject of numerous research studies (Archer, 2010; Vincent, Rollock, Ball, & Gillborn, 2012).

Socioeconomic background (or socioeconomic status – SES) has been widely identified as one of the strongest predictors of school engagement (Archambault et al., 2009; Janosz, Archambault, Morizot, & Pangani, 2008). Gender, too, has consistently been shown to be an important predictor of school engagement, with boys being more likely to report lower levels of engagement than girls (Li & Lerner, 2011; Wang & Eccles, 2012), relating to the greater levels of academic performance usually seen amongst girls at school (Pomerantz, Altermatt, & Saxon, 2002). The existing literature also supports the idea that, overall, minority/migrant children are more likely to experience educational inequalities as they attempt to navigate a process of acculturalisation in the host country (Carrasco, Pàmies, & Ponferrada, 2011; Clycq, Nouwen, & Vandenbrouke, 2014; Gibson, 1998). On the other hand, in more recent years an increasing amount of research has demonstrated a greater level of emotional school engagement (Elffers, Oort, & Karsten, 2012; Wang & Eccles, 2012) or higher aspirations (Behtoui & Neergaard, 2016) amongst young people with a migrant background.

Characteristics such as young persons' developmental stage; relationships with parents, teachers and peers; and the institutional setting they find themselves in at school all contribute to differences in individuals' school engagement. Studies of school engagement have attempted to incorporate these effects by using an ecological framework (Wang & Fredricks, 2014), highlighting the role of school context, families, peers and communities in influencing youth development and outcomes (Quin, 2017).

The importance of context in the study of school engagement is evident, and cross-national research highlights the high degree of variation seen between educational systems and broader cultural and socioeconomic contexts (Crul, Schneider, & Lilie, 2012). For example, because national education systems are the product of generations of cultural and political influence and context-specific policy development, there are differences between countries according to types of academic tracking, existence of grade retention, timing of educational transitions, pedagogical norms and classroom practices. Furthermore, there may be school- and classroom-level effects on individuals' levels of school engagement that cannot easily be accounted for and which may vary significantly within a single school or jurisdiction.

If schools, in particular, do not provide educational environments which are developmentally appropriate for adolescents, then they are unable to motivate students' interest and engagement and, consequently, this will result in negative developmental changes (Udpadyaya & Salmela-Aro, 2013, p. 142).

The RESL.eu survey: school engagement and other key dimensions

The RESL.eu project employed a mixed-methods approach to investigate the mechanisms and processes leading young people to leave education or training early. This chapter uses data from the quantitative survey conducted in seven countries across the EU to identify risk and protective factors of early school leaving. With particular regard to school engagement, the survey sought to build upon existing literature on the relationship between early school leaving and school engagement by identifying those characteristics and factors increasing the likelihood of students to have lower levels of engagement than their peers.

The survey involved at least 1,500 young people in each of the seven RESL. eu countries, within two different research areas per country. The data collection took place in two survey waves. The first wave (spring/summer 2014) surveyed students currently in secondary education,[1] asking a wide range of detailed questions on sociodemographic characteristics as well as behaviours, attitudes and perceptions at school. In most cases, the survey was administered within the schools and colleges using an online interface. The second wave took place two years later (spring/summer 2016) and was based on a much

Disengaged students 21

briefer questionnaire, designed to measure participants' trajectories from school towards further training, higher education or labour market insertion. This was administered via email and telephone, using contact information collected in the first wave.

Overall, 19,586 young people took part in the first wave of the survey, with 7,072 also responding to the follow–up survey two years later. Whilst full academic-year cohorts in schools (two comparable cohorts per country[2]) were targeted to capture a cross–section of the student body in that area, the schools and colleges selected to participate in the first RESL.eu survey were chosen on the basis of being located in areas of relatively high youth unemployment and/or areas with specific demographic or socioeconomic challenges. The final country datasets, therefore, cannot be seen as nationally representative samples of young people. Similarly, the relatively high attrition rate between the first survey and the follow–up survey (retention rate for the overall sample was 36.1%) implies a degree of self-selection bias, whereby those young people who did complete the follow–up survey are more likely to be engaged, and so vulnerable, disengaged or hard-to-reach young people are expected to be under-represented in the sample.

Nonetheless, each sample has a high degree of diversity with regard to personal characteristics and profiles. Of the 19,586 participants in the first survey (Table 1.1), 10,196 (52.4%) were female, 8,828 (45.4%) were in the older cohort, 7,756 (41.2%) had a migrant background (at least one parent born outside of country of survey), and 7,113 (36.3%) had parents working in a manual or elementary occupation. Of the 7,072 young people completing the follow–up

Table 1.1 Demographic characteristics of survey respondents

	Respondents to first survey (N = 19,586)		Respondents to follow–up survey (N = 7,072)	
	N	valid %	N	valid %
Sex				
Male	9,275	47.6%	3,010	42.6%
Female	10,196	52.4%	4,048	57.4%
Year group				
Cohort 1	10,691	54.6%	4,120	58.3%
Cohort 2	8,828	45.4%	2,951	41.7%
Migrant background status				
Native background	11,073	58.8%	4,563	66.2%
Migrant background	7,756	41.2%	2,329	33.8%
Parental occupational status				
Professional	5,176	33.8%	2,095	35.3%
Technical	3,029	19.8%	1,170	19.7%
Manual and elementary	7,113	46.4%	2,675	45.0%

survey (see Table 1.1), 4,048 (57.4%) were female, 2,951 (41.7%) were in the older cohort, 2,329 (33.8%) had a migrant background and 2,675 (37.8%) had parents working in a manual or elementary occupation. Female participants, those in the younger cohort, those who do not have a migrant background and those with parents working in professional occupations, therefore, were over-represented in the follow-up survey. Statistical tests showed these differences to be statistically significant.

Whilst, as discussed earlier, class is consistently recognised as one of the primary predictors of school engagement (Archambault et al., 2009; Janosz et al., 2008), it is also particularly hard to measure in a reliable way through statistical instruments. In the RESL.eu survey, parental occupational status was included in the questionnaire, as a proxy indicator of SES. This was coded according to the International Standard Classification of Occupations (ISCO-08), on the basis of students' responses to the questions 'What is your father's main job?' and 'What is your mother's main job?' The higher status occupation between respondents' fathers and mothers was used as parental occupational status, which was then aggregated into a three-group classification (see Dumont, 2008; Keeley, 2009). Responses to these questions relied on students' ability accurately to recall and sufficiently describe their parents' jobs; therefore, this variable has a low reliability and was subject to high levels of missing data (21.8% in the first wave; 16.0% of respondents to the second wave), which must be taken into consideration when interpreting the findings presented here.

Survey items relating to students' attitudes to school were analysed for dimension reduction and to establish in which configuration these sets of items most logically fit together (a detailed description and discussion of the factor analysis undertaken is provided in Kaye, D'Angelo, Ryan, & Lőrinc, 2015). From this analysis, school engagement emerged as a second-order factor (with mean scores ranging from 1 to 5); a composite of six first-order factors: school belonging, importance of education, academic self-regulation, academic resilience, compliance behaviour at school and attentiveness at school. Descriptive statistics for the school engagement scale are detailed in Table 1.2 for each of the country samples. The reliability coefficient indicates a good level of internal consistency for the school engagement scale (with an overall Cronbach's alpha

Table 1.2 Descriptive statistics for school engagement scale

	N	Mean	St Dev	Min	Max	Cronbach's α
Belgium	2,188	3.68	0.47	1.81	5.00	0.82
Netherlands	2,142	3.51	0.50	1.57	5.00	0.81
Poland	2,838	3.57	0.46	1.00	4.95	0.82
Portugal	1,957	3.67	0.44	1.67	4.86	0.81
Spain	3,358	3.75	0.48	1.48	5.00	0.84
Sweden	1,683	3.63	0.54	1.24	4.95	0.82
UK	2,586	3.73	0.50	1.38	5.00	0.86
All countries	**16,752**	**3.65**	**0.49**	**1.00**	**5.00**	**0.83**

Disengaged students 23

of 0.83) and is reliable across the seven samples (Cronbach's alpha coefficients between .81 and .86).

When linking the results of the two waves of the survey, it emerged that respondents identified as early school leavers at the time of the second wave were more likely to have reported, in the first wave, a level of school engagement significantly lower than their peers. This is the case in each of the country datasets and confirms one of the key hypotheses of our study, that is, that young people's level of school engagement can be used as a means of identifying those students who are more at risk of leaving school early.

Exploratory factor analysis also led to the identification of several other multi-item scales, which measured a wide range of participants' behaviours, perceptions and relationships. These included psychological measures of aspects of one's self-perception, for example, self-esteem – one's subjective self-value, as measured using six items from the Rosenberg self-esteem scale (1965) – and academic self-concept – an individual's self-perceived ability to succeed within the context of their academic career (Bong & Skaalvik, 2003), as measured using six items adapted from previous studies (Liu & Wang, 2005; Perry et al., 2001). Both scales displayed good internal consistency (self-esteem: $\alpha = .83$; academic self-concept: $\alpha = .73$).

Other scales related to participants' perceived levels of support they received from their teachers (eight items; $\alpha = .89$); their parents (eight items; $\alpha = .89$) and their peers (five items; $\alpha = .89$). These measures comprised a number of items asking students to rate the extent to which their teachers, parents and peers would provide support or advice were they in need of it. Such items included, for example: 'If I'm having a social or personal problem, my [teachers/parents/friends] would have advice about what to do', and were derived and adapted from the Interpersonal Support Evaluation List (Cohen & Hoberman, 1983).

Measures of students' educational aspirations and the perceived expectations of their parents and teachers in relation to the highest level of qualification they expect to attain were reported by participants according to their own national educational qualification system. These were subsequently converted into the International Standard Classification of Education (ISCED) so that equivalent levels of qualification could be established for analysis. In addition, students self-reported the average grades (on a 5-point scale) that they received over the previous academic year, and their own level of truancy from school over the same period (ranging from 0 = never to 4 = five or more days per month, on average).

Peer aspirations were measured on a scale by which higher aspirations amongst students' friendship groups – measured as the extent to which their peers feel it is important to attend class, study hard, get good grades and continue education beyond upper secondary level – were equated to friends placing greater value on education and focusing more towards academic success (see Ream & Rumberger, 2008).

On the basis of the particular operationalisation of school engagement described earlier, we proceeded to develop a multivariate regression model to identify the main variables explaining its variability, that is, those dimensions that can be used to predict the level of school engagement of a student. Analysis was carried out for each of its six components. Whilst these sub-dimensions are explored in greater detail elsewhere (Kaye et al., 2017), in this chapter, for limits of space, our findings focus on the multidimensional concept of school engagement. Nonetheless, exploring participants' overall level of school engagement is of particular relevance for policy and practice, allowing us to identify key areas of intervention for the promotion of overall student engagement.

Findings: a statistical model of school engagement

Preliminary analysis of the dataset showed that a considerable proportion of the variability of school engagement was explained by some of the other composite scales measured in the questionnaire, including measures of perceived support from teachers, parents and peers and students' educational expectations and their neighbourhood environment, as well as self-reported levels of truancy and academic grades. Variables related to background demographic and socioeconomic characteristics were found to have negligible coefficients or to be statistically insignificant. The model-building procedure used a forward selection stepwise regression analysis, with variables within each of five subsets (demographic variables, individual behaviour/attitudes, relationship with teachers, relationship with parents, and relationship with peers) being retained if their associated p-values were less than 0.05. This produced an overall regression model comprising 15 predictors[3] and with an overall explanatory power of 52.3% (R^2 = 0.523). However, several of these scales had very small coefficients and, when the model was applied to individual national datasets, were significant only in a minority of samples.

Hence, the final model presented in this chapter (Table 1.3) includes only the five scales accounting for most of the explanatory power and which were

Table 1.3 Multiple linear regression on school engagement

Explanatory variables	Standardised coefficients
Sociodemographic factors	
Female	.093**
Migrant background	−.036**
Parents' SES: manual/elementary	.011
Self-perception and support scales	
Teacher support (positive)	.350**
Academic self-concept	.307**
Peer aspirations	.183**
Parents' educational expectations	.154**
Self-esteem	.140**
Model R^2	**.485**

Note: Statistically significant at the (**) p < .01 level.

significant in all or most of the country samples; namely: academic self-concept, self-esteem, teacher support, parents' educational expectations and peer aspirations. This model also includes – as 'control variables' – the three sociodemographic characteristics identified in the literature as most relevant in understanding the processes leading to school engagement/disengagement. As discussed previously, these are gender, migration background and class – the latter measured through the proxy of parents' occupational status. The coefficients thus calculated indicate a moderate, but statistically significant role for gender, that is, being female has a positive association with school engagement. The coefficient for migrant background, although also significant, has a very weak negative correlation for the model overall; this is the result of the aggregation of different effects at the level of individual datasets. In other words, the correlation is positive in some national samples and negative in others. Finally, estimated parents' SES is not a statistically significant variable within this particular model (sig. = 0.074). Overall, the model based on the aggregate RESL. eu dataset has a total explanatory power close to 50% (R^2 = 0.485), largely on the basis of the five self-perception and support scales.

Comparison between the country datasets

When applied on the level of individual country samples, our final statistical model provides a high level of explanatory power, accounting for between 42% (Netherlands) and 55% (UK) of the variation in school engagement (Table 1.4). Perceived teacher support and academic self-concept emerge as the most important predictors of students' level of overall school engagement in all the country samples. Peer aspirations were also consistently found to be a significant factor in the models. Interestingly, the relative importance of parental expectations for one's educational attainment varied considerably across countries, although it was found to be statistically significant in all country samples except for the Netherlands.

On a country level, certain sociodemographic characteristics contribute to a greater or lesser extent to the predictive power of the final model. In particular, being female is correlated with higher levels of school engagement in all country samples; migrant background was associated with lower levels of school engagement in some countries, whilst in others the reverse was true; and social class, as measured by parents' occupational status, was found not to be a significant predictor in the model for almost all country samples (see Table 1.4).

However, whilst statistically significant, the coefficients show that the extent to which students' sociodemographic characteristics contribute to the overall predictive model is of only marginal relative importance. Whilst gender, migration background and SES have been shown to be important structural markers for engagement at school in the literature (Archambault et al., 2009; Gibson, 1998; Janosz et al., 2008; Li & Lerner, 2011), our model shows the overriding importance of indicators of students' self-concept and perceived support. Furthermore, with regards to school engagement, the predictive power of student

Table 1.4 Multiple regression analysis on school engagement by country of survey, standardised coefficients

Explanatory variables	Belgium	Netherlands	Poland	Portugal	Spain	Sweden	UK
Sociodemographic factors							
Female	.104★★	.099★★	.075★★	.142★★	.135★★	.094★★	.080★★
Migrant background	.035	.059★★	−.045★★	.039★	.016	.081★★	−.003
Parents' SES: manual/elementary	.015	−.009	.021	−.025	−.006	.046★	−.025
Self-perception and support scales							
Teacher support (positive)	.335★★	.376★★	.363★★	.314★★	.334★★	.395★★	.364★★
Academic self-concept	.255★★	.292★★	.314★★	.316★★	.373★★	.292★★	.357★★
Peer aspirations	.203★★	.132★★	.203★★	.182★★	.164★★	.174★★	.179★★
Parents' educational expectations	.085★★	.034	.069★★	.081★★	.126★★	.055★	.033★
Self-esteem	.192★★	.127★★	.171★★	.156★★	.126★★	.130★★	.144★★
Model R^2	**.431**	**.415**	**.525**	**.448**	**.514**	**.517**	**.548**

Note: Statistically significant at the (★★) p < .01 and (★) p < .05 levels.

Disengaged students 27

characteristics lies in their intersection with factors that reveal more about an individual's experiences and attitudes.

Protective factors for school engagement

The multivariate analysis of the RESL.eu survey data – both at aggregate and country level – indicates that reporting positive teacher-student relations and having a positive self-concept within the academic context correlate with higher levels of engagement at school. Having peers with high aspirations, focused towards succeeding academically, is also a predictor of school engagement. Students who report that their parents expect them to achieve higher-level qualifications are also more likely to be engaged. Finally, school engagement is correlated with young people's overall level of self-esteem.

All these factors can be broadly grouped into two domains: on the one hand, key personal relationships; and on the other hand, an individual's self-perception.

As far as personal relationships are concerned, perceived 'teacher support (positive)' was found to have the greatest influence on young people's level of school engagement. Previous research has also found that higher-quality teacher-students relationships are associated with better student engagement in the long term (Quin, 2017). Our finding confirms this and, furthermore, indicates that the relationship between teachers and students is important, not just on an instructional level but also to provide a source of social or pastoral support.

'Peer aspirations' is also a key factor in our model. This is defined as the influence of young people's peer group relations on the extent to which they are engaged at school. The role of friendship group relations, however, is a complex one (Holt, Bowlby, & Lea, 2013). Students can receive negative reinforcement from friends engaged in undesirable or deviant behaviours at school just as easily as academically engaged peer groups can provide a support network towards greater educational success. The role of peer aspirations in our empirical model confirms that those students with peers who have high aspirations, focused towards succeeding academically, also report higher levels of school engagement.

Parents are clearly another key factor in adolescents' development, and this relationship has been shown to influence how young people behave at school (Harris & Goodall, 2008). In particular, the importance placed on achieving 'good' educational qualifications can be seen as part of a set of values, transmitted from one generation to the next. The positive effect of this on school engagement is included in the model and confirms that students who perceive their parents' educational expectations for them as higher are also more likely to be engaged at school.

Academic self-concept is a much-used construct within educational psychology (Byrne, 1996; Shavelson, Hubner, & Stanton, 1976) – which refers to an individual's self-perceived academic ability and the extent to which they feel themselves to be 'a good student'. Unsurprisingly, our model infers that having a more positive academic self-concept has a strong bearing on the extent to which young people are engaged at school. This relationship clearly has a bidirectional pathway, such that those young people who report high levels of school engagement are also more likely to have a more positive impression of themselves as 'a good student'.

Finally, self-esteem, a long-established psychological construct (Rosenberg, 1965), refers to an individual's overall feelings of self-worth. Self-esteem is particularly important for adolescents at a time when they are undergoing significant self-identity development (Harter, 1990). Having high self-esteem can play an effective protective role in promoting school engagement, whilst conversely low self-esteem can reinforce negative self-perceptions within an academic environment, leading to disengagement. This relationship is represented in the model and comprises the only predictor that is not explicitly related to young people's academic sphere.

Discussion and implications for policy and practice

The statistical model produced on the basis of the RESL.eu aggregate dataset (i.e. the seven national samples combined) indicates that the key factors predicting school engagement include, on the one hand, self-perceptions (regarding both the academic and non-academic level) and on the other the relationships with important 'others': peers, parents and, above all, teachers. Although differences exist within each of the datasets collected amongst specific samples in each of the countries, these dimensions are indeed the key predictors for each of the specific student samples, as confirmed by running the regression model at the level of individual samples.

This seems to suggest the absolute importance of self-perceptions and personal relations in the individual pathways determining levels of school engagement, well beyond the predictive power of specific demographic and socioeconomic characteristics and irrespective of the national contexts and school settings. Of course, this does not mean that these dimensions are not relevant – on the contrary, as discussed in the earlier sections, the contextual element and the ways in which young people interact with it on the basis of their social, demographic and economic background is crucial. There is indeed a considerable proportion of the variability in school engagement levels which is accounted for by individual profiles as well as by the specificity of the local and national settings within which young people study and live, including school and classroom-level effects. The interplay between these is so complex that a statistical model cannot easily disentangle the role of each of these individual factors on its own. What our model helps us to identify, however, are those dimensions which seem to matter for every young person, those which can be the centre of policy, pedagogical and pastoral support interventions at local and even international levels in order to promote school engagement.

To this extent, these findings provide important food for thought for policy makers and practitioners. As revealed throughout our fieldwork, very often

Disengaged students   29

schools and local authorities focus on demographic and school-related characteristics to identify those at risk of low school engagement. In some cases, they have been implementing monitoring systems to identify and target young people who correspond to particular profiles. Whilst these approaches can be meaningful and in some cases effective, our research highlights the importance of integrating such interventions with risk assessment tools that measure and monitor students' levels of perceived support. The measurements designed as part of the RESL.eu survey – as operationalised in our questionnaire – represent one very practical example of doing this in a systematic way. Already within the life of the RESL.eu project, these measurements have informed collaborations at the local level, for example in the UK, and the production of toolkits across the international consortium working on this European research.

It is important to highlight that what is measured here are the levels of 'perceived' support, as reported by young people in a purely subjective way. However, our longitudinal analysis – consistent with the broader body of existing research – reveals not only how these perceptions correlate with students' self-reported levels of school engagement (also in this case a personal, subjective assessment), but also, how these, in turn, are linked to tangible outcomes, such as higher or lower risk of becoming an early school leaver. In other words, students' perceptions do matter, and teachers should ensure not just that support measures are available (e.g. through dedicated programmes within the schools), but that young people are aware of these and perceive them as an actual source of help. How this is achieved – and indeed how 'support' is put in place and even understood – does vary depending on the local context and circumstances of individuals. Nonetheless, the key recommendations emerging from our work are, firstly, for schools to employ specific tools to assess and monitor the extent to which individuals feel supported. Beyond this, the information collected should be used to develop interventions aimed at promoting a culture of school engagement amongst all students, in addition to specific measures which take into consideration the profiles and circumstances of individual young people.

Notes

1 Students were selected on the basis of academic year groups in relation to both the end of compulsory education in that country and the point at which students would 'usually' be expected to achieve an upper secondary level qualification. Further details of the academic year groups selected for each of the countries is discussed in RESL.eu Project Paper 5 (Kaye, D'Angelo, Ryan, & Lőrinc, 2015).
2 See Kaye et al., 2015.
3 These predictors are (1) positive teacher support; (2) academic self-concept; (3) peer aspirations; (4) parents' educational expectations; (5) self-esteem; (6) level of truancy; (7) teachers' educational expectations; (8) parental control; (9) academic grades; (10) victimisation at school; (11) parental support; (12) negative student-teacher interactions (reverse scored); (13) neighbourhood environment; (14) neighbourhood safety; and (15) educational expectations.

References

Alexander, K. L., Entwisle, D. R., & Olson, L. S. (2001). Schools, achievement, and inequality: A seasonal perspective. *Educational Evaluation and Policy Analysis, 23*(2), 171–191.

Appleton, J. J., Christenson, S. L., & Furlong, M. J. (2008). Student engagement with school: Critical conceptual and methodological issues of the construct. *Psychology in the Schools, 45*(5), 369–386.

Archambault, I., Janosz, M., Fallu, J. S., & Pagani, L. S. (2009). Student engagement and its relationship with early high school dropout. *Journal of Adolescence, 32*(3), 651–670.

Archer, L. (2010). 'We raised it with the Head': The educational practices of minority ethnic, middle-class families. *British Journal of Sociology of Education, 31*(4), 449–469.

Behtoui, A., & Neergaard, A. (2016). Social capital and the educational achievement of young people in Sweden. *British Journal of Sociology of Education, 37*(7), 947–969.

Belfield, C. R., & Levin, H. M. (Eds.) (2007). *The price we pay: Economic and social consequences of inadequate education.* Washington, DC: Brookings Institution Press.

Bong, M., & Skaalvik, E. M. (2003). Academic self-concept and self-efficacy: How different are they really? *Educational Psychology Review, 15*(1), 1–40.

Byrne, B. M. (1996). Academic self-concept: Its structure, measurement, and relation to academic achievement. In Bracken, B. A. (Ed.), *Handbook of self-concept: Developmental, social, and clinical considerations* (pp. 287–316). Oxford: John Wiley.

Carrasco, S., Pàmies, J., & Ponferrada, M. (2011). Fronteras visibles y barreras ocultas. Aproximación comparativa a la experiencia escolar del alumnado marroquí en Cataluña y mexicano en California. *Migraciones (Madrid) 29,* 31–60.

Carter, C. P., Reschly, A. L., Lovelace, M. D., Appleton, J. J., & Thompson, D. (2012). Measuring student engagement among elementary students: Pilot of the student engagement instrument: Elementary version. *School Psychology Quarterly, 27,* 61–73.

Chase, P. A., Warren, D. J., & Lerner, R. M. (2015). School engagement, academic achievement, and positive youth development. In *Promoting positive youth development* (pp. 57–70). New York: Springer International Publishing.

Clycq, N., Nouwen, W., & Vandenbroucke, A. (2014). Meritocracy, deficit thinking and the invisibility of the system: Discourses on educational success and failure. *British Educational Research Journal, 40*(5), 796–819.

Cohen, S., & Hoberman, H. M. (1983). Positive events and social supports as buffers of life change stress. *Journal of Applied Social Psychology, 13*(2), 99–125.

Crul, M., Schneider, J., & Lelie, F. (Eds.) (2012). *The European second generation compared: Does the integration context matter?* Amsterdam: Amsterdam University Press.

Dumont, J-C. (2008). *A profile of immigrant populations in the 21st century: Data from OECD countries.* Paris: OECD Publishing.

Elffers, L., Oort, F. J., & Karsten, S. (2012). Making the connection: The role of social and academic school experiences in students' emotional engagement with school in post-secondary vocational education. *Learning and Individual Differences, 22*(2), 242–250.

Ferguson, B., Tilleczek, K., Boydell, K., Rummens, J. A., Cote, D., & Roth-Edney, D. (2005). Early school leavers: Understanding the lived reality of student disengagement from secondary school. *Final Report submitted to the Ontario Ministry of Education.*

Finn, J. D. (1989). Withdrawing from school. *Review of Educational Research, 59*(2), 117–142.

Finn, J. D., & Rock, D. A. (1997). Academic success among students at risk for school failure. *Journal of Applied Psychology, 82*(2), 221.

Fredricks, J. A., Blumenfeld, P. C., & Paris, A. H. (2004). School engagement: Potential of the concept, state of the evidence. *Review of Educational Research, 74*(1), 59–109.

Disengaged students 31

Gibson, M. A. (1998). Promoting academic success among immigrant students: Is acculturation the issue? *Educational Policy, 12*(6), 615–633.

Harris, A., & Goodall, J. (2008). Do parents know they matter? Engaging all parents in learning. *Educational Research, 50*(3), 277–289.

Harter, S. (1990). Self and identity development. In Feldman, S. S. & Elliott, G. R. (Eds.), *At the threshold: The developing adolescent* (pp. 352–387). Cambridge, MA: Harvard University Press.

Holt, L., Bowlby, S., & Lea, J. (2013). Emotions and the habitus: Young people with socio-emotional differences (re) producing social, emotional and cultural capital in family and leisure space-times. *Emotion, Space and Society, 9*, 33–41.

Janosz, M., Archambault, I., Morizot, J., & Pagani, L. S. (2008). School engagement trajectories and their differential predictive relations to dropout. *Journal of Social Issues, 64*(1), 21–40.

Jimerson, S. R., Campos, E., & Greif, J. L. (2003). Toward an understanding of definitions and measures of school engagement and related terms. *The California School Psychologist, 8*(1), 7–27.

Kaye, N., D'Angelo, A., Ryan, L., & Lőrinc, M. (2015). Students' survey (A1): Preliminary analysis. *Reducing Early School Leaving in Europe, Project Paper, 5*.

Kaye, N., D'Angelo, A., Ryan, L., & Lőrinc, M. (2017). Early school leaving: Risk and protective factors: Findings from the RESL.eu international survey. *Reducing Early School Leaving in Europe*. Retrieved from www.resl-eu.org/deliverables/resl-eu-publications/

Keeley, B. (2009). *OECD insights international migration – the human face of globalisation: The human face of globalisation*. Washington, DC: OECD Publishing.

Klem, A. M., & Connell, J. P. (2004). Relationships matter: Linking teacher support to student engagement and achievement. *Journal of School Health, 74*(7), 262–273.

Lawson, M. A., & Lawson, H. A. (2013). New conceptual frameworks for student engagement research, policy, and practice. *Review of Educational Research, 83*(3), 432–479.

Li, Y., & Lerner, R. M. (2011). Trajectories of school engagement during adolescence: Implications for grades, depression, delinquency, and substance use. *Developmental Psychology, 47*(1), 233.

Liu, W. C., & Wang, C. K. J. (2005). Academic self-concept: A cross-sectional study of grade and gender differences in a Singapore secondary school. *Asia Pacific Education Review, 6*(1), 20–27.

Martin, A. J., & Marsh, H. W. (2006). Academic resilience and its psychological and educational correlates: A construct validity approach. *Psychology in the Schools, 43*(3), 267–281.

McCoach, D. B. (2002). A validation study of the school attitude assessment survey. *Measurement and Evaluation in Counseling and Development, 35*(2), 66–77.

Perry, R. P., Hladkyj, S., Pekrun, R. H., & Pelletier, S. T. (2001). Academic control and action control in the achievement of college students: A longitudinal field study. *Journal of Educational Psychology, 93*(4), 776–789.

Pintrich, P. R., & Zusho, A. (2002). The development of academic self-regulation: The role of cognitive and motivational factors. In Wigfield, A. & Eccles, J. S. (Eds.), *Development of achievement motivation* (pp. 249–284). San Diego: Academic Press.

Pomerantz, E. M., Altermatt, E. R., & Saxon, J. L. (2002). Making the grade but feeling distressed: Gender differences in academic performance and internal distress. *Journal of Educational Psychology, 94*(2), 396.

Quin, D. (2017). Longitudinal and contextual associations between teacher – student relationships and student engagement a systematic review. *Review of Educational Research, 87*(2), 345–387.

Ream, R. K., & Rumberger, R. W. (2008). Student engagement, peer social capital, and school dropout among Mexican American and non-Latino white students. *Sociology of Education, 81*(2), 109–139.

Rosenberg, M. (1965). *Society and the adolescent self-image* (Vol. 11, p. 326). Princeton, NJ: Princeton University Press.

Rumberger, R. W. (1987). High school dropouts: A review of issues and evidence. *Review of Educational Research, 57*(2), 101–121.

Rumberger, R. W. (2011). *Dropping out.* Cambridge, MA: Harvard University Press.

Shavelson, R. J., Hubner, J. J., & Stanton, G. C. (1976). Self-concept: Validation of construct interpretations. *Review of Educational Research, 46*(3), 407–441.

Upadyaya, K., & Salmela-Aro, K. (2013). Development of school engagement in association with academic success and well-being in varying social contexts. *European Psychologist, 18*(2), 136–147.

Vincent, C., Rollock, N., Ball, S., & Gillborn, D. (2012). Being strategic, being watchful, being determined: Black middle-class parents and schooling. *British Journal of Sociology of Education, 33*(3), 337–354.

Wang, M. T., & Eccles, J. S. (2012). Social support matters: Longitudinal effects of social support on three dimensions of school engagement from middle to high school. *Child Development, 83*(3), 877–895.

Wang, M. T., & Fredricks, J. A. (2014). The reciprocal links between school engagement, youth problem behaviors, and school dropout during adolescence. *Child Development, 85*(2), 722–737.

Wang, M. T., Willett, J. B., & Eccles, J. S. (2011). The assessment of school engagement: Examining dimensionality and measurement invariance by gender and race/ethnicity. *Journal of School Psychology, 49*(4), 465–480.

Woolf, S. H., Johnson, R. E., Phillips Jr, R. L., & Philipsen, M. (2007). Giving everyone the health of the educated: An examination of whether social change would save more lives than medical advances. *American Journal of Public Health, 97*(4), 679–683.

2 Pathways to early school leaving in Hungary
Ethnicised inequalities in education and the case of Roma youth

Ágnes Kende and Júlia Szalai

Vague knowledge about early school leaving

Although Hungary has subscribed to the EU-level goal of reducing early school leaving (ESL) to 10 per cent of the 18- to 24-year-old population by 2020, data for the recent years indicate a growing distancing from the desired and targeted indicator.[1] However, the trend of rising ESL rates does not stir alarming interventions or at least public discussions as if the problem fell far away from people's interest. The silence is largely due to the strange status of the idea, for ESL is a dual-faced concept in Hungarian policy-making: it exists in the EU-level policy discussions and negotiations addressing issues of education; however, the concept is not represented amongst the objectives of domestic educational policy.

It has to be considered that while the reduction of ESL is a governmental responsibility, it is the schools on the primary and secondary levels where the problem appears. In principle, these two levels should be bridged by a consistent policy on ESL – however, such a policy has not been drafted so far. Amongst the many difficulties hindering its development, lack of knowledge about the major causes and manifestations of ESL is a key problem, for schools do not collect data on dropouts (they do not even systematically follow the departing students), and they do not use the data on absenteeism or grade retention or the number of overage students for any other than internal purposes. Much in accordance with the central interest in admissions to higher-level institutions, schools focus on streams of competition and meritocratic measures of performance. ESL as a phenomenon concerning young adults seems to be out of the schools' horizon: they struggle to help the 14- to 15-year-old youth to accomplish the compulsory eight years of primary education and assist them to access the secondary level amidst ever more heated competition. In this context, dropping out or worsening performance is considered as a problem affecting only lower-class – especially Roma – students. As such, it is conceived of as a 'particular issue' that justifiably remains away from mainstream concerns and also falls out of general policy interest (Fazekas, Köllő, & Varga, 2008, Fehérvári, 2015).

In this environment, experience that individual schools accumulate about the multi-faceted causes of a gradually arising path towards leaving education early remains enclosed within the institutions. Even if they know a lot about the problem, schools are reluctant to recognise their own responsibilities. In the prevailing views that most teachers share, the problems of low-performing students and the involved occurrences of absenteeism, truancy, grade retention and even dropping out follow from the 'faulty' ways of how parents bring up their children, and should be resolved at home (Fehérvári, 2015). This widespread attitude contributes to the personification of ESL, and strengthens a fragmentary approach that, in turn, works against developing social and political interests in tackling the problem on the national policy level (Széll, 2015).

While the above explain the lack of systematic research about ESL, studies about the rigid hierarchies in education that contribute to intense competition and sharp selection on all levels and that tend to squeeze the most disadvantaged students into the poorest-quality segment of the system provide the background to frame the processes of ESL. Recent research on the increasing inequalities in education, and more specifically, on the groups of students suffering the greatest disadvantages in schooling and facing the highest risks of dropping out before completing at least the secondary level help us to better understand the causes and the mechanisms of fatal school failures and marginalisation (Fazekas et al., 2008, Hajdu, Kertesi, & Kézdi, 2014, Fehérvári, 2015). The studies unanimously call attention to the deep ethnic divide in public education that hits Roma children and youth in the first place. The risks of Roma failing and dropping out are much higher than the indicators of all other groups, also including their non-Roma peers living in poverty and deprivation (Hajdú, Kertesi, & Kézdi, 2014).

By relying on the existing evidence about the highly selective nature of the Hungarian school system, in what follows, we aim to present those *structural*, *institutional* and *personal* factors and mechanisms that produce and reproduce the ethnic divide and that work as alarming risks of drifting Roma youth towards ESL. Our *structural analysis* focuses on how the selective mechanisms reproduce inequalities between and within schools and how they contribute through segregation to the racialisation of the disadvantages of Roma students. We also introduce some of the consequences on the educational potentials and pathways of Roma students. On the *institutional level* we show how racial and social inequalities affecting the schools are mediated in the processes of instruction and socialisation. In this context we discuss how responsibilities for students' school failures are shifted to the families and how such a personification of the problem on the institutional level affects continuation and educational career. Finally, we turn to the *home conditions* of Roma students and show how extreme poverty deprives them of the possibilities of engaging in schoolwork and school-related activities. In conclusion, we briefly discuss how *the three levels interact* and how they reinforce deprivation and disadvantage on ethnic grounds.

Structural and regional inequalities
in comparative perspective

To draw a meaningful comparison between the life chances of a Roma student coming from a very poor family and a non-Roma student (most likely from a middle-class background), the different sources of inequalities in the educational system have to be considered. Because of structural problems of the system at the macro level, the opportunities of the two children are to a great extent determined by school segregation which, in turn, is a result of institutional racism at the meso level and tensed ethnic differences and cultural conflicts in the classroom at the micro level.

Although by some formal criteria the Hungarian educational system can be considered as comprehensive (children attend a preschool/kindergarten from the age of 3 and then they continue in primary and lower secondary schools – the first eight grades – more or less together before choosing different school tracks at the upper secondary level), it is also one of the most selective systems in OECD countries (OECD, 2015). Since the introduction of the law allowing for the free choice of school in 1985, children from financially privileged households often choose between various education options, whereas children from poorer families mostly stay at their district's state public schools, which are often located in run-down buildings in remote areas. Regarding the furnishings and the available learning materials, the classrooms are poorly equipped, and the class teachers are frequently overloaded and ill prepared for providing extra individual attention that could help their most disadvantaged Roma students towards integration into the school's community (Havas & Liskó, 2005, Varga, 2008). This, of course, has far-reaching implications for the children's performances and their attitudes towards learning. Research in pedagogy and educational sociology recurrently demonstrate that good integration in schools influences further development throughout life. Children belonging to the Roma minority who attend socially and ethnically diverse schools tend to go on to higher education in much larger numbers than their ethnic peers who attend segregated settings homogenised by students' poor socioeconomic backgrounds (Fox & Vidra, 2013; Kertesi & Kézdi, 2013a, 2013b, Havas & Zolnay, 2011).

Besides, the Hungarian educational system is not as comprehensive as it appears at first sight, since in addition to the dominant form of eight grades, students in the fifth and seventh grades can apply to certain selected high-quality general secondary schools where they are expected to pass the very competitive entrance examination specific for these institutions. (It follows that, while the majority spend four or five years in upper secondary education, certain admitted groups attend the best quality track of general secondary schools in the elite sub-system that offers six or eight years of schooling according to the institution's choice). The departing gateways allow for an early selection amongst the students, most often by increasing the privileges of children

36 *Ágnes Kende and Júlia Szalai*

coming from families with high social status. Furthermore, free choice involves selective entrances with a high degree of 'white flight' (i.e. middle-class non-Roma students leave schools where the rate of the Roma children reaches 25–30 per cent). The increasing number of religious schools also adds to the deepening of selection because of their special rules for the admission of children. Typically, church schools are chosen by middle-class families or by local elite groups, while Roma children attend the ever-more abandoned public schools. The ratio of students studying in church schools has increased from 4.9 to 13.8 per cent between 2001 and 2014, and the rate of increase has been especially high after 2010 (Herman & Varga, 2016). At the same time, selection is also present within state-funded kindergartens and schools, where differences in favour of urbanised settings and the concurrent advantages in the social composition of children strongly determine the quality of the institutions (Kertesi & Kézdi, 2013b).

The percentage of Roma students in public education can only be assessed by relying on estimations of the school management. According to these estimations, the proportion of Roma students has increased from 12 per cent to 15 per cent between 2006 and 2013 (Papp, 2013). Growth in the rate of Roma students is uneven amongst the different regions in Hungary: as indicated by the data, it is higher in counties with a higher-than-average percentage of members of the Roma population. This trend has intensified non-Roma families' attempts at 'white flight' and segregation. Despite all the political efforts between 2002 and 2010 for strengthening school integration, the number of segregated public schools with more than 50 per cent of Roma students has increased since 2000 and even doubled during the past ten years (Papp, 2013).

In sum, the unstoppable current of segregation is the prime factor behind increasing educational inequalities. However, by providing better-quality schooling for students of higher social status, the school system clearly further intensifies the social differences between the students while infusing these differences with the social and cultural meanings of ethnicity (Szalai, 2016).

Departing educational experiences[2]

The kindergarten is more or less the only type of educational institution where a Roma child has a good chance to share daily life with non-Roma peers, as the phenomenon of 'white flight' is not as strong in this educational phase as on the primary school level. However, even if a Roma child had attended a kindergarten from the age of 3 or 4, it is very unlikely that the child went to any kind of daycare under the age of 3 (Balás, Baranyai, Herczeg & Jakab, 2016). According to researchers, if disadvantaged children participate in high-quality early childhood intervention services, their life chances are definitely positively affected. (Magnuson, Ruhm, & Jane, 2007; Sylva, Melhuish, Sammons, Siraj-Blatchford, & Taggart, 2004). But villages where most Roma children live do not provide the conditions for such services. Thus, even before entering a primary school, Roma children accumulate significant disadvantages that neither

Pathways to early school leaving in Hungary   37

kindergartens nor primary schools are prepared to compensate for (Kertesi & Kézdi, 2013b).

When entering the primary level, the Roma child will be enrolled into a school that most probably will be a highly segregated one in a village; what is more, it well may be an outright ghetto school.[3] Here our student will spend a minimum of eight years, though, because of the high grade retention rate in these schools, quite probably he completes this school level in more than eight years or never at all. As today in Hungary schooling is compulsory until 16 years of age, the Roma child who started school at the age of 6 or 7 will, at best, finish the primary and lower secondary schools with little chance to continue studies beyond his sixteenth birthday when formal compulsion expires. Because of low performance results and poor self-esteem as shaped by accumulated failures, the only track the Roma child can or will approach is the vocational school track (Fazekas et al., 2008). If the child succeeds in completing his studies in due time, he will conclude schooling at the age of 17 with a certificate in hand that, because of shortcomings of the training, does not qualify him for finding a rewarding job that provides reputation, a satisfactory salary and a chance for upward mobility (Havas & Liskó, 2005).[4]

At the same time, a non-Roma child has a good chance of receiving early childhood services before entering kindergarten, because working mothers' babies are much more likely to be accepted by nursery institutions than those of unemployed or inactive parents. Even better, if the parents can afford it, the child will be cared for in a private childcare arrangement which usually provides rich programmes founded on modern child development studies and is abundantly equipped with toys, books and other amenities. From here, the child will continue in a well-chosen kindergarten which will provide similarly good conditions (Fazekas et al., 2008).

After kindergarten, especially the middle- or upper-middle class non-Roma children will have outstanding opportunities to get into a school in which quality indicators of pedagogical work are above the average; hence, even if illness or family problems may have temporarily slowed down the non-Roma child's development, he certainly will be carefully compensated by the school. After completing primary and lower secondary education, it is very likely that our non-Roma student will access a general or a technical secondary school from where he has a good chance to successfully apply to a college or university. Let us add, because of the segregated educational landscape, our middle-class student most probably will not have any Roma classmates or schoolmates during his entire school career (Havas & Zolnay, 2011).

As illustrated by our two cases, Roma and non-Roma students tend to have sharply departing experiences during the eight years that they spend in primary school. Some of the key consequences of segregation have been pointed out. Here let us address two additional problems that contribute to the departures. The first is the heavy pressure on primary schools to apply meritocratic principles in their work and in this way prepare their students for heated competition on the secondary level, which is meant to 'cream out' the best students who are 'worth' being educated to meet the knowledge requirements of an open, globalised market (Havas & Zolnay, 2011). The second problem partly follows from the first. The schools' orientation towards meritocratic competition has intensified some problematic aspects of teaching: the lack of personalised ways of instruction and the deficiencies of individualised support that would originate in observing the students' needs.[5] Instead, all those (and not only the Roma students) who become laggards or who are classified as 'problem students' are hopelessly left behind, and they enter a vicious circle. Through transference by order to another class or school, they are sooner or later squeezed into segregated arrangements which then justify the seriously lessened provisions that they receive. This is how the personal meets the structural by pushing Roma children to the losing side where segregation will lock them into a prison of disadvantages (Budapest Institute, 2011). The low level of teaching is amongst the most serious ones: teachers with other options tend to refuse teaching in segregated schools or classes. This way children get even less from schooling than what they theoretically could and slowly they become the forgotten generation (Havas & Zolnay, 2011). As a result of these patterns, we can say that Roma children lag behind from the moment they start school and receive little help to catch up (Fazekas et al., 2008). Consequently, they find themselves deprived of free choice: after completing the primary school, they are oriented towards the vocational track, where their missing basic skills are not developed at all and where adjustment to the demands of the market remains very poor (Havas & Liskó, 2005; Kertesi & Kézdi, 2013b).

Departures on the secondary level in the light of policy changes

To better understand selection amongst the different secondary school tracks and the increase in dropout events, it is necessary to introduce the policy and legislative changes since the new conservative government came into power in 2010.

The government accepted four strategic documents since 2010: the National Public Education Act 2011; the National Social Inclusion Strategy 2011 and 2014; the Strategy for Lifelong Learning 2014; and the National Strategy for Preventing School Leaving without a Qualification 2014. Despite the promise of national strategies to decrease segregation all across the country and on the different educational levels, school segregation is now tacitly acknowledged (and strengthened) by law. This is most obviously demonstrated through promoting the foundation of church schools with extra governmental finances and discretionary requirements on admission and also through the open strengthening of meritocratic selection by introducing streaming at an early age. At the same time, there are no signs of initiating a serious, committed government strategy for the benefit of the most disadvantaged students, whether regarding their social integration or their career opportunities. The highly unequal access to the various forms of secondary-level schooling draws up rigid barriers around

Pathways to early school leaving in Hungary 39

inclusive arrangements, limits movement amongst the various formations, and designates given pathways that conclude with leaving education behind at an early stage (Szalai, 2016).

The three types of schools at the secondary level are predominantly shaped by the needs and expectations of distinct social classes: the *gymnasium* (general secondary school concluding in matriculation) reflects the needs, aspirations and strivings of the upper and upper-middle classes; the secondary technical school responds to the efforts and needs of the lower-middle class and the established working class; and vocational schools serve mainly those coming from the less educated, lower ranks and especially from poor socioeconomic backgrounds. This latter type of school does not offer pathways of transference either towards the two other secondary tracks, or towards institutions that would render general knowledge for assisting successful entrance into the labour market (Szalai, 2016).

Recent legislative changes made the tracking system at the secondary level more inflexible and more disadvantageous for those coming from lower social ranks and contributed to an increase in their risk of dropping out. Inflexibility of the system is an important factor behind early school leaving: those failing in a given vocational school hardly have the opportunity to try elsewhere; the only option they see is leaving (Fehérvári, 2015). Before lowering the compulsory schooling age from 18 to 16 years (in 2012), the extended period in education compelled Roma students to spend a significantly longer time in education. Even students with low motivation had to spend some years in a vocational school until the age of 18, and this fact alone helped in acquiring some skills while it also increased opportunities for students to develop higher self-esteem. There was also a possibility of transference between the vocational and the secondary technical track in order to gain a diploma of matriculation. As a result of relaxed rules in the 2011 Act on Public Education, many students do not even start upper secondary education, as they have already turned age 16 while attending the lower secondary grades. Since 2013, the vocational education and training (VET) system provides three professional training years, that is, one fourth less than before. Measured in duration, the shortened curriculum offers theoretical education only for a third of the length under the preceding rules. The lowered compulsory school age has increased the chance of dropping out already at the beginning of the training (Fehérvári, 2015).

There are further risks inherent in the new system. At the age of 14 years (in the eighth grade) it is too early to choose a professional career, whilst the last chance to claim within-school transference into another professional track is in October in the ninth grade. This means that, should a student change his mind later, he cannot claim a change but must wait a full academic year to start on the new track from scratch. In sum, fewer people start vocational training in the new structure, and their chances of finishing the programme are worse. At the same time, it is also harder for students to continue studies after completing training and because of the lower quality of instruction, it is harder to get an adequate job. The indicators for Roma children getting jobs after concluding training have worsened in a larger proportion than for their non-Roma peers (Mártonfi, 2015).

According to the main findings of Martonfi's research,[6] developmental programmes that prepare students for the labour market and the schools' efforts to offer attractive perspectives prove more efficient in preventing students from dropping out than any other measures introduced in the VET system. Interviews with students who participated in the study reveal that they feel hopeless; completing studies in a vocational school is not a solution, because the number of training courses on offer is very limited and usually they are of very low quality, furthermore, the available jobs pay only a very low salary. In the case of Roma youth, strong labour-market discrimination further decreases motivation for getting a vocational certificate. There are only a few second-chance after-school programmes that are aimed at tackling educational disadvantages (such as the so-called Study Hall programme),[7] but even these programmes have no significant impact on reducing drop-out rates (Kende, 2017).

Personal conditions and relations

As it was pointed out earlier, because the Hungarian education system strongly influences how families' socioeconomic conditions affect students' performance and educational career, a full picture of the inequalities between Roma and non-Roma youths calls for a glance at families' personal circumstances. This implies the need to take a closer look at the material conditions and pertinent micro-level relations for complementing the foregoing institutional discussion.

Approximately 70 per cent of Roma families live in impoverished conditions, and Roma are the largest group amongst the poorest of the poor who face destitution and extreme social exclusion. Inequalities in income and wealth hit Roma the hardest: compared with those in the middle and upper positions of the income distribution, indicators of 20 to 40 times difference in per capita income point to sharp deprivation (Szívós & Tóth, 2013). Having more children than the average, and, simultaneously, being long-term unemployed, Roma parents seriously struggle to provide for the basic needs of their family. Lack of proper clothing, consumption of cheap but unhealthy food, no heating even on freezing winter days and the spreading of all kinds of diseases, especially amongst children, are frequently occurring aspects of Roma daily life (Kende, 2017). Roma children affected by these conditions often cannot show up at school simply because they do not have the proper shoes and coats or because they are ill. Absenteeism that is widely explained by the schools as resulting from disengagement and lack of proper parental care is often nothing more than a manifestation of deep and chronic poverty (Fehérvári, 2015; Szalai, 2016). However, not having formalised contacts with the local welfare agencies, schools have very limited tools at hand to intervene for ascertaining material support that would be of fundamental help for their poorest Roma students (Fazekas et al., 2008).

The most troubling implication of widespread and chronic poverty that deeply affects Roma child development is children's involvement in adult duties

Pathways to early school leaving in Hungary   41

at an early age (Fazekas et al., 2008; Szalai, 2016). Given that most Roma parents do not have any hope for re-employment, the adults will seize all opportunities to engage in gainful work. Therefore, parents do not have control over their time and such a situation forces them to shift household duties, childcare or care for the elderly or the ill to their children, who are often not older than 7 or 9 or 11 years of age. In addition, both girls and boys have to help in agricultural or construction tasks that often require efforts beyond their physical capacity. Needless to say, these work engagements frequently conflict with school schedules, providing yet another factor leading to absenteeism and dropping out. A lasting consequence is the shortening of the years of childhood, which exists in sharp contrast to the peaceful and gradual maturation of the middle-class child (Fazekas et al., 2008). Schools are usually reluctant to acknowledge the indicated 'irregularities'. This is not due only to teachers' prejudices: they do not see a way to relate to their 'ill-behaving' students other than to be rigorous in requiring completion of homework and observing the rules of the house – their positions and remunerations depend on achieving this success. Yet again, the institutional and authoritative separation of the domains of work, welfare and schooling induces school mechanisms that push Roma children towards disengagement and that increase the risks of early school leaving (Szalai, 2016; Kende, 2017).

Despite the sharply deteriorating living conditions of the majority of Roma (Havas & Zolnay, 2011), it has been because of a significant change in the attitude of the community over the past decades that schooling has become a norm even for the poorest. Apart from the above indicated constraints that they see as incidental, parents expect their children to regularly visit school at least until the completion of the first eight grades. They would even support continuation if a good vocational school appeared on the horizon (Havas & Zolnay, 2011). Although teachers often complain that Roma parents do not show up frequently enough at parent-teacher conferences, many teachers would be ready to advise on the child's further educational prospects in response to parents' requests. However, the encounters usually come late and do not alter the negative ideas of the school personnel about the Roma community (Kende, 2017). Prejudices are strong and widespread; blaming the 'negligent' Roma child and his 'uninterested' and 'risk-loaded' family works as a mechanism for shifting responsibilities to the private domain and in this way legitimising the built-in inclination of the school system for observing and serving middle-class needs (Havas & Zolnay, 2011; Szalai, 2016).

The micro world of the classroom involves similar tensions. Motivated often by hatred towards Roma as an undifferentiated populace, parents in non-Roma settings mediate deeply prejudiced views to their children from a very early age on. In such an atmosphere it is hardly a surprise that bullying and harsh treatment are frequent occurrences that Roma children face at school, regardless of whether they attend mixed or separated classes. Conflicts might grow large and require intervention by staff, who are inclined to blame the Roma party. Interviews with Roma children often bring up the felt injustice as the most important factor in early alienation from schooling (Papp, 2013).

42 Ágnes Kende and Júlia Szalai

Humiliation as induced by majority responses to the inextricable manifestations of poverty and ethnic 'otherness' and the unbroken experience of being refused have severe impacts on Roma children's identity formation. Low degrees of self-respect and internalisation of the degrading opinions of important adults and some respected non-Roma classmates gradually build up self-devaluation and self-denial (Neményi & Vajda, 2014). Usually, Roma parents and the community do not have enough strength and agency to countervail these developments. At the same time, disturbances in identity development easily find their expressions in turning away from the humiliating agents, most specifically, from schools. This way the micro-level conditions and the relationships built on their ground easily come together with the earlier described macro- and meso-level tendencies. By mutually reinforcing each other, the involved factors impregnate the status and self-perception of Roma children at school while they generate early disengagement from schooling that later takes its route to ESL.

Conclusions

Roma families suffer multi-faceted discrimination in key areas of living, such as education, employment, housing and health. Accumulation of the discriminative occurrences induces almost unbridgeable multiple disadvantages: elimination of discrimination in one area does not result in improvements in other areas (Kende, 2017). Given these circumstances, the disadvantages of a Roma child start well before entering the educational system. The discussion in this chapter sought to present how the disadvantaged life chances of Roma children are determined from almost the very first moments of their lives, and how the sharp departure from the conditions of their more fortunate peers affects their later educational opportunities.

This chapter aimed to single out those most important structural features of the Hungarian educational system and also those key processes at the various stages of schooling that, together, lead to major inequalities between students from different social backgrounds and that represent a high risk of early departure from education in the case of the most disadvantaged Roma students. The discussion revealed that the risks of school failures concluding later in early leaving appear in the closing years of primary education and in vocational training. It was demonstrated that ethnic segregation is the primary factor behind dropping out or distancing from education through absenteeism. In vocational schools, the inadequacy of the training and the fact that students cannot acquire meaningful and useable qualifications are what instigate early leaving en masse. A closer look at the students who are facing the risks of early leaving revealed high rates of poverty, early take-up of heavy workloads that hinder healthy child development, a pressure of unemployment, and disturbed relationships between parents and the schools (Papp, 2013).

The risks are faced primarily by Roma students – so much so that early school leaving is considered by professionals and also by policy makers as an issue specific to Roma. Such a characterisation influences public policy. ESL

Pathways to early school leaving in Hungary 43

is meant to be tackled by changes in the attitudes of the Roma community towards supporting education and learning. With this attitude in the background, no comprehensive policies have been shaped to tackle dropping out, absenteeism or truancy as early manifestations of the later risks of ESL. These phenomena are handled on the individual level, and the methods of combating them usually build on penalisation and shame. Therefore, the applied measures hardly are efficient to stop the process and to turn it around. Instead, they deepen alienation and add to thickening the wall between the school and Roma students and their families.

To understand the differences in the educational and life chances between Roma and non-Roma students, a multi-level approach had to be introduced. *Micro-level racialisation* in schools is framed by the departing familial socialisations and the shared cultural values that are manifested in the classroom positions of the individual children coming from various ethnic and social groups. These positions are shaped by interactions with students from other social groups, and they are significantly influenced by local environmental conditions.

Meso-level institutional racialisation recognises the accumulated disadvantages that have been faced in the series of interrelated educational experiences and that have been produced by routine institutional operations, regardless of intentionality of the individual actors.

The *macro-level structural conditions* provide the societal framing through which the meso-level institutional processes and practices are enacted. Hence, the modern state acts through its apparatuses for providing the definition, regulation, management, economic controls and mediation of racial relations that then shape the manifestations of race and racist exclusion (Phillips, 2011).

Informed by the interplay of the three levels, Roma students face multiple deprivations, one of which is the inability of the mainstream educational system to compensate for social inequality and providing upward mobility for them. Given the prevailing regulations of free school choice, it is impossible to implement a consistent policy of equality in education (Varga, 2008). At the *macro level* it means that about one third of each student-generation leaves education without having received the basic skills required to make it in the labour market (OECD, 2015; Kende-Osztolykán, 2015).

Integration versus segregation of Roma children in schools is one of the most debated and contested issues at the institutional level (meso level) in the Hungarian public discourse, going far beyond the remits of policy actors in the field. However, in reality, little has been done so far; thus, Roma students remain on the losing side:

> School systems that reward academic achievement in their admissions policies effectively shift Roma children out into schools with lower rates of educational attainment. The result is that Roma pupils are concentrated in the same (underperforming) schools even in areas where they may be otherwise (residentially, locally) integrated.
>
> (Fox & Vidra, 2013)

At the *micro level*, chronic poverty, poor housing and inherent health risks are deeply influencing the educational chances of Roma children and also the families' relations to the school. Framed by the institution's micro world, Roma students tend to have poor performance results or, mainly in primary schools, they are frequently faced with grade retention. These tendencies are deepened by the children's low self-esteem that is shaped, amongst other factors, by the often degrading attitude of the school. As the teachers do not believe in him, the child also does not believe in himself. The lowering of esteem and trust at both ends destroys the remnants of the child's chances for applying with realistic likelihood into an upper secondary school that provides a diploma of matriculation (Neményi & Vajda, 2014). Roma parents hardly are in a position to turn around the process in their struggles for better schooling for their child. Like the child, they are also victims of the so-called Pygmalion effect of accepting the teachers' judgement who, due to their assumed limited capabilities, orient the Roma child towards a VET school as the only path open to him.

However, the vocational school often proves to be a dead-end, while it is a point of ultimate departure between the Roma and the non-Roma students. Firstly, these schools are but loosely integrated into the upper secondary school system: because of the prevailing policy, transference towards the other two school types is blocked. This way the departure in educational and life chances becomes institutionally acknowledged: vocational schools as the 'schools for Roma' provide certificates of qualification but without a diploma of matriculation, while the secondary general and technical schools open the gate towards higher education. Secondly, most of the training programmes serve the needs of certain powerful groups of the old working class while they remain insensitive to newly emerging challenges and claims of the labour market (Havas & Liskó, 2005). The consequences are rather severe. As soon as reaching the end of compulsory schooling, the majority of Roma youth leave the training (Mártonfi, 2015). However, the departure very often involves farewell to education as such. Therefore, it is not an exaggeration to state that the VET system in its current form is the major producer of early school leavers. Besides channelling Roma students towards the low segments of the labour market and into serving as members of a 'reserve army' of oscillating employment, the systemic separation on the secondary level also underscores and legitimises the departing social (class) positions to the benefit of non-Roma youth.

Lacking public and political discourse about the structural and institutional embedding of the educational failures of Roma students deprives the stakeholders of education of understanding the true nature of the problem. Instead, 'disinterest', 'negligence' and 'behavioural deficiencies' of the Roma parents and children are seen as the major causes of the accumulated disadvantages, and these are perceived also as the key factors of the sharp inequalities that hinder the educational and life chances of Roma youth in comparison to their non-Roma peers (Havas & Zolnay, 2011). Given the very weak state of empowering civil initiatives and proper civic protection, the Roma community tends to internalise the negative attitudes of the non-Roma public and thus rarely makes any attempts to stand up for self-protection. However, personification and the prevalence of behavioural argumentations work as further potent factors: poor performance, reduced educational opportunities and growing occurrences of early school leaving remain enclosed into the micro worlds of the Roma families and the community. This way the lack of a dialogue towards mutual understanding contributes to frame ESL as an exclusively 'Roma problem' of a marginalised community. This situation does not appear likely to change in the short run; currently there is very little pressure on public policy to reconsider the exclusionary trends in education and to initiate policies that observe equal opportunities and equity as their cornerstones. A betterment of the case of Roma could be expected only after such a turn-around.

Notes

1 With a slight tendency of increase, the ratio of ESL was oscillating between 10.5 and 11.5 per cent in the 2010–2014 period, while a clear worsening is indicated by the 11.9 per cent rate for 2015.
2 Following Putnam's method (2015), the Roma and non-Roma exemplary student cases were developed for comparative purposes. The cases were amalgamated from the most typical characteristics that recent research has identified along the lines of ethnicity and socioeconomic position (Kertesi & Kézdi 2013b; Hajdú et al., 2014; Kende, 2017).
3 Ghetto schools represent the extreme cases of segregated schools, with more than 80 per cent of Roma (and poor) students in their student population.
4 Vocational training is supposed to prepare students for direct access to the labour market, but because of recent regulations that shortened the training time and that restructured the curricula by eliminating the bulk of general subjects, the quality of the programmes has deteriorated in most fields (Fazekas et al., 2008).
5 The way of instruction in primary and secondary schools is still ruled by the century-old routines of 'Prussian-style teaching', that is, by a rigid hierarchy between teachers and students; the dominance of one-way communication; a focus on transferring 'ready-made' blocs of knowledge; and the total lack of interactions.
6 Martonfi's study has been the only research on early school leaving in Hungary so far. The research addressed how changes in Hungarian legislation have impacted the educational outcomes of disadvantaged pupils and Roma youth since 2011. The results come from 150 interviews and a survey in 37 classes.
7 The Study Hall programme was set up in the 1990s to ensure a successful learning career and a path to further education for children whose social backgrounds and educational circumstances do not typically allow for these. In the Study Hall programme, the students – mainly of Roma origin – are given a second chance through an extra after-school curriculum. The target group of the Study Halls is students mainly from the fifth to eighth grades, before they approach the different types of upper secondary schools.

References

Balás, G., Baranyai, Z., Herczeg, B., & Jakab, G. (2016). *Affects of the 'sure start' program.* Budapest: Hétfa.
Budapest Institute. (2011). *School quality and segregation in Hungary.* Budapest: Budapest Institute. Retrieved from www.budapestinstitute.eu/uploads/bi_fio_case_study1_segregation_2609111.pdf

46 *Ágnes Kende and Júlia Szalai*

Fazekas, K., Köllő, J., & Varga, J. (Eds.) (2008). *Green book for the renewal of the Hungarian public school system.* Budapest: Ecostat.

Fehérvári, A. (2015). Trends of dropout and early school leaving. *Neveléstudomány, 3,* 31–47.

Fox, J., & Vidra, Z. (2013). *Applying tolerance indicators: Roma school segregation.* Retrieved from http://cadmus.eui.eu/bitstream/handle/1814/26140/2013-21-Roma_Indicators.pdf?sequence=1

Hajdu, T., Kertesi, G., & Kézdi, G. (2014). *Roma youth in secondary education.* Budapest: MTA KRTK.

Havas, G., & Liskó, I. (2005). *Segregation of Roma students in primary schools.* Budapest: FKI.

Havas, G., & Zolnay, J. (2011). Stock-taking of Sisyphus: Integration policy in education. *Beszélő, 16*(6), 88–113.

Hermann, Z., & Varga, J. (2016). *State, municipal, religious and foundation schools: Shares, student composition and student performances.* Retrieved from www.tarki.hu/hu/publications/SR/2016/15hermann.pdf

Kende, Á. (2017). *Involving others: Assessing efforts to improve the schooling experience of Hungarian Roma children through focused teacher training and afternoon schooling programs.* Budapest: CEU CPS.

Kertesi, G., & Kézdi, G. (2013a). Ethnic segregation between Hungarian schools: Long-run trends and geographic distribution. *Hungarian Statistical Review.* Special number, *16,* 18–45.

Kertesi, G., & Kézdi, G. (2013b). *School segregation, school choice and education policies in 100 Hungarian towns.* Budapest: Institute of Economics, CERS, HAS – Department of Human Resources, Corvinus University. Retrieved from www.econ.core.hu/file/download/bwp/bwp1312.pdf

Magnuson, K. A., Ruhm, C., & Waldfogel, J. (2007). Does Prekindergarten improve school preparation and performance? *Economics of Education Review, 26*(1), 33–51.

Mártonfi, G. (2015). *Dropouts and ghosts: Legislative changes affecting the education of disadvantaged pupils: Roma children and youth in Hungary.* Budapest: Roma Education Fund, Manuscript.

Neményi, M., & Vajda, R. (2014). Intricacies of ethnicity: A comparative study of minority identity formation during adolescence. In Szalai, J. & Schiff, C. (Eds.), *Migrant, Roma and post-colonial youth in education across Europe: Being 'visibly different'* (pp. 103–120). Houndsmills, Basingstoke: Palgrave Macmillan.

OECD. (2015). *Education at a glance 2015.* Paris: OECD Publishing.

Papp, A. Z. (2013). Added pedagogical value depending on the rate of Roma students in the Hungarian school system. In Bárdi, N. & Tóth, Á. (Eds.), *Identity and fragmentation: Discussions on cultural distinction* (pp. 69–88). Budapest: MTA TK KI.

Phillips, C. (2011). Institutional racism and ethnic inequalities: An expanded multilevel framework. *Journal of Social Policy, 40*(1), 173–192.

Putnam, R. (2015). *Our kids: The American dream in crisis.* New York: Simon and Schuster.

Sylva, K., Melhuish, E., Sammons, P., Siraj-Blatchford, I., & Taggart, B. (2004). *The effective provision of pre-school education: Final report of the EPPE project.* London: Institute of Education, University of London.

Szalai, J. (2016). *Early school leaving: The Hungarian experience.* Budapest: CEU CPS.

Széll, K. (2015). *School efficiency and teachers' attitudes.* Budapest: OFI.

Szívós, P., & Tóth, I. Gy. (Eds.) (2013). *Inequalities and polarisation in Hungarian society.* Budapest: TÁRKI.

Varga, J. (2008). Institutional structure and financing in the school system. In Fazekas, K., Köllő, J., & Varga, J. (Eds.), *Green book for the renewal of the Hungarian public school system* (pp. 235–259). Budapest: Ecostat.

3 Shaping the policies towards early school leaving in Portugal, Sweden and Poland

Helena C. Araújo, Eunice Macedo, Alireza Behtoui, Hanna Tomaszewska-Pękała, Paulina Marchlik, Anna Wrona and Cristina Rocha[1]

Introduction

Increasing interactions between supranational, national and local institutions reflect the introduction of new forms of educational governance/regulation. These include the reconfiguration of education by means of supranational decision-making, and the production of guidelines and programmes by international organisations. The role of the nation state concerning the definition, steering and implementation of policies and public action goes hand in hand with an increasing intervention of other entities and actors, accountable to different governing bodies. This multiple-scale governance (Dale, 2007; Enjolras, 2008; Gordon & Stack, 2007), where different arenas of action and influence are not necessarily in a hierarchical relation, refers to the (de)fragmentation of decision-making from the states to European institutions and the assertion of sub-national levels of governance (Hooghe & Marks, 2001). Efforts to coordinate education policies, including those involving early school leaving (ESL), are part of the EU's soft regulation by means of instruments such as the Open Method of Coordination, which leads to increased standardisation. This form of soft law includes the provision of funds and the harmonisation of evaluation systems, such as the European Qualification Framework (EQF). This is put in motion by means of governance networking, which involves organisations, associations, agencies and committees in charge of implementation processes. National governments have both used opportunities and faced constraints arising from the multiple-scale governance to carry out re-nationalisation policies (Musselin & Paradeise, 2009), aimed at pursuing national goals by designing and implementing specific national policies that recontextualise the European guidelines.

This chapter focuses on educational policies and measures that contribute to the political construction of ESL in three EU countries as well as the ambiguities and tensions inherent in this process. We explore the similarities and differences as well as the relationships between these policies and measures in Portugal, Sweden and Poland. These countries have quite diverse positions in the EU in what concerns the rates of ESL. Even if great progress has occurred in the past decades, Portugal still has one of the highest rates of ESL in Europe.

48 *Helena C. Araújo et al.*

Sweden has been in quite a comfortable position as its ESL rate is lower than the European average, and the Polish rate is significantly below the European average. A set of interrelated questions are at the core of this chapter: 1) What are the views of policy makers and other educational stakeholders on ESL in the three countries? 2) What is the nature of the measures to confront ESL? And 3) Are there any similarities and/or differences amongst the three countries?

Dynamics of Europeanisation and national contexts and policies

Based on the theoretical proposal referred to above, we take into consideration the relationship of education with the dynamics of Europeanisation, as well as the affirmation of new roles for the member states, as entities (amongst others) that interact with *multiple-scale governance* resulting in potential compromise or conflict. According to Roger Dale (2007), the interaction between national and European scales should be seen in the framework of a relationship of complementarity, allowing, for instance, the analysis of the rise of parallel discourses. This means there is a process of cooperation where some tensions may arise.

The convergence intended by the Lisbon Agenda 2000 (Commission of the European Communities, 2001) has influenced the consolidation of the EU dimension in education. The coordination structures and processes provide a *common grammar* (Magalhães, Araújo, Macedo, & Rocha, 2013; Magalhães, Veiga, Ribeiro, Sousa, & Santiago, 2013), which frames the educational reforms, and is based on "governance by 'opinion formation': the capacity of the EU to initiate and influence national discourses about educational issues" (Balzer & Martens, 2004, p. 7) under the influence of opinion-makers and the proliferation of common views. This 'thematic' governance involves not only the content but also the means that provide materiality to the models and concepts to be disseminated as "one of the most powerful modes of governance that are being managed in Europe" with a view to accountability and comparability (Nóvoa, 2002, p. 144).

Comparing education policies across European countries brings to evidence that their pace of implementation and their very nature are diverse and not necessarily converging. However, the *political grammar* that legitimates the reforms enables some degree of convergence, by means of the concepts that are used both nationally and internationally to 'talk' about education. The efficiency of these soft political instruments relies on the fact that they put national reputation under scrutiny. Lack of compliance to the strategic European objectives brings *naming, blaming and shaming* in international comparisons (Araújo, Magalhães, Rocha, & Macedo, 2014).

Still informing the Europe 2020 Strategy (European Commission, 2010), the Lisbon Agenda (Commission of the European Communities, 2001) represented an important landmark as it brought education to the fore in the European agenda in an unprecedented way. The Commission recommended that states commit to a system of goal setting and evaluation processes to assess and compare the performance and achievement of educational objectives (Commission of the European Communities, 2001). ESL was clearly recognised by the Commission as a serious concern. Across countries, the Ministers of Education agreed to reduce the rate to 10% by 2020. The ministers further agreed that the focus should be primarily on schooling and disadvantaged groups, striving to promote successful training for every young person, and supporting their aspirations and capabilities.

EU organisations, platforms and initiatives recommended that member states develop policies addressing ESL. It was further recommended that this effort ought to encompass the incentive to complete secondary education; tighter coordination between general education and vocational training; elimination of barriers blocking the return of early school leavers to education and training; better conditions for lifelong learning; and early identification of youngsters at risk of ESL, amongst other measures. It also included strategies for encouragement of school inclusion; support to students at risk of ESL; enhancement of the quality of education; strong school and educational leadership; adequate teacher training; linking ESL to lifelong learning; and promoting awareness of the advantages of education and training amongst disadvantaged groups (Commission of the European Communities, 2001).

Methodology

This paper relies on the content analysis of official documents and secondary data produced at the European and national levels (Portugal, Sweden and Poland) as well as on the consultation of various stakeholders – altogether, six focus group discussions and 24 individual interviews were organised in three countries. Informants included policy makers; central, regional and local authorities; and experts of various educational and employment institutions. Additionally, in each country, four focus schools were selected in one of the two research areas where interviews with the principals (12) and focus group discussions with school staff (close to 60 participants) took place.

This chapter addresses some results of this research to produce a comparative framework of some of the measures that various institutions implement to confront ESL and of the ways in which each country complies, resists or ignores the European *grammar* and guidelines. With these concerns, the questions already referred to may be rephrased as such: What are the effects of the European policy framework in each country? Are there signs of a *common grammar*? And if this occurs, how is it shaped?

Education and social measures regarding ESL in the three partner countries

Taking the EU concerns and targets into account, this section focuses on the measures implemented in the three partner countries. Since the 2000s, in general, the countries experienced changes with regard to ESL, which may be

50   *Helena C. Araújo et al.*

related to the different position of each member state within the EU. Concerning this matter, the deep financial and economic crisis after 2008 has to be taken into account. Policies designed by local actors to deal with specific and institutional issues related to ESL are considered here.

Portugal

In Portugal, ESL was identified as a political issue early in the 2000s. Considering the ongoing grade repetition and school failure, especially amongst the most disadvantaged groups, ESL remains a social and educational concern despite its reduction from 44.2% in 2001 to 13.7% in 2015. The focus on ESL is common to the preambles and texts of many policy initiatives (e.g. the extension of compulsory education to grade 12, or the age of 18). Research shows that the focus on raising the qualifications of the population has had positive effects, in line with the EU guidelines and in response to the average Portuguese results in international comparative assessments such as the Programme for International Student Assessment (PISA).

Between 2000 and 2010, there was growing investment in education in terms of the attempt of modernisation particularly by means of technological innovation, and Europeanisation as we detail subsequently. In this vein, several educational and social changes reshaped the field of education and paved the way for concern about reducing ESL. Around 2005, there was emphasis on the effectiveness of the extension of compulsory schooling in parallel with measures to consolidate the public school, such as financial support to low-income families, particularly to postpone children's entry into the labour market. Following European educational policy, meaningful examples are: 1) improvement and expansion of upper secondary and post-secondary vocational education and training as well as providing skills for the labour market, by means of partnerships amongst schools, enterprises and other stakeholders; 2) the New Opportunities Programme aimed at adult training and youth education, including certification and recognition of competencies; and 3) modernisation of school facilities.

A milestone in education (in 2009) was the extension of compulsory education up to the age of 18 or the completion of grade 12, which went hand in hand with other political measures targeted at optimising secondary school, reducing dropout rates and increasing young people's skills and qualifications.

Since 2011, the worldwide 'crisis' has had a strong impact on Portugal: increasing economic problems, political instability, volatility of labour, deterioration of quality of life, general impoverishment of the population and a sharp rise in emigration. Budgetary reductions affected the education and training systems, jeopardising the universality and quality of public education, including higher education and scientific research. Tensions between the normative prescription of compulsory schooling and the social and political capacity to ensure its effective universality became increasingly visible. Vocational education has been presented as a 'solution' for low performers in mainstream education, and an early vocational pilot programme was launched in 2012 to provide work skills to students as young as 13 years old (Macedo, Araújo, Magalhães, & Rocha, 2015). Because it segregated 'vulnerable' students at an early age in the vocational track, this programme was abolished in 2016, with the change in the national governance and the greater concern about social and educational inclusion (see Araújo, Macedo, Santos, & Doroftei, forthcoming). There seems to be a clash between political intentions and practice as was argued by some of the respondents:

> EU educational policies related to ESL aim to provide training to young people, and the organisation of different responses with contemplative dimensions; and a qualification that, if they wish, allows them to enter the labour market. . . . I evaluate this type of initiative very positively. However, there is a mismatch between affirming the concern to find solutions to combat ESL and the rationality of the solutions that are in place. From professional courses to vocational courses, which are exemplary in this regard, there is clear concern not to exclude those who have greater difficulties.
> (Director of Vocational Training, Institute of Employment)

Launched in 1996 and currently in its third generation, the Programme Educational Territories of Priority Intervention (TEIP) is a political practice of positive discrimination in school and the community in areas of greater socio-cultural disadvantage to reduce ESL, absenteeism and indiscipline. This programme was picked up and expanded after the EU initiatives, in line with the English model of the Educational Priority Areas, in the 1970s, and the *Zone d'Éducation Prioritaires* (ZEP), in France in the 1980s.

Since 2015, with a socialist government in Portugal, supported by left-wing parties, educational policies have been more focused on equality and inclusion, the learning processes and human development. Amongst several measures already taken, worth mentioning are the abolition of national exams in the fourth and sixth grades, along with substituting assessment in schools that allows for the adoption of compensatory measures, the implementation of conditions for childhood education, and the implementation of the teacher tutor, who is responsible for an holistic support to individual students according to their identified needs. The political intention of implementing students' enrolment in vocational education should also be highlighted, by reducing the stigmatising character of these courses while at the same time making it more attractive to young people.

Trying to comply with the EU knowledge-based economy and highly competitive knowledge society, Portugal followed the EU mandates and somehow used them for re-nationalisation (Musselin & Paradeise, 2009), which recontextualises the European guidelines.

Sweden

Upper secondary school in Sweden, grades 10 to12 (*gymnasium*), is optional and young people can choose whether or not to attend it. Only students between

52 *Helena C. Araújo et al.*

16 and 20 years of age can attend *gymnasium*; those older than 20 have the possibility of completing upper secondary education in 'adult education' (*Komvux*). All education in Sweden is free and is funded entirely by municipal budgets, which are derived from local taxes and the national government's municipal equalisation system. However, regional economic differences and priorities, which affect how much money each municipality can spend per pupil, can vary by as much as 5,300 Euros.

There are different regular national programmes of three years' duration to choose from, some of which are preparatory for tertiary (*academic* and *professional*) education – with 57.3% of total students in the 2015–2016 school year –and others, which are vocational (about 24.2%). Entrance requirements vary between programmes, but all students must earn a pass grade in Swedish, English and Mathematics in their final year of compulsory education (grade 9) to be able to enter a national upper secondary programme. Students who do not qualify for a national programme follow a separate, special programme – an *introductory programme* – after the successful completion of which they can graduate to a national programme. In the 2015–2016 school year (according to statistics published by the National Agency for Education), about 18.5% of pupils [100 − (57.3 + 24.2) = 18.5] participated in these introductory programmes.

Early school leavers are mainly young people from the latter group, those who attend an introductory programme. These pupils study mainly in segregated schools in poor neighbourhoods of Swedish cities.

As our interviews with teachers and school principals indicate, there is social and ethnical segregation of schools, as a consequence of a complex process (Behtoui, 2017a, 2017b). This includes rising income inequality over the previous four decades, together with changes in housing policy in the 1990s – which involved prioritising private housing over rental apartments – that resulted in housing segregation becoming more widespread. Additionally, between 1990 and 1994, a number of educational reforms were carried out. Decentralisation, the shifting of *responsibility for schooling from* central government to the municipalities, is to be highlighted. During the 1980s, the ideological tenets of neoliberalism and the ideals set out in the New Public Management agenda gained ground in education policy (Lundahl, 2002; Lundahl, Arreman, Holm, & Lundström, 2013). As 'freedom of choice' became the overriding principle in official discourses on education, the ethos of equality lost its appeal. Parents were given the right to decide which school their children should attend, and a voucher system was introduced, giving parents the right of choosing between public and private schools (Bunar, 2008). Reforms in the field of education, combined with intensified segregation in the housing market, led to severe socioeconomic and ethnic school segregation, a serious problem for educational outcomes of students in these segregated schools. Nowadays, Sweden's urban landscapes are marked by overlapping patterns of ethnic and economic segregation.

Even though there are many students who do not complete upper secondary schools in Sweden before they are 25 years old (OECD, 2012), as Lundahl, Lindblad, Lovén, Mårald, and Svedberg (2017, p. 39) write, a common

ESL policies in Portugal, Sweden and Poland   53

belief amongst Swedish politicians is that early school leavers "are young people who at some point of time decide to drop out of school". Therefore, ESL up to now has not been a serious political issue and the problem has not been explicitly in focus. Heretofore, the only educational policy for preventing ESL has been concentrated around 'compensatory spending programmes' – that is, spending more amounts of money on highly segregated schools to improve the life chances of the children of poor families (both native-born and children of immigrants). But these measures have had limited success. Extra money in place of more effective measures for desegregation of schools (so that children of lower social strata with less-educated parents are able to attend the schools with middle-class families) has produced no achievement gain for children in these schools (for more detailed explanations see Chapter 13 in this book).

Alternative learning pathways have been more successful in helping early school leavers in Sweden, offering them a way to discover a new educational environment characterised by more flexibility, more mature students and a more diverse student population (see Björklöf & Behtoui, forthcoming). The last proposal announced by the Social Democratic minister of secondary schools (April 2017) to tackle the escalating problem of ESL is the following: The government has directed the National Agency for Education to design shorter occupational packages for students in the introductory programmes to enable them to get a job in the labour market. These occupational packages shall consist of practical courses from national vocational programmes and be planned together with industry representatives who have knowledge of which vocational skills are in demand.

If there has not hitherto been explicit national policy initiatives to prevent or compensate for ESL, there are a number of local initiatives as illustrated by the principal of a vocational upper secondary school in Stockholm:

> In our school the students have many difficulties. . . . Many of them were not able to complete compulsory school; last year, 38% attended the introductory programme, because they lack sufficient knowledge from compulsory school. It is partly because the majority . . . had parents with low socioeconomic status and some of them have different neuropsychiatric diagnoses. Most who completed the compulsory schools chose the vocational programme rather than theoretical . . . they see themselves as failures and feel they cannot handle theoretical studies.

The school referred to has the highest number of teachers per student in Stockholm: more than eight adults per 100 students. A counsellor works 80% of a full work week in this school and student health care is well developed. Classes are small: theoretical subjects contain 20 students at most, and vocational subjects no more than 12. Study plans have been adjusted. The teaching has clear time frames and a definite structure.

There are also a number of other local initiatives outside schools in Stockholm, including alternative learning. One such project is the Youth Centre,

54   *Helena C. Araújo et al.*

assigned to arrange education for youth under 20 years old who do not proceed to upper secondary school or who leave school early (Fischbein & Folkander, 2000). Other projects are designed to help early school leavers carry on with either studies or work. Since 2009, there has been a project called "Youth In" (*Unga In*) in Stockholm, financed by Swedish municipalities and the European Social Fund. Youth In is directed at youth aged 16 to 24 years who neither study nor work. The project attempts to meet them in their own neighbourhoods to motivate and offer them an opportunity to change their situation and either go back to school or find a job.

Regarding the perception of ESL amongst politicians in Sweden, we argue that a common belief is that early school leaving is mainly the result of an individual decision of young people who are tired of school and have no motivation to complete it. About measures to counter this problem, we have mentioned 'compensatory spending programmes', namely extra money to the schools in marginalised areas (but without serious effects), as well as more recent small measures such as 'shorter occupational packages'.

Poland

As a country with one of the lowest ESL rates in Europe, Poland set up its own national goal to decrease its level to 4.5% by 2020. A few years ago, it seemed that Poland would reach this goal without much difficulty, but unlike the rate of persons not in education, employment or training (NEETs), which was three times higher (15.5% in 2015), the national ESL rate remained almost constant throughout the previous decade, oscillating between 5% and 6%. Therefore, some experts hold the opinion that both "the halt in the decrease of the rate in recent years, as well as its very low level in comparison with the EU, may mean that we have approached the real borderline of improvement" (Sysco, 2015, p. 72). The analyses written for the implementation of the European Social Fund are highly optimistic about the necessary tools to tackle ESL that exist in Poland. Some analysts argue that there exists a system of both gathering and analysing data about ESL, which enables monitoring the situation as well as creating targeted policies and an evidence-based framework for such policies (RPO WD, 2014).

However, an analysis of Polish policy documents, reports and academic literature clearly indicates that in Poland, like in the majority of European countries, there is no comprehensive strategy for preventing ESL (GHK, 2011; Tomaszewska-Pękała, Marchlik, & Wrona, 2015). The documents do not refer to this issue in terms of an urgent challenge of the national education or social policies. Some strategies that can be linked to coping with this phenomenon are described in the Lifelong Learning Perspective (LLLP, 2013) and Human Capital Development Strategy 2020 (SRKL, 2013). They stress the development of qualifications and competencies at different stages of life, starting from early childhood, as well as the development of qualifications at different stages of education.

Interestingly, the rationale for the lack of an education policy specifically directed towards ESL is justified by the argument that the main priority is to provide education for all rather than focus on measures addressed to specific at-risk groups, which is somehow different from the dominant European discourse:

> We could teach the EU to put less emphasis on those groups that are already outside the system and vulnerable groups which are almost lost. . . . Better and faster results can be achieved by investing in those who are still at school and do everything so they do not suddenly stop. What saves us is not a high level of services for the ones at risk, but the fact that we have a common system of education for all children.
>
> (Expert from Ministry of National Education)

An incentive for central and regional governments to pay attention to the problem of ESL was created by the implementation of the European Social Fund (ESF), 2014–2020. Following Regulation 1304/2013 (European Parliament and Council, 17 December 2013), the central and regional authorities issued a set of documents regulating the priorities of the ESF allocation. Amongst them is the priority to support labour market instruments and services addressed to people who leave the educational system early (SZOOP POWER, 2016).

Polish education can be called a system 'under construction' as it has been experiencing reforms since 1989, starting from a decentralisation process (1990–1999) and development of non-state education, through various structural reforms. Especially important was the introduction of lower secondary schools in 1999, which expanded the length of the uniform general education curriculum and delayed the selecting of vocational or general education tracks. Other reforms included: curricular reforms, implementation of standardised examinations at the end of primary (abolished in 2016) and lower secondary schools (since 2002, abolished in 2016 as the schools are being phased out), external vocational exams and upper secondary school final examinations (Matura) (since 2005–2006), ending with an unsuccessful reform of lowering the school starting age (2009–2016). Also, the far-reaching reform of vocational and continuing training took place to increase the link with the labour market. Adult vocational and technical supplementary schools gradually closed to be replaced by shorter vocational training schemes, that is, vocational qualification courses.

Internal criticism of the educational system – opposition to the lowering of school age, aversion to external exams that may lead to test-driven education, poor evaluation of the functioning of lower secondary schools – was used in the last election by the current government headed by the conservative Law and Justice party. Currently, since 2016, a reform is being implemented, restoring the structure of education from the period of the Polish People's Republic and introducing a new curriculum at each educational stage.[2] There is "significant uncertainty over the outcomes of this reform. The establishment of lower secondary schools and the resulting extension of common general education to nine school years . . . are often seen as the major reason explaining the significant improvement of PISA results in Poland" (IBE, 2014; see European Commission, 2016). Surprisingly, this improvement did not affect the popular view that Polish schools offered poor education and that the education reforms introduced over the past 15 years were not successful: "This opinion strikingly runs counter to any evidence collected from international and national studies that suggests the opposite — that the lower secondary schools are probably the strongest part of the system. . . . This contradiction between evidence, expert views and the popular opinion is key to understanding the recent proposal for reforms of the present government" (Białecki, Jakubowski, & Wiśniewski, 2017, p. 8).

Elements of the design of the educational system that, according to our interviewees, 'immunise' Poland against a high ESL rate are lack of selectivity, a long cycle of general education, compulsory education until age 18, well-developed second-chance schools, compulsory teacher training, and the prevalence of upper secondary and tertiary education. Institutional solutions also provide support for students with special educational needs or students with behavioural problems. These systemic arrangements — combined with high educational aspirations, the belief in the value of education and its importance for upward social mobility, and the undoubted benefits resulting from holding a higher education diploma — have created a favourable climate for raising the level of education of the Polish society.

Youth with ESL and NEET status in Poland are directly subject to the social sector provisions. The social policy measures aimed at ESL are described in the Plan of Implementation of Youth Guarantee (RGdM, 2016), the main responsible state organisation being Voluntary Labour Corps (VLC). VLC combines second-chance education with work opportunities for its pupils through job placements and partially refunding employers for the cost of employing young people.

Looking at the context of Warsaw, there have been many initiatives directed at the prevention of social and educational exclusion, and indirectly focused on ESL. One example is a large social revitalisation programme (*Blok, podwórko, kamienice — ożywiły się dzielnice*) implemented in one of the districts of Warsaw. It involved various non-governmental organisations working with institutions such as schools, psychological and pedagogical assistance centres, and community centres (Araújo et al., 2014; Marchlik & Tomaszewska-Pękała, 2013).

Contrary to the assumptions and rationale presented by the Ministry of Education expert, the representative of the local administration emphasised the importance of programmes targeting particularly vulnerable groups such as immigrant communities, the Roma community and those at risk of social exclusion. Because the number of foreign and immigrant children in the schools is growing, in cooperation with the Welsh city of Cardiff, Warsaw carried out a project on the integration of immigrant students and their families through education (*Caerdydd – Warsaw Integracja Project*). In addition, there are programmes to prepare teachers to work in a multicultural environment (Araújo et al., 2014; Marchlik & Tomaszewska-Pękała, 2013).

Tendencies, similarities and differences in the three countries

Even if national specificities can be identified in both the countries' pathways and current realities concerning education, in line with the EU 2020 general and country-specific targets and recommendations, all three countries report deep changes in their national educational and training systems. They point to both the emphasis on the articulation between education and labour, in particular through vocational education and training, and the engagement of traditionally more distant stakeholders in education. Concerns about social inclusion can be identified from time to time in each country.

The three countries' socio-political and economic contexts, including their diverse positions within the EU, have accounted for the way in which they managed to implement change in education and training systems. Besides reports of job scarcity, insecurity and low pay affecting young people from particular sub-groups, the countries have been through national socio-political changes.

After experiencing a more conservative approach to education between 2011 and 2015, Portugal has recently changed its political direction and concerns are returning to the political agenda to concentrate on reducing social inequalities and social exclusion through education, even if within strict financial restrictions. Left-wing Swedish political parties aim to combat the extremely segregated school system as the main reason for catastrophic educational outcomes in marginalised neighbourhoods. These parties are part of the government but have no majority in the Swedish parliament. Consequently, many of the suggested reforms (such as making education compulsory up to the age of 18) have been blocked by right-wing and extreme right parties. In Poland, the impact of the new reform introduced at the end 2016 is difficult to predict. The reform has put the focus on returning to the 'classical' system of education, with a strong division between subjects. The establishment of a new kind of two-stage sectorial vocational school allows youngsters to obtain both professional and academic qualifications and to pursue higher education. This can help increase the attractiveness of vocational education.

When looking at the level of local stakeholders, the picture seems more nuanced. The educational concern with youth development and empowerment become more visible and may be explained by the contexts and the relationships of greater or lesser proximity to the practice of the interviewees. Even if the EU influence on ESL policies and measures is neither visible nor recognised by some actors, the soft introduction and development of EU ideas is present in all countries involved where a *common grammar* is identified. There is a widespread view that education is a national responsibility, an idea that may stem from the fact that the EU does not have the power to legislate on

58 *Helena C. Araújo et al.*

education. More or less rhetorical changes were stimulated by the EU and were used even in countries where ESL is not identified as a priority.

Final remarks

The development and implementation of educational policies and political instruments dealing with ESL after the Lisbon Strategy (2000) involve the reconfiguration of educational governance and regulation within the *globally structured agenda for education*. The educational debate has different accents. On the one hand, proponents of non-academic vocational tracks stress that not all pupils want to pursue university and must have the opportunity to attend educational tracks that interest them. This argument maintains that this reform will increase completion rates. Others are critical of this approach, underlining that weaker knowledge in academic subjects decreases the possibility of students continuing on to higher education and reproduces former social inequalities. Europeanisation takes place based on countries' diverse interpretation and implementation of a *common grammar*. This is embodied by means of the national policy and under the framework of programmes of cooperation, support, research and development set by different international organisations and with EU funding, evaluation systems and soft law.

Together with migration processes and labour market volatility, the sociopolitical and economic crisis has reshaped the ways in which different countries address the problem of ESL and try to make the best of EU funding schemes concurrently with the rhetorical resistance to EU ideas and the implementation of their guidance. Taking into account the multiple-scale governance of education as well as the three national specificities, in terms of the educational systemic structure and educational policy and practices, the three countries can learn from one another and provide potential contributions to the European political and intellectual dialogue and learning.

In this paper, in line with the Lisbon Strategy and the Europe 2020 Strategy, the fact that education is seen simultaneously as a factor of economic competition and of social cohesion is brought to the fore. Tensions between social and educational goals and new labour market needs are present in varying degrees. In the vein of the EU guidelines towards social inclusion, educational and social concerns about equality of opportunities and educational development should be the object of wider political debate and implementation policies.

Notes

1 The Portuguese Team acknowledges the relevant contribution of Professor António Magalhães in the analysis of education policies towards ESL.
   The Polish part of this scientific paper was financed from the funds for science in the years 2013–2018 allocated for the international co-financed project.
2 The new reform, which started in 2016, includes the elimination of compulsory schooling for 6-year-olds, the abolition of the exam at the end of primary school, the phasing out of lower secondary schools and their transformation into an eight-year primary school, and the newly established types of secondary schools.

References

Araújo, H. C., Macedo, E., Santos, S., & Doroftei, A. (forthcoming). Tackling early school leaving: Glances of principals in Portuguese upper secondary schools. *European Journal of Education*.

Araújo, H. C., Magalhães, A., Rocha, C., & Macedo, E. (2014). *Policies on early school leaving in nine European countries: A comparative analysis*. Antwerp: University of Antwerp.

Balzer, C., & Martens, K. (2004). *International higher education and the Bologna process: What part does the European Commission play?* Paper presented to the epsNet 2004 Plenary Conference, 18–19 June. Political Science after the EU Enlargement: Challenges to the Discipline. Prague: Charles University.

Behtoui, A. (2017a). Social capital and the educational expectations of young people. *European Educational Research Journal, 16*(4), 487–503.

Behtoui, A. (2017b). *Swedish young people's after-school extra-curricular activities: Attendance, opportunities, and consequences*. Paper presented in 13th Conference of the European Sociological Association. Athens, Greece.

Białecki, I., Jakubowski, M., & Wiśniewski, J. (2017). Education policy in Poland: The impact of PISA (and other international studies). *European Journal of Education, 52*(2), 167–174.

Björklöf, M., & Behtoui, A. (forthcoming). El abandono escolar prematuro en Suecia. In Carrasco, S., Timmerman, Ch., & Pàmies J. (Eds.), *El abandono escolar prematuro en Europa: Realidades, políticas y prácticas desde una perspectiva comparada*. Madrid: Síntesis.

Bunar, N. (2008). The free schools 'riddle': Between traditional social democratic, neo-liberal and multicultural tenets. *Scandinavian Journal of Educational Research, 52*(4), 423–438.

Commission of the European Communities. (2001). *European commission white paper. A new impetus for European youth*. Brussels: Commission of the European Communities. Retrieved from http://ec.europa.eu/youth/documents/publications/whitepaper_en.pdf (accessed on 13.06.2017).

Dale, R. (2007). Globalization and the rescaling of educational governance. In Torres, C. A. & Teodoro, A. (Eds.), *Critique and Utopia: New developments in the sociology of education in the twenty-first century* (pp. 25–42). Plymouth: Rowman & Littlefield Publishers.

Enjolras, B. (2008). Two hypotheses about the emergence of a post-national European model of citizenship. *Citizenship Studies, 12*(5), 495–505.

European Commission. (2010). *Europe 2020: A strategy for smart, sustainable and inclusive growth*. Retrieved from http://ec.europa.eu/eu2020/pdf/COMPLET%20EN%20BARROSO%20%20%20007%20-%20Europe%202020%20-%20EN%20version.pdf

European Commission. (2016). *Education and training monitor 2016 – country analysis, Poland*. Retrieved from https://ec.europa.eu/education/sites/education/files/monitor2016-pl_en.pdf (accessed on 25.04.2017).

Fischbein, S., & Folkander, M. E. (2000). Reading and writing ability and drop out in the Swedish upper secondary school. *European Journal of Special Needs Education, 15*(3), 264–274.

GHK Consulting Ltd. (2011). *Reducing early school leaving in the EU*. Brussels: European Parliament, Directorate General for Internal Policies (Policy Department B: Structural and Cohesion Policies).

Gordon, A., & Stack, T. (2007). Citizenship beyond the state: Thinking with early modern citizenship in the contemporary world. *Citizenship Studies, 11*(2), 117–133.

Hooghe, L., & Marks, G. (2001). *Multi-level governance and European integration*. Lanham: Rowman & Littlefield.

IBE. (2014). *Raport o stanie edukacji 2013. Liczą się nauczyciele* [Report on the State of Education in 2013: Teachers matter]. Warsaw: Educational Research Institute.

60 *Helena C. Araújo et al.*

LLLP. (2013). *Life-long learning perspective.* Warsaw: Ministerstwo Edukacji Narodowej. Retrieved from https://men.gov.pl/wp-content/uploads/2014/01/plll_2013_09_10zal_do_uchwaly_rm.pdf (accessed on 25.04.2017).

Lundahl, L. (2002). Sweden: Decentralization, deregulation, quasi-markets and then what? *Journal of Education Policy, 17*(6), 687–697.

Lundahl, L., Arreman, I. E., Holm, A. S., & Lundström, U. (2013). Educational marketization the Swedish way. *Education Inquiry, 4*(3), 497–517.

Lundahl, L., Lindblad, M., Lovén, A., Mårald, G., & Svedberg, G. (2017). No particular way to go: Careers of young adults lacking upper secondary qualifications. *Journal of Education and Work, 30*(1), 39–52.

Macedo, E., Araújo, H. C., Magalhães, A., & Rocha, C. (2015). La construcción del abandono temprano de la escuela como concepto político: Un análisis en la sociologíde la educación. *Profesorado, Revista de Curriculum y Formación del Profesorado, 19*(3), 28–42.

Magalhães, A., Araújo, H. C., Macedo, E., & Rocha, C. (2015). Early school leaving in Portugal: Policies and actors' interpretation. *Educação, Sociedade e Culturas, 45*, 97–119.

Magalhães, A., Veiga, A., Ribeiro, F. M., Sousa, S., & Santiago, R. (2013). Creating a common grammar for European higher education governance. *Higher Education: The International Journal of Higher Education Research, 65*, 95–112.

Marchlik, P. & Tomaszewska-Pękała, H. (2013). Policy Analysis ESL & Field Description. *Final Report Poland.* WP2–2. Faculty of Education. University of Warsaw.

Musselin, C., & Paradeise, C. (2009). France: From incremental transitions to institutional change. In Paradeise, C., Reale, E., Bleiklie, I., & Ferlie, E. (Eds.), *University governance: Western European comparative perspectives* (pp. 23–49). Dordrecht: Springer.

Nóvoa, A. (2002). Ways of thinking about education in Europe. In Nóvoa, A. & Lawn, M. (Eds.), *Fabricating Europe: The formation of an education space* (pp. 131–155). Dordrecht: Kluwer Academic Publishers.

OECD. (2012). *Equity and quality in education: Supporting disadvantaged students and Schools.* OECD Publishing. Retrieved from http://dx.doi.org/10.1787/9789264130852-en

RGdM. (2016). *Realizacja Gwarancji dla Młodzieży w Polsce w 2015 r.* [Implementation of Youth Guarantee in 2015]. Warsaw: Ministerstwo Rodziny, Pracy i Polityki Społecznej, Departament Rynku Pracy.

RPO WD. (2014). *Regionalny program Operacyjny Województwa Dolnośląskiego 2014–2020* [Regional Operational Programme of Lower Silesia 2014–2020]. Wrocław: Urząd Marszałkowski Województwa Dolnośląskiego.

SRKL. (2013). *Strategia Rozwoju Kapitału Ludzkiego 2020* [Human Capital Development Strategy 2020]. Warsaw: Ministerstwo Pracy i Polityki Społecznej.

Sysco. (2015). *Early school leaving: Monitoring and prevention solutions: Monitoring systems.* Eurocultura, Mazowiecki Kurator Oświaty, Sysco Business Skills Academy, Sysco Polska. Retrieved from www.syscopolska.pl/pliki_ftp/O1_Monitoring%20systems_EN.pdf (accessed on 25.04.2017).

SZOOP POWER. (2016). *Detailed description of the priority axes of the operational program knowledge education development 2014–2020.* Warsaw: Ministerstwo Rozwoju.

Tomaszewska-Pękała, H., Marchlik, P., & Wrona, A. (2015). Between school and work: Vocational education and the policy against early school leaving in Poland. *Educação, Sociedade & Culturas, 45*, 75–98.

4 The individual and economic costs of early school leaving

Marie Gitschthaler and Erna Nairz-Wirth

Introduction

This chapter sheds light on the negative individual and economic costs of early school leaving (ESL). In Europe alone there are currently more than four million early school leavers (European Commission, 2016), that is, young people between the ages of 18 and 24 who have no upper-secondary qualifications and are not enrolled in education and training. Almost 60% of these young people are unemployed and face the risk of becoming socially excluded (EUROSTAT, 2016a).

One of the causes of the increasing exclusion of early school leavers may be seen in relation to the educational expansion, which led to displacement processes both in the educational system and on the labour market. At the same time the demand for unskilled workers is decreasing because of technological progress (e.g. digitization) and the ongoing transition to a knowledge and service economy. The continuing globalization and outsourcing of unskilled tasks to low-wage countries aggravate the situation of early school leavers. While labour market theory often explains this process using the displacement argument, studies show that stigmatization processes also need to be taken into account, for example, the perceptions towards early school leavers as a homogenous group of low-qualified people who are not capable of meeting today's societal and entrepreneurial expectations (Nairz-Wirth, Gitschthaler, & Feldmann, 2014; Nairz-Wirth, 2011; Solga & Kohlrausch, 2013; Solga, 2002). Additionally, the global economic crises have also worsened the situation for many young people, transforming the labour market into an even more precarious field, above all in the lower income segment.

This can be illustrated using Austria and Sweden as examples. Both countries have very low early school leaving rates (Austria: 7.0%, Sweden: 7.5% in 2016) (EUROSTAT, 2016b), yet the risk of exclusion is higher in those countries than the EU average (Nairz-Wirth, Gitschthaler, & Feldmann, 2014; Nairz-Wirth, 2011): while in the EU–15 this risk is on average 1.9 times higher for early school leavers than for people with an upper secondary qualification, it is 2.5 times and 2.9 times higher in Austria and Sweden, respectively (EUROSTAT, 2017).

ESL became one of the key policy targets of the European Union under the Lisbon Strategy 2000. The target aimed at reducing the average ESL rate below

10% by 2010. However, only nine EU member states managed to reach this target in 2010, namely Croatia (5.2%), Austria (8.3%), Slovakia (4.7%), Czech Republic (4.9%), Slovenia (5.0%), Poland (5.4%), Luxembourg (7.1%), Lithuania (7.9%) and Sweden (6.5%). In 2016 the average ESL rate for the EU-28 was still above 10%. This means that the European target has not yet been reached, which is why the demand for a reduction in ESL rates is one of the headline targets of the EU 2020 strategy.

The first part of this chapter provides an overview of the current status of research in this field, which is followed by an overview of the key findings in the research of the costs of ESL, with a focus on the following areas: individual employment and income, public transfer payments, crime, healthcare and economic growth. These parts draw mainly on studies conducted in the United States and Australia, where research on the negative impact of ESL has a long tradition. European studies are still rather rare, mainly because of a lack of available data. A common thread that runs through all the studies is that tremendous costs could be avoided if long-term measures to prevent ESL were sufficiently implemented on multiple levels. The particular need for structural measures is confirmed by cost-benefit analyses, some of which are presented in the last part of this chapter. The chapter concludes with a summary and a brief outlook.

Current status of research into the costs of early school leaving

The most comprehensive study in this field was carried out in the course of a project at the Teachers' College at Columbia University with the title "An excellent education for all of America's children" (Levin et al., 2012; Levin, Belfield, Muennig, & Rouse, 2007). H. M. Levin had already published a study (Levin, 1972) on the high costs of ESL 30 years ago. Even at that time he referred to the huge fiscal and social costs to national economies of inadequate education, which manifest themselves in the form of loss of income, higher transfer payments and higher expenditure in the justice system, as well as reduced political participation and intergenerational mobility. Further notable follow-up studies on this topic include those by the Alliance for Excellent Education (2015) on the theme of "Every child a graduate" for the United States, by Hankivsky (2008) and the Canadian Council on Learning (2009) for Canada and the Allen Consulting Group (2003) for Australia.

In the case of Europe, only a few studies are available to date that are comparable to those mentioned above. Notable country-specific exceptions are provided by Anspal et al. (2011), Bertelsmann Stiftung (2012), Brunello and Paola (2014), Calero and Gil-Izquierdo (2014), and Psacharopoulos (2007). In "The Costs of School Failure – A Feasibility Study", Psacharopoulos (2007) presents a multi-step plan for calculating the costs of inadequate education in Europe. In the spirit of the seminal work by Belfield and Levin (2007), Bertelsmann Stiftung (2012) provides a study on the social costs of inadequate education for Germany. Anspal et al. (2011) calculate the subsequent costs of ESL for income levels, social transfers, the justice system and healthcare in Estonia. Calero and

Individual and economic costs of ESL 63

Table 4.1 Overview of the private, social and fiscal costs of early school leaving

Cost category	Cost element
Private	Higher unemployment incidence
	Higher unemployment duration
	Lower initial and lifetime earnings
	Lower own health status
	Higher own discount rate
	Less risk aversion
	Less lifelong learning participation
	Lower quality of life for children
	Lower life satisfaction
Social	Increased criminality
	Lower positive spill-over effects on co-workers
	Lower rate of economic growth
	Lower intergenerational effects on children and parents
	Lower public health status
	Higher unemployment
	Lower social cohesion
Fiscal	Lower tax revenues
	Higher unemployment and welfare payments
	Higher public health expenditures
	Higher criminal justice expenditure

Source: Psacharopoulos (2007).

Gil-Izquierdo (2014) refer to the additional gross domestic product (GDP) that could be generated in Spain from a reduction in ESL. Brunello and Paola (2014) also present a literature review which focuses on the calculation methods used in international studies.

Table 4.1 provides an overview of the private, social and fiscal costs of ESL. Private costs are tied to the individual and can mostly be observed directly, while social costs affect society and are mostly not observable directly (e.g. a lower social cohesion). Moreover, as Table 4.1 shows, many of these costs may overlap with one another (e.g. unemployment is both a private and a social issue).

In the following sections we describe in more detail some of the key research findings into the costs of ESL, focusing on the following aspects, as mentioned in the introduction to this chapter: employment and income, public transfers, crime, healthcare and economic growth.

Costs of early school leaving for employment and income

The positive correlation between education and personal income is a well-researched topic (e.g. Kiefer, 1985; Levin et al., 2007; OECD, 2016; Rouse, 2007). In OECD member countries, people of working age with an upper secondary level qualification earn one fifth more than those without such a qualification. As expected, people with a tertiary-level qualification earn the most – on average 55% more than those with an upper secondary qualification (OECD, 2016, p. 125). However, a higher level of education not only has an impact on direct income, but also it brings other advantages such as improved working conditions and employer healthcare schemes. Furthermore, economic losses from a lower level of education stem not only from reduced income (personal costs) but also from correspondingly lower income tax revenues for the state (public cost). The study by Rouse (2007) on the "Labor market consequences of an inadequate education" in the United States shows that with an average annual income of USD 12,000, high school dropouts earn 50% less per year than high school graduates (ibid., p. 111), totalling USD 260,000 less than the latter over the course of their lifetimes. For the treasury, this corresponds to loss of income tax revenues of USD 60,000 per dropout (ibid., p. 116). Overall, Rouse concludes, "The combined income and tax losses aggregated over one cohort of 18-year-olds who do not complete high school is more than USD 156 billion, or 1.3 percent of GDP" (2007, p. 120).

Costs of early school leaving for public transfer payments

Early school leavers are more frequently reliant on public transfer payments than their counterparts with a higher level of education. Allmendinger, Giesecke, and Oberschachtsiek (2012) calculate the potential savings for the treasury of a reduction in education poverty based on lost additional revenues (income tax, unemployment contributions) and lost savings (unemployment benefits, transfer payments). Their model reduces the figures for young people who have at best a lower secondary qualification by modelling two scenarios: Scenario I reduces the figures for low-qualified young people by 20 percentage points and Scenario II by 50 percentage points. The calculations show that the potential savings after 35 years are approximately EUR 600 million (for Scenario I) or EUR 1.6 billion (for Scenario II).

Waldfogel, Garfinkel, and Kelly (2007) analyze the reliance of early school leavers in the United States who are single mothers on state transfer payments in relation to their educational level. They calculate the potential savings for three welfare benefits – TANF[1] (Temporary Assistance for Needy Families), "food stamps" and housing assistance – under the assumption that each single mother has at least graduated from high school. Their sample comprised some 10 million single mothers, with non-high school graduates constituting the largest group for all three welfare benefits. Waldfogel et al. (2007) calculated an annual savings potential for TANF, "food stamps" and housing assistance at USD 7.9 billion to USD 10.8 billion, under the premise that all single mothers were high school graduates.

Costs of early school leaving for the justice system

The great bulk of empirical literature focuses on the link between education and the risk of crime (Freeman, 1996; Gilpin & Pennig, 2015; Grogger, 1998;

Individual and economic costs of ESL 65

Lochner & Moretti, 2004; Machin, Olivier, & Sunčica, 2011; Moretti, 2007; Witte & Tauchen, 1994). The most popular approaches to explaining the influence of education on crime can be grouped into three strands: income, time and risk aversion. Although there are types of crime which are linked to a higher level of education ("white collar crime"), statistics show that older and better-educated people commit fewer crimes (Entorf & Sieger, 2012; Lochner, 2004). An explanation for the lower crime rate is that people with higher socioeconomic status (SES) have to contemplate higher opportunity costs in the case of incarceration compared with those in lower income groups (Becker, 1993; Entorf & Sieger, 2012; Freeman, 1996; Grogger, 1998; Lochner & Moretti, 2004; Machin et al., 2011).

A central argument common to such studies is that:

> education and training increase human capital levels and market wage rates, which raises the costs of planning and engaging in crime. Human capital investments also increase the costs associated with incarceration, since they increase the value of any time foregone. The fact that training and learning occur throughout life implies that the opportunity costs of crime should generally rise with age just as they rise with educational attainment.
>
> (Lochner, 2004, p. 811f)

There is also a correlation between crime risk and the "time" factor, whereby it is argued that young people who attend educational institutions have less time to commit crimes (Gilpin & Pennig, 2015; Machin et al., 2011; Tauchen, Witte, & Griesinger, 1994). Another explanation for lower crime rates amongst higher-educated people is that they are considered to be more risk averse, which means that they weigh the possible negative consequences of criminal behaviour for their future (e.g. incarceration, loss of work and social relationships) more heavily than those with low education levels (Entorf & Sieger, 2012; Groot & Van den Brink, 2010).

Except for the studies by Lochner and Moretti (2004) or Machin et al. (2011), little research has been conducted into whether there is a causal link between education and crime (Entorf & Sieger, 2012, p. 75). Indeed, Lochner and Moretti (2004) and Moretti (2007) note that a causal effect of school education on crime is extremely difficult to verify statistically, given the possible spurious correlations:

> persons who grow up in poor, inner-city neighbourhoods may be more likely to drop out of school and at the same time may be more likely to engage in criminal activities. As a result, one might observe a negative correlation between crime and education even if education has no causal effect on crime. In other words, the correlation between education and crime might be causal but might simply reflect the influence of disadvantaged family background, bad peer influence, and poverty in general.
>
> (Moretti, 2007, p. 143)

Entorf and Sieger (2012) call attention to the possible influence of other relevant factors such as unemployment, financial situation, debts, personal maturity, acceptance of rules, drug/alcohol abuse and social relationships on engagement in criminal activities.

A negative correlation exists between an increase in the length of compulsory education and incarceration rates (Entorf & Sieger, 2012; Lochner & Moretti, 2004; Machin et al., 2011). In an empirical analysis for Great Britain, Machin et al. (2011) use the increase in the school leaving age from 15 to 16 years in England and Wales in 1972 to demonstrate the potential of education to reduce crime. This rise in the school leaving age by just one year significantly reduced the number of property crimes. The authors even suggest a robust causal statistical influence of education on property crimes, which account for around 70% of all crimes. Entorf and Sieger (2012, p. 73f.) draw similar conclusions for Germany. They use the composition of the prison population to demonstrate that a large proportion of violent crimes (e.g. robbery, assault, murder) and property crimes (e.g. burglary, larceny, murder) are committed by people with a low level of education. Specifically, an analysis of the prison population by level of education shows that 46% have only completed lower secondary education and 17% have no lower secondary education at all. The percentage of inmates who did not complete lower secondary education is particularly high (25%) amongst those convicted of criminal assault or theft.

Lochner and Moretti (2004) and Moretti (2007) analyze the economic costs of crime by male Americans based on level of education. In particular, they calculate a potential savings for the justice system of a 1% rise in the high school graduation rate in a study group of 20- to 60-year-olds. These calculations indicate an annual savings potential of more than USD 1.4 billion (Moretti, 2007, p. 155).

Machin et al. (2011) estimate the net savings potential for Great Britain's justice system of a 1% reduction in the share of people with no school qualifications at GBP 23 to 30 million over a ten-year period. Anspal et al. (2011, p. 73) calculate an annual savings potential for Estonia of EUR 1.4 million to EUR 2 million if the share of people having only compulsory-level schooling were to be halved.

It should be noted here that studies of the crime risk of early school leavers could lead to further stigmatization of this group. It therefore cannot be stressed often enough that these studies merely show that there is a higher risk of members of this group engaging in criminal activities given their frequently multi-causal problems. Furthermore, "white collar crime" (synonymous with economic crimes), which calls for a higher level of education, is a topic that is often ignored in research (Lochner, 2004).

Costs of early school leaving for healthcare

Better-educated individuals have a higher life expectancy because of a higher chance of practicing a healthy lifestyle. Research shows that people with upper-secondary education certificates live approximately six to nine years longer than early school leavers (Chetty, Stephner, & Cutler, 2016). Another reason that explains this fact is that wealthier people face a lower risk of suffering from illness or disability in a variety of forms.

The link between education and health is often generally described as follows: Higher education leads to better social participation (e.g. labour market integration and income), which in turn effects health-related resources such as living conditions (e.g. housing) and health-related behaviour (e.g. smoking) (Cutler, Huang, & Lleras-Muney, 2015; Feinstein, Sabates, Anderson, Sorhaindo, & Hammond, 2006; Mielck, Lüngen, Siegel, & Korber, 2012). Numerous empirical studies refer to the interdependencies between SES, living conditions and health-related behaviour, which make it difficult for researchers to define cause-effect relationships in empirical models (Chetty et al., 2016; Feinstein et al., 2006; Mielck et al., 2012).

A handful of studies faced this challenge and explored the individual and economic costs of ESL for the health sector. A study in the United States (Muennig, 2007) analyses healthcare expenditure according to education level ("high school dropouts", "high school graduates" and "college graduates"). We calculate that each additional high school graduate yields $39,000 of savings in lifetime government health insurance costs (Muennig, 2007, p. 136). For Estonia, Anspal et al. (2011, p. 37) calculate healthcare savings of EUR 53.4 million if the ESL rate for 2011 were halved.

The influence of education and income levels on life expectancy is well documented – for example, studies for the United States by Chetty et al. (2016), Meara, Richards, and Cutler (2008), and Pijoan-Mas and Rios-Rull (2014), and for Europe by Avendano et al. (2010), Boháček, Crespo, and Mira (2015), and Majer, Nussfelder, Mackenbach, and Kunst (2011). Boháček et al. (2015) show significant differences in life expectancy depending on education level and location in Europe for people over age 50. This difference is highest in Eastern European countries. In Estonia, for example, the difference in life expectancies of people with upper secondary and lower secondary education is 8.4 years. The lowest difference is found in Northern Europe (e.g. 1.4 years in Denmark).

Costs of early school leaving for the economy

All calculations of the economic costs of ESL are guided by the basic concept of endogenous growth theory, namely that high human capital creates innovations in the form of new technologies and ideas and thus stimulates economic growth (Barro, 2001; Bills & Klenow, 2000; Krueger & Lindahl, 2001). The OECD study on *The High Cost of Low Educational Performance* (Hanushek & Wößmann, 2010) also estimates loss in economic growth through inadequate education. The scenarios used in the study estimate the economic effects of an average rise in PISA scores (by just 25 points). Based on the assumption that no education reform is carried out, France would realize a GDP of USD 3,638 billion in 2042. Were France to succeed in raising its PISA score, its GDP forecast for the same year would rise by USD 111 billion, that is, by approximately 3%. The effects of better education in the present therefore extend well into the future. Translated to all OECD countries, the authors (Hanushek & Wößmann, 2010, p. 24) forecast a rise in GDP of USD 115 billion by 2090.

A study carried out for Spain (Calero & Gil-Izquierdo, 2014) simulates the effect of a total prevention of ESL on economic growth. The calculations cover a 20-year period and indicate a rise in GDP of up to 17%. Based on data for 2013, the Alliance for Excellent Education (2015) likewise estimates a potential annual increase in GDP of up to USD 11.5 billion for the United States had a high school graduation rate of 90% been achieved in that year, that is, if 610,000 more students had graduated from high school.

Early school leaving: cost–benefit analysis

Discussions on the urgency of education reforms feature regularly in education science and policy publications in the European Union. One aspect which is often highlighted is the fact that even small reforms in the educational system can have significant economic effects. The cost-benefit analyses presented show that selective reforms such as improvements in early childhood education and care, parental involvement and school-community programmes are particularly effective.

Prime examples here include the High/Scope Perry Preschool Program launched in 1962 in Ypsilanti, Michigan, with 123 Afro-American children from socially disadvantaged families. The goal was to break down the link between poverty and ESL by improving the conditions for cognitive, socio-emotional and physical development. This should also serve to reduce problems such as delinquency, poverty or teenage pregnancy. Calculations show that the benefits far exceed the costs – often by a factor of seven to 12 (Belfield, Nores, Barnett, & Schweinhart, 2006; Heckman, Moon, Pinto, Savelyev, Yavitz, 2010; Temple & Reynolds, 2015). Another preschool programme that receives equally positive assessments is the Chicago Child-Parent Center. Founded in 1967, the programme focuses in particular on parental involvement, outreach measures and health/nutrition services. Calculations for the preschool sector show a cost-benefit ratio of USD 11 per USD 1 invested in the programme (Reynolds et al., 2011; Temple & Reynolds, 2015). These benefits would result above all from the reduced need for placement in special education programmes, secondary education retention, more students graduating from high school and reductions in both juvenile and adult crime rates (Temple & Reynolds, 2015).

Building effective relationships between schools and the community (school-community ties) is considered as important for the quality of learning. Thus, people (e.g. volunteers) and organizations (e.g. non-governmental organizations) from the regional community are involved in many recognized ESL prevention programmes and are encouraged to participate in improving the school situation and thus indirectly the development of the region (Downes, Nairz-Wirth, & Rusinaite, 2017; Fiore, 2011; Mac Iver & Mac Iver, 2009).

Individual and economic costs of ESL 69

One such particularly comprehensive programme is City Connects. The programme, which aims to assist both students and schools alike, was launched in 1999 and is currently offered at 25 elementary and middle schools in six U.S. states. Students who participate in the scheme are provided with access to an individualized set of services designed to support their needs from the learning, social, emotional, family and health perspectives. At a school level, the City Connects programme establishes connections between schools and various community agencies and service providers. It also helps to ensure that students receive more targeted and efficient learning support by streamlining the corresponding referral and management processes. A cost-benefit analysis for Boston shows that social benefits of USD 3 are achieved for every USD 1 invested (Bowden et al., 2015).

The tutoring programs that have been in place in many schools in the English-speaking world for decades are also considered to be particularly effective when it comes to reducing early leaving. Evaluations show that tutoring (by specially trained students) triggers a significant rise in performance and improvement in motivation amongst low-performance students (Downes et al., 2017; National Dropout Prevention Center, 2017; Ritter, Barnett, Denny, & Albin, 2009). A particularly well-evaluated tutoring programme implemented in the United States to improve the reading skills of pre-school and elementary-school children is provided by the non-profit organization Reading Partners. In this programme, volunteer tutors donate a few hours of their time each week to help young children with reading difficulties. A cost study shows that the programme costs USD 3,610 per student, of which only 20% has to be covered by the schools. The remaining costs are borne by the volunteers and by the Reading Partners non-profit organization (Jacob, Armstrong, Willard, Bowden, & Pan, 2015).

Another key factor in determining student performance and therefore also the risk of ESL is teacher quality (Brunello & Paola, 2014). Teachers, school leaders and other educational staff are key actors in the implementation process of school reforms. A precondition for this is, however, that these actors are highly professionalized and supported for creating inclusive learning environments (Barile et al., 2012; Nairz-Wirth & Feldmann, 2017).

The programmes described earlier represent just a selection of many good practices. A deciding factor in their selection as examples was the very good results accorded to them by evaluation studies. For many such measures, no such data are available – often for cost reasons. At a European level, a variety of programmes evaluated on a smaller scale are included in the European Toolkit for Schools. A similar platform for the United States is the National Dropout Prevention Center.

Prevention matters: summary and outlook

This article illustrated the enormous costs of ESL for both individuals and society as a whole. Most of the studies presented were conducted in the United

States and Australia, where research in this field has a much longer tradition than in Europe. An increasing amount of research is being conducted on the costs of ESL in Europe, which is mainly inspired by the seminal work of H. M. Levin. But comparative studies are still rare for Europe because of the lack of both a standardized European definition of poor education and adequate data (e.g. health sector).

All studies presented in this article are based on estimates and forecasts for specific countries, and therefore cannot be transferred easily to other countries. Furthermore, forecasting labour market and economic trends always comes with a certain level of uncertainty. Nonetheless, with all due caution and scepticism towards such calculations, the individual and economic costs of a misguided education policy cannot be underestimated. Indeed, all the studies mentioned in this article confirm the link between education and various indicators such as personal income, income tax, public transfers, crime risk, health and GDP. Nevertheless, there are also intangible and non-material costs (e.g. social isolation, stigmatization), which are very difficult to compute in monetary terms, but which should be taken into account (Hankivsky, 2008; Nairz-Wirth et al., 2014; Nairz-Wirth, 2011).

Research shows that ESL could best be tackled by supporting disadvantaged families and communities and by implementing long-term scientifically supported prevention and intervention programmes in kindergartens and schools. The section on cost-benefit analysis clearly illustrates that long-term benefits of prevention/intervention measures (such as high-quality preschool education) are seven to 12 times more effective and less cost-intensive than programmes that are implemented at a later stage of education.

Last, but by no means least, we stress that it is not just about reducing ESL and the costs entailed. The whole issue needs to be understood in its full impact on the different spheres of social life. It is apparent that inadequate integration of young people into the education and employment systems entails a number of socio-political challenges. Recent data show that ESL now stands at 10.7% in the EU. There are still more than 4.4 million early school leavers across Europe, and about 60% of these are either inactive or unemployed, which means a reproduction of social inequalities, a threat to social cohesion, and less confidence in society and its institutions (Council & Commission of the European Union, 2015). For young people themselves ESL negatively affects their chances to live a self-determined life and to realize personal, educational and career aspirations (Nussbaum, 2006).

Note

1 TANF was introduced in the 1990s to help needy families (two thirds of whom are single mothers) achieve self-sufficiency. The qualification criteria and amounts received are determined individually at the state level (see www.acf.hhs.gov/programs/ofa/tanf/about.html).

References

Allen Consulting Group. (2003). *The economy-wide benefits of increasing the proportion of students achieving year 12 equivalent education: Modelling results.* Sydney: Australia: Allen Consulting Group.

Alliance for Excellent Education. (2015). *The economic benefits of increasing the high school graduation rate for public school students in the United States of America.* Retrieved from http://impact.all4ed.org/#national/increased-investment/all-students

Allmendinger, J., Giesecke, J., & Oberschachtsiek, D. (2012). Folgekosten unzureichender Bildung für die öffentlichen Haushalte. In Bertelsmann Stiftung (Ed.), *Warum sparen in der Bildung teuer ist: Folgekosten unzureichender Bildung für die Gesellschaft* (pp. 39–72). Gütersloh: Verlag Bertelsmann Stiftung.

Anspal, S., Järve, J., Kallaste, E., Kraut, L., Räis, M-L., & Seppo, I. (2011). *The cost of school failure in Estonia.* Retrieved from www.centar.ee/uus/wp-content/uploads/2011/03/2012.03.29-Cost-of-school-failure-in-Estonia-final-technical.pdf

Avendano, M., Kok, R., Glymour, M., Berkman, L., Kawachi, I., Kunst, A., & Mackenbach, J. (2010). Do Americans have higher mortality than Europeans at all levels of the education distribution? In Crimmins, E. M., Preston, S. H., & Cohen, B. (Eds.), *International differences in mortality at older ages: Dimensions and sources* (pp. 313–332). Washington, DC: The National Academies Press.

Barile, J. P., Donohue, D. K., Anthony, E. R., Baker, A. M., Weaver, S. R., & Christopher, C. H. (2012). Teacher–student relationship climate and school outcomes: Implications for educational policy initiatives. *Journal of Youth and Adolescence, 41*(3), 256–267.

Barro, R. J. (2001). Human capital and growth. *The American Economic Review, 91*(2), 12–17.

Becker, G. S. (1993). *Ökonomische Erklärung menschlichen Verhaltens.* Tübingen: Mohr Verlag.

Belfield, C. R., & Levin, H. M. (Eds.) (2007). *The price we pay: Economic and social consequences of inadequate education.* Washington, DC: Brookings Institution Press.

Belfield, C. R., Nores, M., Barnett, S., & Schweinhart, L. (2006). The high/scope perry pre-school program: Cost-benefit analysis using data from the age-40 follow-up. *The Journal of Human Resources, 41*(1), 162–190.

Bertelsmann Stiftung. (Ed.) (2012). *Warum sparen in der Bildung teuer ist: Folgekosten unzureichender Bildung für die Gesellschaft.* Gütersloh: Verlag Bertelsmann Stiftung.

Bills, M., & Klenow, P. J. (2000). Does schooling cause growth? *American Economic Review, 90*(5), 1160–1183.

Boháček, R., Crespo, L., & Mira, P. (2015). *The educational gradient in life expectancy in Europe: Preliminary evidence from SHARE.* Retrieved from www.cemfi.es/~pijoan/Work_in_Progress_files/FRB_12.pdf

Bowden, A. B., Belfield, C. R., Levin, H. M., Shand, R., Wang, A., & Morales, M. (2015). *A Benefit-cost analysis of city connects.* Retrieved from http://cbcse.org/wordpress/wp-content/uploads/2015/08/CityConnects.pdf

Brunello, G., & Paola, M. (2014). The costs of early school leaving in Europe. *IZA Journal of Labor Policy, 3*(22).

Calero, J., & Gil-Izquierdo, M. (2014). Too much to pay: An estimation through micro-simulation techniques of the monetary costs of early school leaving in Spain. *Journal of Simulation, 8*(4), 314–324.

Canadian Council on Learning. (2009). *No 'drop' in the bucket: The high costs of dropping out. Canadian Council on Learning.* Toronto. Retrieved from http://en.copian.ca/library/research/ccl/lessons_learning/no_drop_bucket/no_drop_bucket.pdf

Chetty, R., Stepner, M., Abraham, S., Lin, S., Scuderi, B., Turner, N., . . . Cutler, D. (2016). The association between income and life expectancy in the United States, 2001–2014. *Journal of the American Medical Association, 315*(16), 1750–1766.

Chetty, R., Stepner, M., & Cutler, D. (2016). Relationships between income, health behaviors, and life expectancy-reply. *Journal of the American Medical Association, 316*(8), 880–881.

Council and Commission of the European Union. (2015). *Joint Report of the Council and the Commission on the implementation of the strategic framework for European cooperation in education and training (ET 2020)*. New priorities for European cooperation in education and training, (2015/C 417/04). Retrieved from http://eur-lex.europa.eu/legal-content/EN/TXT/HTML/?uri=CELEX:52015XG1215%2802%29&from=EN

Cutler, D. M., Huang, W., & Lleras-Muney, A. (2015). When does education matter? The protective effect of education for cohorts graduating in bad times. *Social Science & Medicine, 127*, 63–73.

Downes, P., Nairz-Wirth, E., & Rusinaitė, V. (2017). *Structural indicators for inclusive systems in and around Schools*, NESET II report. Luxembourg: Publications Office of the European Union.

Entorf, H., & Sieger, P. (2012). Unzureichende Bildung: Folgekosten durch Kriminalität. In Bertelsmann Stiftung (Ed.), *Warum sparen in der Bildung teuer ist: Folgekosten unzureichender Bildung für die Gesellschaft* (pp. 73–104). Gütersloh: Verlag Bertelsmann Stiftung.

European Commission. (2016). *European semester thematic Fiche early Leavers from education and training*. Brussels. Retrieved from http://ec.europa.eu/europe2020/pdf/themes/2016/early_leavers_education_training_201605.pdf

EUROSTAT. (2016a). *Education and training in the EU – facts and figures: Distribution of early leavers from education and training by labour status, 2015*. Retrieved from http://ec.europa.eu/eurostat/statistics-explained/images/0/0c/Early_leavers_from_education_and_training_statistics_ET2016_08_09.xlsx

EUROSTAT. (2016b). *Frühzeitige Schul- und Ausbildungsabgänger: Anteil der Bevölkerung zwischen 18 und 24 Jahren, der höchstens die Sekundarstufe durchlaufen hat und keine weitere allgemeine oder berufliche Bildung erfahren hat*. Retrieved from http://ec.europa.eu/eurostat/tgm/mapToolClosed.do?tab=map&init=1&plugin=1&language=de&pcode=t2020_40&toolbox=types

EUROSTAT. (2017). *Unemployment rates by sex, age and highest level of education attained*. Retrieved from http://appsso.eurostat.ec.europa.eu/nui/submitViewTableAction.do

Feinstein, L., Sabates, R., Anderson, T. M., Sorhaindo, A., & Hammond, C. (2006). What are the effects of education on health? In OECD, Centre for Educational Research and Innovation (Ed.), *Measuring the effects of education on health and civic engagement proceedings of the Copenhagen symposium* (pp. 171–313). Paris: OECD Publishing.

Fiore, D. J. (2011). *School-community relations*. Larchmont, NY: Eye on Education.

Freeman, R. (1996). Why do so many young American men commit crimes and what might we do about it? *Journal of Economic Perspectives, 10*(1), 25–42.

Gilpin, G. A., & Pennig, L. A. (2015). Compulsory schooling laws and school crime. *Applied Economics, 47*(38), 4056–4073.

Grogger, J. (1998). Market wages and youth crime. *Journal of Labor Economics, 16*(4), 756–791.

Groot, W., & Van den Brink, H. M. (2010). The effects of education on crime. *Applied Economics, 42*(3), 279–289.

Hankivsky, O. (2008). *Cost estimates of dropping out of high school in Canada*. Canadian Council on Learning. Simon Fraser University. Retrieved from www.ccl-cca.ca/pdfs/Other Reports/CostofdroppingoutHankivskyFinalReport.pdf

Individual and economic costs of ESL   73

Hanushek, E. A., & Wößmann, L. (2010). *The high cost of low educational performance: The long-run economic impact of improving PISA outcomes.* Paris: OECD Publishing. Retrieved from www.oecd.org/edu/school/programmeforinternationalstudentassessmentpisa/thehigh costofloweducationalperformance.htm

Heckman, J. J., Moon, S. H., Pinto, R., Savelyev, P. A., & Yavitz, A. (2010). The rate of return to the high scope Perry preschool program. *Journal of Public Economics, 94*(1–2), 114–128.

Jacob, R. T., Armstrong, C., Willard, J., Bowden, B., & Pan, Y. (2015). *Mobilizing volunteer tutors to improve student literacy: Implementation, impacts, and costs of the reading partners program.* Retrieved from www.mdrc.org/publication/mobilizing-volunteer-tutors-improve-student-literacy

Kiefer, N. M. (1985). Evidence on the role of education in labor turnover. *The Journal of Human Resources, 20*(3), 445–452. Retrieved from www.jstor.org/stable/145895

Krueger, A. B., & Lindahl, M. (2001). Education for growth: Why and for whom? *Journal of Economic Literature, 39*(4), 1101–1136.

Levin, H. M. (1972). *The costs to the nation of inadequate education: A report for the select committee on equal educational opportunity, U.S. senate.* Washington, DC: U.S. Government Printing Office.

Levin, H. M., Belfield, C., Hollands, F., Bowden, A. B., Cheng, H., Shand, R., . . . Hanisch-Cerda, B. (2012). *Cost-effectiveness analysis of interventions that improve high school completion.* Center for Benefit-Cost Studies of Education Teachers College, Columbia University. Retrieved from http://citeseerx.ist.psu.edu/viewdoc/download?doi=10.1.1.437.742&rep=rep1&type=pdf

Levin, H. M., Beldfield, C., Muennig, P., & Rouse, C. (2007). *The costs and benefits of an excellent education for all of America's children.* Teachers College, Columbia University. New York. Retrieved from https://academiccommons.columbia.edu/catalog/ac:204241

Lochner, L. (2004). Education, work, and crime: A human capital approach. *International Economic Review, 45*(3), 811–843.

Lochner, L., & Moretti, E. (2004). The effect of education on crime: Evidence from prison inmates, arrests, and self-reports. *The American Economic Review, 94*(1), 155–189.

Machin, S., Olivier, M., & Sunčica, V. (2011). The crime reducing effect of education. *The Economic Journal, 121*(552), 463–484.

Mac Iver, M. A., & Mac Iver, D. J. (2009). *Beyond the indicators: An integrated school level approach to dropout prevention.* Mid-Atlantic Equity Center. The George Washington University Center for Equity and Excellence in Education. Arlington. Retrieved from http://diplomasnow.org/wp-content/uploads/2013/06/dropout-report-8-11-09.pdf

Majer, I., Nussfelder, W., Mackenbach, J., & Kunst, A. (2011). Socioeconomic inequalities in life and health expectancies around official retirement age in 10 Western-European countries. *Journal of Epidemiology and Community Health, 65*(11), 972–979.

Meara, E. R., Richards, S., & Cutler, D. M. (2008). The gap gets bigger: Changes in mortality and life expectancy, by education, 1981–2000. *Health Affairs, 27*(2), 350–360.

Mielck, A., Lüngen, M., Siegel, M., & Korber, K. (2012). Folgen unzureichender Bildung im Bereich Gesundheit. In Bertelsmann Stiftung (Ed.), *Warum sparen in der Bildung teuer ist. Folgekosten unzureichender Bildung für die Gesellschaft* (pp. 133–170). Gütersloh: Verlag Bertelsmann Stiftung.

Moretti, E. (2007). Crime and the costs of criminal justice. In Belfield, C. R. & Levin, H. M. (Eds.), *The price we pay: Economic and social consequences of inadequate education* (pp. 142–159). Washington, DC: Brookings Institution Press.

Muennig, P. (2007). Consequences in health status and costs. In Belfield, C. R. & Levin, H. M. (Eds.), *The price we pay: Economic and social consequences of inadequate education* (pp. 125–141). Washington, DC: Brookings Institution Press.

Nairz-Wirth, E. (2011). Early school leaving: Stigma and diversity. *Diversitas*, (1), 41–48.

Nairz-Wirth, E., & Feldmann, K. (2017). Teachers' views on the impact of teacher – student relationships on school dropout: A Bourdieusian analysis of misrecognition. *Pedagogy, Culture & Society*, *25*(1), 121–136.

Nairz-Wirth, E., Gitschthaler, M., Feldmann, K. (2014). *Quo Vadis Bildung? Eine qualitative Längsschnittstudie zum Habitus von early school leavers*. Abteilung für Bildungswissenschaft, Wirtschaftsuniversität Wien. Retrieved from www.wu.ac.at/fileadmin/wu/d/i/bildung swissenschaft/Forschung/Publikationen/quovadis2010.pdf

National Dropout Prevention Center. (2017). *The 15 effective strategies for dropout prevention online courses: Mentoring/tutoring*. Clemson, SC: National Dropout Prevention Center.

Nussbaum, M. (2006). *Frontiers of justice: Disability, nationality, species membership*. Cambridge, London: Belknap.

OECD. (2016). *Education at a glance 2016: OECD indicators*. Paris: OECD Publishing.

Pijoan-Mas, J., & Rios-Rull, J. V. (2014). Heterogeneity in expected longevities. *Demography*, *51*(6), 2075–2102.

Psacharopoulos, G. (2007). *The costs of school failure – a feasibility study: European commission*. European Expert Network on Economics of Education. Retrieved from http://cesifo gruppe.info/fr/dms/EENEE/Analytical_Reports/EENEE_AR2.pdf

Reynolds, A. J., Temple, J. A., White, B. A., Ou, S-R., & Robertson, D. L. (2011). Age 26 cost-benefit analysis of the child-parent center early education program. *Child Development*, *82*(1), 379–404.

Ritter, G. W., Barnett, J. H., Denny, G. S., & Albin, G. R. (2009). The effectiveness of volunteer tutoring programs for elementary and middle school students: A meta-analysis. *Review of Educational Research*, *79*(1), 3–38.

Rouse, C. E. (2007). Consequences for the labor market. In Belfield, C. R. & Levin, H. M. (Eds.), *The price we pay: Economic and social consequences of inadequate education* (pp. 99–124). Washington, DC: Brookings Institution Press.

Solga, H. (2002). 'Stigmatization by negative selection': Explaining less-educated people's decreasing employment opportunities. *European Sociological Review*, *18*(2), 159–178.

Solga, H., & Kohlrausch, B. (2013). How low-achieving German youth beat the odds and gain access to vocational training – insights from within-group variation. *European Sociological Review*, *29*(5), 1068–1082.

Tauchen, H., Witte, A. D., & Griesinger, H. (1994). Criminal deterrence: Revisiting the issue with a birth cohort. *Review of Economics and Statistics*, *76*(3), 399–412.

Temple, J. A., & Reynolds, A. J. (2015). Using benefit-cost analysis to scale up early childhood programs through pay-for-success financing. *Journal of Benefit-Cost Analysis*, *6*(3), 628–653.

Waldfogel, J., Garfinkel, E., & Kelly, B. (2007). Welfare and the costs of public assistance. In Belfield, C. R. & Levin, H. M. (Eds.), *The price we pay: Economic and social consequences of inadequate education* (pp. 160–174). Washington, DC: Brookings Institution Press.

Witte, A. D., & Tauchen, H. (1994). *Work and crime: An exploration using panel data*. Working Paper No. 4794. National Bureau of Economic Research. Cambridge, MA. Retrieved from www.nber.org/papers/w4794

Part II

Youngsters' perspectives on early school leaving and schooling

5 A narrative approach exploring youngsters' experiences of schooling and leaving school early in Flanders (Belgium)

The stories of Simon and Karim

Rut Van Caudenberg, Noel Clycq and Christiane Timmerman

Introduction

"*Just, like, during the summer holiday*", Simon, a 21-year-old middle-class youngster of native Flemish origin, tells us during our RESL.eu-fieldwork in 2015 when we ask him when he left mainstream secondary education. "*Because I had a C-certificate* [grade retention] *again, and then I decided to go to adult education*", he continues, "*my parents were like 'that's also a possibility'. I had never really considered it and then we looked into it together, and it seemed interesting. At school they hadn't really given me many tips about what I could do; they said 'just repeat the year'. I could have done that, but that's what they'd already told me every year.*" A few weeks later we interview Karim, a 21-year-old working-class youngster of Moroccan origin. When we ask him the same question, he starts to recount how he had already repeated his sixth year after failing six courses even though a schoolmate who failed five courses was allowed to pass onto the next year. "*I accepted that*", he says, "*so then I repeated my year. At the end of the school year I failed two courses, and yet they gave me a C-certificate* [grade retention] *again. That's when I tried to challenge it. It didn't work. I had no more motivation to go on. I'm 21 years old! I thought to myself, 'I'm not going to keep repeating the sixth year'. So I thought, 'well, I'm going to quit and I'm going to the examination commission* [system of self-study but with formal qualification]'. *That was the only option left actually.*"

When reflecting on the moment they left school early, Simon and Karim show a significant similarity in that they both refer to being confronted with grade retention at multiple times in their educational trajectory as an important trigger for their decision to leave school. In that sense, these accounts speak to a common finding that grade retention is an important predictor of early school leaving (ESL) (Lamote et al., 2013). At the same time, however, when looking at the way both youngsters interpret receiving this 'C-certificate' and how they react to it, the accounts suggest a more complex reality. Simon left secondary education after receiving a C-certificate while at the same time enrolling in adult education. While he believes staying in mainstream education and repeating the year was also an option, following his parents' advice to change to (non-mainstream) adult education seemed like a more '*interesting*' alternative. Karim, on the other hand, did not think he deserved the C-certificate and had '*no more motivation*' to continue. He envisioned a situation of endless grade repetition and did not see another option than leaving school and going to the examination commission, where he could obtain his diploma via a system of self-study. Why is it that these two youngsters experience a similar event, namely being confronted with grade retention in the form of a C-certificate, in such different ways? And what do these divergent experiences reveal about how youngsters' social position in the socially and ethnically stratified Flemish education system shapes their understanding of schooling and leaving school early?

In this chapter, we address these questions by digging deeper into the school narratives of Simon and Karim, two youngsters categorized as early school leavers, not having obtained their ISCED 3–level qualification of upper secondary education. We foreground the voices of these youngsters, thereby giving legitimacy to the experiences and unique points of view of those who – despite the growing attention to and large body of research on early school leaving – still remain largely absent in policy and research debates (Clandinin et al., 2010; Smyth & Hattam, 2004). It is not our intent to represent the stories told by the two boys as typical or representative of the 11% of early school leavers in Flanders (Belgium) (Flemish Ministry of Education and Training, 2017), nor do we consider them as specific or contradicting archetypes of 'early school leavers'. Instead, we argue that listening carefully to the individual stories of these youngsters when they make sense of schooling provides us with a window through which to look at "the intersection of personal life, social institutions and social structure" (Laslett, 1999, p. 400). Looking into the schooling experiences of youngsters who left school early allows us to explore what it means for them to be in school, and can lead to a more detailed understanding of what is happening when they (choose to) leave school early (see e.g. Smyth & Hattam, 2004; Gallagher, 2002; Hodgson, 2007). As schooling experiences are co-constructed within social settings that are characterized by particular relationships, hierarchies of power and status, and specific rules and normative practices (Brown & Rodriguez, 2009), an in-depth exploration of the youngsters' narratives may reveal how these issues play out (differently) and shape their relationship with school and education more generally. Furthermore, by comparing the narratives of two youngsters who speak from different locations in terms of their migration background, socioeconomic status and educational trajectory, we can learn about the diversity and complexity of the phenomenon of ESL, thereby moving beyond overly generalized and stereotypical understandings of the 'early school leaver'. Before turning to the stories of Simon and Karim, we first briefly describe the broader educational context in which these narratives emerge.

Situating the narratives: social and ethnic stratification, educational inequality and early school leaving in the Flemish education system

In Flanders, compulsory education starts at the age of 6 and ends at the age of 18. Although there exists the possibility of home schooling, in practice nearly all children and young people receive their education in formal educational settings; consequently, schools take up a central place in their lives. Overall, education is highly valued, and being successful in education is considered necessary to become successful in the labour market and in one's personal life (Clycq, Nouwen, & Vandenbroucke, 2014). The dominant narrative of Flemish education suggests that it is a democratic, meritocratic and neutral system of equal access and opportunity. Yet, research continuously shows that strong social and ethnic stratification processes have an important influence on students' educational trajectories and negatively impact specific social groups, in particular those whose backgrounds do not fit with the Flemish native middle class whose norms and culture are commonly reflected in school policies, practices and curriculum (see e.g. Groenez, Nicaise, & De Rick, 2009; Duquet, Glorieux, Laurijssen, & Van Dorsselaer, 2006; Clycq et al., 2014). Indeed, PISA data indicate that Flanders continues to show one of the largest socioeconomic inequalities when it comes to educational opportunities (Jacobs & Danhier, 2017). In an education system characterized by early and rigid tracking into hierarchically structured tracks with different levels of social prestige, which allows almost exclusively for downward mobility between those tracks, educational inequality and socio-ethnic segregation is persistent and intergenerational. Moreover, because schools and teachers in Flanders have a high level of autonomy to evaluate their students, social bias can influence these evaluations and consequently affect youngsters' educational trajectories (Spruyt, Laurijssen, & Van Dorsselaer, 2009; Stevens, 2012). Overall, these social and ethnic stratification processes reveal themselves in the fact that students with an ethnic minority background and/or from families with lower socioeconomic status (SES) are largely overrepresented in the lower-esteemed vocational track, more often experience grade retention and are more likely than their native middle-class peers to leave secondary education without a diploma (Van Landeghem, De Fraine, Gielen, & Van Damme, 2013). Moreover, because of the power inherent in the dominant narrative of meritocracy, the way in which educational practices and teacher dispositions shape students' educational experiences and (unintentionally) contribute to alienating and excluding particular students remains mostly unnoticed (Valencia, 2010; Nouwen & Clycq, 2016). Research shows that the fact that students with an ethnic minority background tend to be less 'successful' in education and consequently considered more 'at-risk' is often attributed to individual students and their families, who are believed to lack the necessary features to be successful in education (see e.g. Clycq et al., 2014; Van Praag, Stevens, & Van Houtte, 2016; Stevens, 2012). In policy practice and

80 *Rut Van Caudenberg et al.*

discourse regarding ESL as well, the focus continues to be primarily on the individual student and his/her parents who need to be held accountable for the student's educational behaviour (Clycq, Nouwen, Van Caudenberg, & Timmerman, 2015). It is against this background that we analyse the school narratives of Simon and Karim. As argued earlier, by listening to how these two youngsters – who occupy different social positions in terms of their migration background and SES – make sense of schooling within a context of social and ethnic stratification, we can illuminate how this broader context plays a role in the youngsters' individual experiences.

Data and methods

The two youngsters whose narratives are foregrounded in this chapter are part of a larger sample of 18 youngsters living in a large, multi-ethnic city in Flanders (Belgium) who left mainstream secondary education without an upper secondary education diploma and with whom several in-depth semi-structured interviews were carried out between August 2015 and October 2016 in the framework of the RESL.eu project. Half of the youngsters were enrolled in an 'alternative learning arena', that is, adult education or part-time vocational education and training, at the time of the first interview, while the other half were not attending any educational institution. Simon belongs to the former group and Karim to the latter. Both youngsters were interviewed twice, with approximately nine months in between each interview. Interviews touched upon a range of topics (educational trajectories, work experience, aspirations, social networks, leisure activities, etc.). For this study, we focused on the sections of the interviews that related to the youngsters' experiences with (secondary) education and leaving school early.

To analyse the data, we applied thematic narrative analysis in which the focus was on the *content* the narratives communicate, rather than on their *structure* (Riessman, 2008). In the representation of the data we seek to give explicit room to the voices of the youngsters by turning interview transcripts into 'narrative portraits' as a method of textual representation developed by Smyth and McInerney (2013), who build on the work of Lawrence-Lightfoot (see e.g. Lawrence-Lightfoot, 2005). By preserving the integrity and richness of the data relevant to the study and the choice of words of the respondents, this method "rejects flat and stereotypical explanations for school success and failure" and holds the capacity to "convey the emotions, depth of feelings, and intellectual reasoning young people express about their schooling" (Smyth & McInerney, 2013, p. 6). The construction of narrative portraits is inherently an interpretative process; therefore, we do not claim to represent 'authentic' voices of the youngsters but rather our interpretation of how they retrospectively narrate their experience with schooling and leaving school early. Nonetheless, using the words of the youngsters – despite being translated into English – preserves the uniqueness of their voice and the way they recount their experiences. Moreover, the richness of the data that can be found in the narrative portraits allows us to illuminate underlying processes and mechanisms that may be crucial in the youngsters' educational trajectories and schooling experiences, but that remain invisible in studies concerned with identifying general patterns or creating conclusive knowledge.

Findings

Simon and Karim were both 21 years old when we first met them, and both lived in the same multi-ethnic, predominantly working-class urban neighbourhood. Simon is of native Flemish origin and the only child of divorced parents. He recently moved into what he calls a student flat above his father's apartment, for which he pays him monthly rent. Both his parents have a higher education degree and hold managerial positions. Karim, on the other hand, is the child of Moroccan immigrants and lives with his parents and three of his four siblings. At home he usually speaks Dutch with his siblings and Moroccan Arabic with his parents. His father is retired but used to work in construction as a manual labourer, whereas his mother works as a cleaning lady. Simon had been in mainstream education until the age of 19, after which he changed to adult education. Karim stayed in school until the age of 21 and had only recently left mainstream education when we first spoke to him. Our findings indicate that both youngsters thoughtfully and critically reflect on their time in secondary education, and voice their thoughts on a system that shaped their schooling experience. At the same time, a close reading of their stories shows the diverging social realities in which both youngsters construct their understanding of schooling and leaving school early. In this section, we start from the narrative portraits of both youngsters to explore how Simon comes to see his schooling experience mainly as an individual story of lack of motivation, while for Karim it is a story embedded in an education system of unequal educational opportunities and unfair treatment.

"I think motivation was the biggest problem": Simon's story

I left school and went to adult education when I was in the fifth year. I actually would have had to repeat the fifth year for the third time. I still did human sciences [academic track] in the third and fourth year but then I got a B-certificate and repeated the year but at a different school. Then I got a B-certificate and I went to art school [artistic track] where I got a B-certificate. Then I repeated the fifth year but went to commerce [technical track]. If in mainstream secondary education you have to repeat the year, you have to repeat everything even if you only failed two courses, for example. So then it's like the stuff you actually already know, you have to repeat it. For instance, I've always been bad at French, always. Very often it came down to French and one or two other courses that I had to repeat everything and then I used to get really mad at French. . . . During the year I always tried to cooperate very much and it all went pretty good,

I thought. But then there are the exams. I really think that's a pity that a few weeks can actually ruin an entire year. But those are the rules of the school, right. That's how the system works. I don't think it's the job of the school to hold on to their students. I think it's more their job to actually show them like, 'look, these are all the possibilities, and did you already take a good look at all of that'?

As a student I was a bit of a class clown, someone who just tried to have fun. I always participated in the lessons and stuff, when it interested me, but I also talked a lot, I drew a lot during class, did stuff on my phone, played games with classmates when the teacher wasn't looking. . . . I never had a fight with the teachers. They were always very hopeful for me, well, most of the time. And every year at the end of the year, the same explanation: 'Look, we believe in you but you just have to try harder'. I really didn't do a lot, but I also was like, 'Look, schoolwork is for when you're at school. Why am I doing this at home and why is my whole life all of a sudden revolving around this'. The teachers tried to keep me in school. But, for example, extra classes, I never really went to them. That was my own fault. They did try to invite me. . . . I think motivation was the biggest problem. My parents really tried to motivate me. For me it was either really interesting and then it all went perfectly, or I was like, 'What use will this have in my life? I don't think this is important enough'. And that's entirely my own fault, I think. Although there are some things that I think could be a little different. Like, for instance, the modular system [from adult education]. I thought that was much easier to find motivation for. . . . You just think like, 'Yes, OK, just finish this module and then that's also finished'. I also think that's why the modules are so much better, because you will be less likely to quit.

Like most students in Flanders (see e.g. Groenez et al., 2009), Simon started his secondary education career in the highly esteemed academic track, and when confronted with his first B-certificate in his fourth year, he first repeated his year to be able to remain in the academic track before starting to 'stream down' the educational waterfall. When he received a B-certificate again, he went to the artistic track and then to the technical track. However, he left mainstream education before streaming down to the lowest-esteemed vocational track. Simon describes an educational trajectory he mainly associates with grade retention and rigid and early tracking. He criticizes the fact that the linear system of mainstream education (as opposed to the modular system of adult education) obliges students to repeat an entire school year, even when they fail only a few courses, which in his experience implies having to repeat '*stuff that you actually already know*'. He felt that having difficulties with only a few courses obstructed his educational progress; consequently, these courses became the object of his frustration ('*I used to get really mad at French*'). Moreover, the strong emphasis on having to score well on the exams, in his experience, overshadowed the efforts he had made during the school year. However, despite his implicit critiques of these particular systemic features of the education system,

Simon does not question that those are the rules by which one has to play, but rather accepts that that is '*how the system works*'. He considers that schools should not necessarily focus on trying to keep their students, but rather inform them about what other possibilities to obtain a diploma are out there. In doing so, he frames his decision to change to adult education not as an act of 'early school leaving' but one of choosing another way towards getting his diploma. Simon reported never having had a conflictual relationship with his teachers while attending mainstream education. On the contrary, even though he describes himself as a '*bit of a class clown*', who did not always pay attention in class, in his experience his teachers remained '*hopeful*', repeatedly voicing their belief in him and trying to keep him in school. In this context, in which the system is perceived as working the way it is supposed to work and teachers as doing their jobs the way they are supposed to do them, Simon comes to see his struggles mainly as an individual problem of motivation. Once he changed to adult education, where the linear system was replaced by a modular system, finding this motivation turned out to be easier, which is why according to Simon '*you're less likely to quit*'. In other words, for Simon, leaving school (or not) is a matter of finding the necessary motivation, and – although he still mainly sees that as an individual matter ('*that's entirely my own fault*') – particular ways of organizing schooling are considered to either hinder (linear system) or facilitate (modular system) this. By the time we interviewed Simon for a second time, he had obtained his upper secondary education diploma via adult education. When asked about what it was like to (finally) have his diploma, he reacted as follows:

> I had expected much more of it. Finally done with it, and then it was like, 'Ah, OK'. There was this ceremony, but nothing special or anything. You know, for the people who organize it it's the same thing every year, right, people who graduate. To be honest I also missed half of the ceremony because I was too late and I also didn't think it was very interesting. For me it was actually just like, 'Now I have my diploma, now I can get on with my life'. It was mainly that. I think my studies just took much longer than they should've taken. I think I could've done more with my life by now. Just a real pity that I made so little effort to get the motivation for it. . . . When people ask about my studies I have to disappoint them. That it just didn't work out for me. That studying is not for me.

By stating that '*now I have my diploma, now I can get on with my life*', Simon suggests that not obtaining this diploma had never really been an option for him. He considers graduating from secondary education not particularly a big deal but rather something people do all the time ('*it's the same thing every year, right, people who graduate*'), and something he needed to get over with. The fact that he did not get his diploma in what is considered the 'normal' way – that is, after six years of mainstream secondary education – makes him feel like he wasted time and is disappointing people when they hear about his educational trajectory.

84 *Rut Van Caudenberg et al.*

"Sorry for saying so, but they've got a fucked-up system": Karim's story

Why I started secondary education in BSO [vocational track]? Corruption. 'Hup hup BSO', that's how I got there. The teachers probably don't feel like explaining the difference between educational tracks, so they say, 'That's an allochthone [person with migration background]; he probably won't make an effort so we send him to BSO; that's a good track for him'. I don't think that's OK. I actually would have liked to try ASO [academic track] or TSO [technical track]. . . . I spent year 1 in [School 1]. I had family who went to that school but it was very far, so if I just missed one tram I was too late and that can also influence the outcome at the end of the year: 'You came too late too often'. Year 2 I went to [School 2], I was in a class with three, four fun guys. So that was very distracting. I saw that my grades were going down, I just didn't realize it was because of my friends. So then I went to [School 3], top year, the teachers were great. Then year 4 also in [School 3] but at a different campus and everything changed; stricter teachers, stricter rules. I really went through a lot there, [including] fights with teachers. I thought, 'I'm never going to make it', but they gave me an A-certificate and then I thought, 'The best thing I can do now is to change schools because say I stay here, maybe they will get me next year and make me repeat my year'. So then I went to [School 4], a Catholic school so a bit more difficult. As expected, I got my first C-certificate there. . . . And then to [School 5] and that's where my educational career ended.

I'm someone who gets distracted easily. But when the teacher spoke to me privately, then I could concentrate on that during the next classes. But that didn't happen most of the time. They mostly shouted through the classroom. . . . When I thought I was being mocked, I talked back to them. Then I was told to leave. That was often a problem. . . . Teachers who purely abuse their power. 'We'll see who will laugh at the end of the year, we'll see how your grades will be.' My grades . . . they make them lower. I really went through a lot of situations. More and more frustrations. The teachers always said that I'm someone who contradicts a lot. But actually I just have my honour. 'You're the teacher, you should be teaching us. You don't have to belittle us. That's not how it works.' They always get the final word. Sorry for saying so, but they've got a fucked-up system. In the end they're playing with your future. They don't care. It's easy to simply give a C-certificate. [School 5] is actually a pretty good school. But it's the teachers who change that – who ruin the school. And I think it's a shame. . . .

I'm working for a car rental company now, but I'm trying to get a full-time job. Once I have that, I'm going to combine it with the central examination board, so that I can get my diploma. I can't go around without a diploma. My whole family has a diploma. My mother wouldn't be proud of me. Suppose I find a perfect job, then there'd still be some part of me saying, 'No, you need to get your diploma'. I think it's a very important document. I want to be able to proudly tell people, 'Yes, I've graduated'.

> Because for most people, I'd say racists and the like, they look at you like, 'Do you have a diploma? No?' Then they think, 'Ah, he's on welfare. He's from that neighbourhood. It's one of those people'. But when you say, 'Yes, I've graduated. I've got my diploma', then they would look at you in a more positive light. And I would like that.

For Karim, mainstream secondary education did not start where he would have liked it to start – or at least that is how he looks back on it, that is, a more highly esteemed track than the vocational track he was advised to follow by what he considers to be prejudiced teachers within a broader ('*corrupted*') system that holds negative images about the educational attitudes and capabilities of ethnic minority students. Even though the actual advice of the teachers and the motives behind it remain unclear, Karim's perception of being considered unfit for higher esteemed tracks because he is an '*allochthone*' suggests that he is aware that teachers often (unconsciously) subscribe to stigmatizing views regarding members of ethnic minority groups (particularly of Moroccan and Turkish background) as having low educational motivation and counterproductive attitudes (see e.g. Nouwen & Clycq, 2016). Consequently, he comes to see his start in the vocational track as a result of unequal educational opportunities rather than as a matter of educational interests or skills. After starting his first year in secondary education, Karim describes a trajectory that involved frequent school changes as a result of disciplinary actions, in an attempt to get away from 'distracting friends' and to find a school where he could have a good relationship with his teachers. The fact that even after receiving an A-certificate – allowing him to pass on to the next year in the same educational track – he still decided to change schools because he did not have a good relationship with his teachers and did not trust that they would give him a fair chance ('*maybe they will get me next year and make me repeat my year*') suggests that Karim considered the relationship with his teachers to be crucial for his own successful progress through school. However, establishing a good relationship with his teachers was difficult, as he experienced these primarily as relationships of unequal power dynamics and conflict. In his experience, teachers did not treat him in a respectful manner ('*they mostly just shouted through the classroom*') and abused their institutional power and authority to give him lower grades than what he thought he deserved. Karim resisted to what he experienced as unfair and condescending treatment by '*talking back*'. However, what for him was about defending his '*honour*' and resisting a stigmatized identity was treated as mere deviant behaviour by his teachers ('*the teachers always said I'm someone who contradicts a lot*'), which led to '*more and more frustrations*'. In his experience the teachers ultimately did not care about him, played with his future and ruined what was actually a 'good school'. The relationship with his teachers strongly influenced Karim's connection with school and the critique he developed about an education system that he came to consider as '*fucked up*'. In Karim's experience, unfair, prejudiced and condescending teachers who have all the power made him feel he no longer could succeed in this system. Consequently, for Karim, leaving school early becomes about feeling pushed out by (yet another) C-certificate but at the same time also about criticizing what he perceives as an illegitimate system of unequal educational opportunities and unfair treatment. Nevertheless, although Karim questions the legitimacy of the education system, he does not question the importance of a diploma. On the contrary, he still holds very strongly to the idea of obtaining his upper secondary education diploma and hopes to achieve this via the examination commission, thus without having to attend an educational institution. The value he attaches to this diploma is not so much about having an entry ticket to the labour market; rather he comes to interpret it as a symbol of personal achievement ('*I want to be able to proudly tell people, "Yes, I've graduated"*') and a way to protect himself against discriminatory and racist perceptions and practices, and a way to challenge stereotypes.

Discussion

We started this chapter with the observation that two youngsters experienced and reacted to a similar event, namely being confronted with grade retention, which consequently 'triggered' their early school leaving, in a very different way. While for Simon leaving school and going to adult education instead seemed like a more *interesting* option than repeating his year in mainstream secondary education, for Karim leaving school seemed like the *only* option. The aim of our study was to explore why these youngsters came to experience this event in different ways, and what these diverging experiences reveal about how their social positions in a socially and ethnically stratified education system shaped their understanding of schooling and leaving school early. Our findings indicate that, while both youngsters criticize the education system, the form and extent of this criticism differs considerably. For Simon, the education system is perceived as a neutral and fair system that in itself is not questioned but that poses particular challenges because of specific systemic features. As a Flemish native, middle-class youngster, he 'escapes' teacher bias based on ethnicity as 95% of the teachers have a Flemish ethnic origin, and he continuously receives the message that he can succeed in education but just needs to try harder. Consequently, he comes to interpret his struggles in mainstream education mainly as an individual matter of a lack of motivation. In an attempt to find this motivation, Simon turns to a different, more '*interesting*', educational setting where he eventually manages to obtain his diploma. Simon's schooling experience is one in which he upholds the meritocratic ideal put forward by the dominant narrative, and sees individual effort to be the key to educational success. The fact that – even with an upper secondary education diploma – he considers his own educational journey to be a personal 'failure' suggests how he constructs his perceived lack of investment in school in a social context that takes educational success as a given as well as a necessity in order to maintain one's privileged middle-class position (Ball, 2003). Karim, who – unlike Simon – does not belong to the dominant group, on the other hand, expresses a more profound critique of an education system that he experiences as a '*corrupt*' and *'fucked-up'* system of unequal educational opportunities and unfair treatment. He feels negatively stigmatized by his teachers and deprived of educational opportunities because of his migration background, and in the end questions what he has come to consider an illegitimate system in which succeeding has become impossible. In this context, leaving school becomes the only option he sees; however, his wish to obtain a diploma remains and becomes a form of resistance to prove people wrong. The process of disidentification with the school environment that we see in Karim's story, and the fundamental role the relationship with his teachers seems to play in this process, show the impact of perceived justice of teacher behaviour on the sense of school belonging and institutional trust (Osterman, 2000; D'Hondt, Van Houtte, & Stevens, 2015). Previous research has shown how teacher behaviour and their expectations of their students tend to be socially biased and that students with a lower socioeconomic and/or migration background are often considered less 'teachable' (see e.g. Merry, 2005; Boone & Van Houtte, 2013). Karim's experience with what he perceives as biased teachers illustrates how these processes of stigmatization play out and influence his schooling experience in which the meritocratic ideal ultimately presents itself as an almost unachievable myth. Nonetheless, Karim's desire to 'prove people wrong' by obtaining his diploma suggests that also for him, educational success remains something for which to strive.

While our study was not designed to make general statements or identify causes of ESL, it shows that paying close attention to the stories of youngsters who leave school early helps to shed light on the complex and diverse ways in which they make sense of schooling and leaving school early. The narrative approach we used allowed us to unravel how schooling experiences unfold and how they are impacted by the social context in which they are shaped. The 'narrative portraits' became analytical lenses to understand the impact of the youngsters' social position, in terms of their migration background, SES and educational trajectory. They reveal the importance of the institutional legitimacy (Erickson, 1987) youngsters attribute to the schools, the teachers and the education system, in which issues of power, privilege and trust play a crucial role. The cases put forward in this chapter illustrate that, if this legitimacy is called into question, then the youngsters' dispositions towards school and towards the options made available to them after leaving school will be more profoundly impacted. Being aware of youngsters' various schooling experiences and critiques and the contexts in which these are shaped is crucial if efforts to tackle ESL are to be effective for all youngsters.

References

Ball, S. J. (2003). *Class strategies and the education market: The middle classes and social advantage.* London: Routledge.

Boone, S., & Van Houtte, M. (2013). Why are teacher recommendations at the transition from primary to secondary education socially biased? A mixed-methods research. *British Journal of Sociology of Education, 34*(1), 20–38.

Brown, T. M., & Rodriguez, L. F. (2009). School and the co-construction of dropout. *International Journal of Qualitative Studies in Education, 22*(2), 221–242.

Clandinin, D. J., Steeves, P., Li, Y., Mickelson, J. R., Buck, G., Pearce, M., . . . Huber, M. (2010). *Composing lives: A narrative account into the experiences of youth who left school early.* Retrieved from https://policywise.com/wp-content/uploads/resources/2016/07/Anar rativeinquiryintotheexperiencesofearlyschoolleaverspdf.pdf

Clycq, N., Nouwen, W., Van Caudenberg, R., & Timmerman, C. (2015). Education in Flanders: Balancing social and economic rationales while tackling early school leaving. *Educação, Sociedade and Culturas, 45*, 13–32.

Clycq, N., Nouwen, W., & Vandenbroucke, L. (2014). Meritocracy, deficit thinking and the invisibility of the system: Discourses on educational success and failure. *British Educational Research Journal, 40*(5), 796–819.

D'hondt, F., Van Houtte, M., & Stevens, P. A. (2015). How does ethnic and non-ethnic victimization by peers and by teachers relate to the school belongingness of ethnic minority students in Flanders, Belgium? An explorative study. *Social Psychology of Education, 18*(4), 685–701.

Duquet, N., Glorieux, I., Laurijssen, I., & Van Dorsselaer, Y. (2006). *Wit krijt schrijft beter: Schoolloopbanen van allochtone jongeren in beeld.* Antwerpen, Apeldoorn: Garant.

Erickson, F. (1987). Transformation and school success: The politics and culture of educational achievement. *Anthropology & Education Quarterly, 18*(4), 335–356.

Flemish Ministry of Education and Training. (2017). *Vroegtijdig schoolverlaten in het Vlaams secundair onderwijs.* Cijferrapport voor de schooljaren 2009–2010 tot en met 2014–2015. Retrieved from http://onderwijs.vlaanderen.be/sites/default/files/atoms/files/VSV_2014-2015_DEF.pdf

Gallagher, C. J. (2002). Stories from the strays: What dropouts can teach us about school. *American Secondary Education, 36*–60.

Groenez, S., Nicaise, I., & De Rick, K. (2009). De ongelijke weg door het onderwijs. *De sociale staat van Vlaanderen, 33*–67.

Hodgson, D. (2007). Towards a more telling way of understanding early school leaving. *Issues in Educational Research, 17*(1), 40.

Jacobs, D., & Danhier, J. (2017). *Segregatie in het onderwijs overstijgen.* Analyse van de resultaten van het PISA 2015-onderzoek in Vlaanderen en in de Federatie Wallonië-Brussel.

Lamote, C., Van Landeghem, G., Blommaert, M., Nicaise, I., De Fraine, B., & Van Damme, J. (2013). Voortijdig schoolverlaten in Vlaanderen: een stand van zaken en een voorstel tot aanpak. In Callens, M., Noppe, J., & Vanderleyden, L. (Eds.), *De Sociale Staat van Vlaanderen* (pp. 13–60). Brussel: Studiedienst van de Vlaamse Regering.

Laslett, B. (1999). Personal narratives as sociology. Featured essay. *Contemporary Sociology, 28*(4), 391–401.

Lawrence-Lightfoot, S. (2005). Reflections on portraiture: A dialogue between art and science. *Qualitative Inquiry, 11*(1), 3–15.

Merry, M. S. (2005). Social exclusion of Muslim youth in Flemish-and French-speaking Belgian schools. *Comparative Education Review, 49*(1), 1–23.

Nouwen, W., & Clycq, N. (2016). The role of teacher-pupil relations in stereotype threat effects in Flemish Secondary Education. *Urban Education, 1*–30, doi:0042085916646627

Osterman, K. F. (2000). Students' need for belonging in the school community. *Review of Educational Research, 70*(3), 323–367.

Riessman, C. K. (2008). *Narrative methods for the human sciences.* Thousand Oaks, CA: Sage.

Smyth, J., & Hattam, R. (2004). *'Dropping out,' Drifting off, being excluded: Becoming somebody without school* (Vol. 22). New York: Peter Lang.

Smyth, J., & McInerney, P. (2013). Whose side are you on? Advocacy ethnography: Some methodological aspects of narrative portraits of disadvantaged young people, in socially critical research. *International Journal of Qualitative Studies in Education, 26*(1), 1–20.

Spruyt, B., Laurijssen, I., & Van Dorsselaer, Y. (2009). Kiezen en verliezen-Een analyse van de keuze na het krijgen van een B-attest in het Vlaams secundair onderwijs als een replicatie van Kloosterman en De Graaf (2009). *Mens en maatschappij, 84*(3), 279–299.

Stevens, P. (2012). An ecological approach to understanding the development of racism in schools: A case study of a Belgian secondary school. In Kassimeris, C. & Vryonides, M. (Eds.), *The politics of education: Challenging multiculturalism* (Vol. 65, pp. 151–168). London: Routledge.

Valencia, R. R. (2010). *Dismantling contemporary deficit thinking: Educational thought and practice.* New York: Routledge.

Van Landeghem, G., De Fraine, B., Gielen, S., & Van Damme, J. (2013). *Vroege schoolverlaters in Vlaanderen in 2010: Indeling volgens locatie, opleidingsniveau van de moeder en moedertaal.* Leuven: Steunpunt Studie- en Schoolloopbanen, rapport nr. SL/2013.05/1.2.0.

Van Praag, L., Stevens, P. A. J., & Van Houtte, M. (2016). 'No more Turkish music!' The acculturation strategies of teachers and ethnic minority students in Flemish schools. *Journal of Ethnic and Migration Studies, 42*(8), 1353–1370.

6 Struggling against the waves or taking another course[1]

School disengagement in the educational trajectories of early school leavers from Warsaw

Paulina Marchlik, Anna Wrona and Hanna Tomaszewska-Pękała

Introduction – early school leaving and school disengagement

School disengagement is a crucial notion in explaining early school leaving (ESL), and the relation between those two concepts seems to be reciprocal. On the one hand, the more disengaged the student, the higher the risk of ESL (Ferguson et al., 2005; Lamb, Markussen, Teese, Sandberg, & Polesel, 2011). On the other hand, ESL is a part or a period in the disengagement process (Hancock & Zubrick, 2015) and can be treated as an indicator of school disengagement, while the frequency and duration of ESL may inform about the strength of the disengagement. Early school leaving may be the turning point or even an end of one's educational trajectory, but often it is not necessarily so. Relying on the results of the qualitative research conducted within the RESL.eu project (Van Caudenberg, Van Praag, Nouwen, Clycq, & Timmerman, 2017), we can reject the conceptualisation of ESL as something 'final' or 'definite'. Periods of ESL are in many cases intertwined with returns to education via mainstream schools (regular, full-time education for youth) or various alternative learning pathways. The moments of *being in* and *being out of* education can form a repetitive cycle. In many respects, the youth leaving school early appear to be very similar to their peers remaining at school, so ESL should be viewed as a periodic, temporary, sometimes even accidental part of the youth's educational trajectory and not a permanent, unchangeable status (Entwisle, Alexander, & Olson, 2004).

Departing from this state of knowledge, the chapter aims to investigate ESL in relation to the school disengagement processes. We argue that ESL, alongside absenteeism, grade retention and other experiences of some young people, can be treated as an observable manifestation of the disengagement process. However, those experiences are not always the result of school disengagement, for example, grade retention might happen to students who are engaged in education but cannot attend school for some other reason.

Theoretical approaches to school disengagement

Basing on the vast body of literature, we consider school disengagement as a construct of a multidimensional nature (Finn, 1989, 1993; Fredricks, Blumenfeld, & Paris, 2004; Johnson, Crosnoe, & Elder, 2001; OECD, 2003), usually used synonymously with low engagement or lack of school engagement (Hancock & Zubrick, 2015). The concept of school engagement was thoroughly examined and established in social sciences (Appleton, Christenson, & Furlong, 2008; Fredricks et al., 2004; Hancock & Zubrick, 2015; Kaye, D'Angelo, Ryan, & Lőrinc, 2017; Van Houtte, 2004). However, a single correct definition of engagement does not exist (Skinner, Kindermann, Connell, & Wellborn, 2009). In this chapter we follow the definition depicting school engagement as a metaconstruct equivalent to the *glue* (Reschly & Christenson, 2012) linking important contexts: home, school, peers and community to students and to outcome areas such as belonging, behavioural participation, motivation, self-efficacy and school connectedness. It relies on the "idea of commitment, or investment" (Fredricks et al., 2004, p. 61) when engaged students invest their time and effort in learning and not simply attend school (Reschly & Christenson, 2012).

In the following analyses we try to combine a few approaches to study school (dis)engagement. We acknowledge that school engagement is embedded in the broader concept of attitude (Breckler, 1984), and that it can be studied as a sort of outcome at a given moment of time, with a focus on its components, usually: behavioural, cognitive and affective or emotional (Appleton et al., 2008; Fredricks et al., 2004; Kaye et al., 2017). However, we also recognise school (dis) engagement as a process within the educational trajectory of the individual in which factors interplay in various configurations and periods of time (Lessard et al., 2008). The latter approach takes into account not only the very relation to the school, but also the out-of-school factors affecting students' attitudes towards education, as well as youngsters' consciousness – emotions and views on what actually happened with their lives.[2] Thus, we conceptualise school (dis)engagement as both a process and an outcome (Appleton et al., 2008; Reschly & Christenson, 2012; Skinner, Furrer, Marchand, & Kinderman, 2008), in which approach certain behaviour or state of the individual can be analysed as an indicator or a facilitator of school engagement (Skinner et al., 2009), depending on the context. For example, "student absenteeism may reflect disengagement from school, but it is also a risk factor for other disengagement indicators such as early school leaving" (Hancock & Zubrick, 2015, p. 5).

Metaphors of turbulent trajectories

We believe that the process of school disengagement is most visible in those educational trajectories which are fragmented, non–linear (*turbulent*), departing from the model assuming direct and uninterrupted movement throughout

92   *Paulina Marchlik et al.*

consecutive education levels: from primary, through lower and upper secondary, to acquiring ISCED 3 qualification. The concept of turbulence has been used by scholars to describe de-standardised life trajectories (Abebe et al., 2016; Elzinga & Liefbroer, 2007; Schapendonk, 2012) and implies "an increasing number of transitions and/or an increasing number of distinct states and/or increasing variation in the timing/duration of events" (Elzinga & Liefbroer, 2007, p. 232). Turbulent educational trajectories may contain periods of long absences, skipping and switching schools, suspension or grade retention – which are often considered indicators of school disengagement (Connell, Halpern-Felsher, Clifford, & Usinger, 1995; Connell, Spencer, & Aber, 1994; Fredricks et al., 2004; Ripple & Luthar, 2000) – as well as ESL incidents and moving to alternative learning pathways. Hence, we argue that *turbulent trajectories* of youth can be used as an observable indicator of the developing school disengagement.

As "most of our normal conceptual system is metaphorically structured" (Lakoff & Johnson, 2008, p. 56), to further illuminate and organise the studied examples of turbulent trajectories, and to make our analysis more figurative, we use the metaphor of a sea journey. We compare upper secondary school education to a sailing ship, being part of which one may encounter various temporary or more permanent turbulences: disturbances and obstacles that make the journey not as smooth as planned. Those turbulences in the journey are not solely related to school factors, but are often connected with factors from other contexts which are beyond the educational setting such as peer group, family life, etc. Thus, similarly to Anne Lessard and colleagues (2008), we distinguished various types of turbulent trajectories (courses of journey), leading to various levels of disengagement – disengagement with the school, with content, with people or with education as such (Hancock & Zubrick, 2015). In the context of the theoretical framework we applied, we set the following research questions: How does the process of becoming disengaged from school develop? What are the most common characteristics (e.g., socioeconomic status, family situation) and experiences disengaged young people share despite individual differences? What are the key risk and protective factors affecting the process of disengagement and/or ESL?

Methodology

The analysis is based on qualitative research – biographical in-depth individual interviews conducted from 2014 to 2016 within the RESL.eu project amongst 40 young people aged 18 to 24 living or studying in Warsaw, all of whom were Polish natives. All interviews were conducted amongst three subsamples of youth according to their status at the moment of the first interview: upper secondary school pupils, students learning in alternative pathways/institutions, and youngsters who left school early.

For this text, five stories were reconstructed based on interviews with one of the subsamples: young people who left school early. They were purposefully selected as illustrations for the distinguished types of turbulent educational

Struggling or taking another course 93

trajectories. However, we do assume that the trajectory types described may also apply to young people who have not necessarily experienced school breaks or periods out of school, especially because our research shows that in many cases young people who were temporarily out of the educational system have returned or are thinking of returning to school or training.

The biographical interviews with youngsters were analysed using the grounded theory approach. The methodology of grounded theory as proposed by Glaser and Strauss (1967) offers an approach to research that develops theories from research grounded in data rather than deduces testable hypotheses from existing theories (Charmaz, 2006). In the grounded theory perspective, the theory is derived from empirical data analysis performed in the course of empirical research, from data directly related to the observed part of social reality. During the analysis we noticed regularities that emerged from the data and therefore we applied the empirically construction approach (Kluge, 2000) to develop a typology of turbulent trajectories we present further in the text.

Youth at risk of ESL and their turbulent educational trajectories: stories of youth

In this part of the text we apply the metaphor of a sea journey. Choosing an upper secondary school, students decide on a type of boat (school type and/or educational track) they are going to board. Each of the boats takes a different course and the sea journey begins. In an ideal situation, all passengers of each boat reach their destination port (ISCED 3 education level). However, sometimes not everything goes as smoothly as planned and some passengers may fall overboard (become early school leavers). What happens to them afterwards? We present five possible situations which we encountered during our research, denominated as: *struggling against the waves, saved by someone, taking another course, cast away, falling in the hands of pirates*. The basis for their distinction was the course of the trajectories until the moment the research took place and the status held at the time of the interviews.

Struggling against the waves – Mariola

This trajectory illustrates the situation of people who, despite a difficult start and many adversities encountered on their way, try not to fall overboard and/ or fight for a possible return on board after falling out. They do not necessarily reach the predefined place or if they do, it may also be only a momentary stop in a further journey.

The example youngster, Mariola, 20, comes from a small town. She grew up in a large, low socioeconomic (SES) family, challenged by divorce, mother's health problems, unemployment, father's alcohol addiction and imprisonment resulting from family violence. In primary school Mariola had no educational setbacks, though she was quite an average student. The school could even be treated as a refuge from the difficult family environment. However, at lower secondary school she experienced peer violence – both verbal and physical. Her story illustrates Hancock and Zubrick (2015) classification of the disengagement levels, as growing disenfranchisement with the particular school did not lead to disengagement with education as such, whose value she still recognised. The critical moment occurred when deserted by her close friends and not feeling safe, Mariola stopped appearing at school and even attempted suicide. The only support she received at school was the principal, who suggested that she change schools. Mariola joined the VLC[3] and trained as a hairdresser, in Warsaw, where she had to commute two hours each way. However, she felt harassed in the workplace, and eventually resigned from her practice. At the new school she also experienced some disengagement because of a poor relationship with very demanding and unsupportive teachers. Despite difficulties, she was able to finish lower secondary school and planned to continue education at a vocational school. However, because of a challenging economic situation at home, she decided to enrol at a school for adults (a weekend course),[4] which enabled her to reconcile work and education. A few months later, she started having health problems and the following hospitalisation eventually resulted in her leaving school. After a few months' break, she decided to enrol at a different school, as she was determined to complete upper secondary school and would like to go to college, like her elder sisters, who had managed to obtain university degrees. The determinants of her engagement in education, and at the same time factors protecting her from permanent ESL, are: her aspiration to achieve more than her parents – to have a better education and a better economic situation in the future – and self-esteem built upon the struggle with difficult experiences: "For me it's a success that I managed to stand up on my two feet; I haven't given up and haven't ended on the bottom." Both self-esteem and educational expectations were confirmed as important correlates of school engagement also in the quantitative research (Kaye et al., 2017).

Saved by someone – Maria

Youngsters who are *saved by someone* have benefitted from some form of support during their journey. This support can be both personal and institutional. However, it is not the availability of support that is the most important but the youngster's internal readiness and willingness to accept it, like in the case of Maria, 20. Her background resembled the previous case: a low SES family, a physically abusive father, divorce, father not paying alimony, mother not able to support her family from a low-paid, unqualified job. Her personal situation is a good illustration of the accumulation of numerous risk factors, which theoretically puts her at higher risk of school disaffection (OECD, 2003). Her school disengagement also started to increase at the beginning of lower secondary education, as a result of physical violence and constant bullying by older girls from the same school. Maria also received no support from the school staff. This led to a long absence and a grade repetition, which further increased her disengagement. It took a form of permanent truancy (in her group of friends, who were similarly disengaged peers), leading again to grade repetition (Day, 2012).

The turning point in her educational trajectory was an intervention of street workers from a youth club, who showed her other, more rewarding ways of spending her free time. Maria emphasises that one of the educators played a key role in her trajectory, which changed her perspective on life: "She showed me that you can do more in life, that you can do something nice." Educators helped Maria to find a new school – despite her difficult financial situation, she went to a non-public school specialising in working with challenging students who have no motivation to learn and often have various special educational needs (e.g. dyslexia, disturbed concentration, hyperactivity). In the new school, she received the emotional and educational support she did not have access to previously and started to overcome her high level of disengagement from school. She successfully completed lower secondary school and continued education in an upper secondary level. However, she got pregnant and had to interrupt schooling to care for the baby. Conflicts with her partner negatively affected her mental health and emotional stability. Nevertheless, she still aimed to complete ISCED Level 3 education. She aspired to go to college and later work with 'difficult' youth to "show them [the difficult youth] onto the right path." Amongst the protective factors helping her to re-engage in education she particularly valued the support she had obtained at the youth club and at the lower secondary school she attended as the last one, and the emotional support from her female family members.

Taking another course – Marek

Youth *taking another course* after having left school, often enrol in a completely different school, change tracks, or take up employment and focus on their professional career options. The latter is also the case for Marek, 21, who comes from a small town near Warsaw. His disengagement trajectory was triggered by a personal tragedy. His father died when he was in the first grade of lower secondary school and his mother had to work more to be able to support her and her two sons, which weakened her parental control. He often played truant, which resulted in him having to repeat a grade. There were some factors that facilitated and increasingly contributed to disengagement in upper secondary school: the long distance from home to school, demanding and unsupportive teachers and, on top of all, a wrong choice of track. Although he was interested in the army, the general track with a military-oriented profile did not suit him. This led to truancy; his educational backlog increased and at the end of the first year he failed two subjects. As he was already 18, the school authorities suggested that he transfer to a different school, which is a common way of dealing with challenging students in Polish secondary schools (Marchlik & Tomaszewska-Pękała, 2016). He enrolled in a weekend course at a school for adults in his home town, which he tried to reconcile with full-time work during the week.

96 *Paulina Marchlik et al.*

He found it really exhausting, so he quit school after one semester (but he managed to complete the first grade). In the meantime, he started living on his own, and, at that time, the family benefit which he received after his father's death (but only as long as he continued his education)[5] was a significant motivation for him to re-enrol at school. However, new career options and a higher salary appeared and he moved to another town. Thus, his disengagement with education was further reinforced by labour market opportunities. The benefit money ceased to be as attractive as it had been previously, and Marek did not look for a school in the new place. Moreover, after two years, having only lower secondary education, he became a manager at a new company and his salary tripled. He does not regret leaving school and believes that "in a way it is better to have a career than finish school." Marek's story reinforces the findings of the previous surveys (e.g. Bernard & Michaut, 2014), showing that the desire to take up a job and earn one's own money as well as being fed up with school can be major motives for leaving education.

Cast away – Marcin

Youngsters belonging to the *cast away* group, in literature are often defined as NEETS (not in education, employment or training) – they do not attend any course or school and they do not work. These young people, unlike those struggling against waves, do not fight to come back after falling overboard. In the case of Marcin, 19, this trajectory of school disengagement was facilitated by a difficult family environment. He grew up without a father figure – his father left during Marcin's childhood. His parents divorced and after a few years his mother found a new partner and soon gave birth to another son. Marcin never liked his stepbrother. One day his baby brother had an accident when he was under Marcin's care. The mother, knowing that Marcin did not accept his brother, suspected deliberate action. As a result, Marcin was sent to a psychiatric hospital, and diagnosed as a depressive type. Later he went to the same hospital again – after a suicide attempt.

Marcin became disengaged from school in lower secondary school. He never liked school, although he could not precisely explain why. He found the lessons boring and he felt school was a waste of time, which can be considered an indicator of disengagement with education. He often played truant, reading books outdoors or looking at animals in pet shops. The school reacted to the absences, immediately asking his mother to make sure her son got to school. But it was difficult for her to reconcile looking after two sons and work, so both school supervision and parental control were not sufficient or ineffective in Marcin's case. Although he did not have problems with learning, because of frequent absences, he often needed to retake exams in the summer. Marcin's mother, feeling that she had no influence on her son, decided to send him to a youth sociotherapy centre.[6] He spent the next years in a number of different boarding schools and care institutions (in the last grade of lower secondary school he attended four different schools). Such a trajectory confirms the previous findings that school absenteeism as well as frequent school changes may lead to school failure, disengagement and subsequent ESL amongst youth in foster care (Zorc, O'Reilly, Matone, Long, Watts, & Rubin, 2013).

When he completed middle school, he was placed in a youth emergency shelter, where he stayed until he reached the age of 18, which meant the end of compulsory education. Without the legal obligation to study, he quickly dropped out of school and looked for a job but, being inexperienced and unqualified, he was only able to find temporary employment. He worked in a few places, the longest employment period in one place was two months.

At the time of the interview he was not working or participating in any kind of training and could not find any motivation to change something in his life: "Someone telling me something is not motivating at all (. . .). A person who could motivate me to do anything does not exist. I think I have big problems with motivation." In addition, his mother, with whom he never had a good relationship, had thrown him out of the house. With no goals in life and no confidence in his abilities, he made very little effort to try and change his situation and he did not see any point in seeking help from local support institutions. Homeless and unemployed, he tried sleeping in the basement of a building, but that led to him getting arrested for break-in and thefts.

Marcin's case illustrates the trajectory of accumulating family, educational and psychological risk factors, eventually leading not only to strong school disengagement and ESL, but also to social exclusion. He lacked important protective factors, which could have been mother's support, social participation, at least one supportive teacher and the ability to ask for help (Lessard, Butler-Kisber, Fortin, & Marcotte, 2014); meanwhile, the measures applied to help him when he was still in education turned out to be inadequate or ineffective.

Falling in the hands of pirates – Mariusz

The educational journey of young people who *fell in the hands of pirates* is interrupted by the appearance of external pull factors which draw them away from learning. Those factors, symbolised by pirates, signify serious disturbances manifested by various risky behaviours such as self-harm, substance abuse (drugs, alcohol), criminal offences, suicide attempts, etc.

Mariusz, 23, comes from a family with a low SES. He grew up without his father and at school he was looking for the acceptance of older boys, who impressed him, so he wanted to prove that he was fit for their company. At the age of 10 he had already been abusing drugs (he tried drugs for the first time when he was 7), so school and studying were not his priority, although he did not have any problems with learning when he was at school. Although drug abuse is sometimes placed as one of the outcomes of negative dispositions towards school (OECD, 2013), Mariusz's story is an example of a contrary situation in which drug abuse triggered various school problems, leading to further disengagement and eventually leaving school. Despite playing truant, Mariusz managed to complete both primary and lower secondary on time since he did not present disruptive behaviours that would clearly indicate the seriousness of his life situation. Later he went to a technical school, but quickly changed to basic vocational school training in the profession of car mechanic, because of his interests and to avoid fines related to the non-fulfilment of compulsory education. He found an apprenticeship in a car repair shop, where he spent most of his time; he preferred work to school and rarely appeared at school.

When Mariusz was 16, his mother lost her job and fell into a severe depression and did not leave home (or bed). Her partner, an alcohol addict, also did not work, and at home there was lack of money for daily expenses, and above all – for food. Mariusz, being a minor, was the sole breadwinner of the family. The owner of the car repair shop where Mariusz worked knew his situation. He became the boy's father figure. Trying to help, he employed the boy illegally and let him work more (also at night) so Mariusz could earn a living for his family (brother, mother, mother's partner). However, because of continuous absenteeism he had to repeat a grade. In total, he spent three years in the first grade and never completed it.

Nevertheless, he considered completion of upper secondary school as normative, and when his younger brother wanted to quit school and go to work to help, Mariusz persuaded him not to do it, because "he was the only one who had it together and was normal in our family." The brother graduated from an upper secondary school, but did not take an external examination (which is not obligatory) and as a result did not obtain a Matura certificate, which would have enabled him to participate in higher education. Still, Mariusz's brother's level of education is the highest in the family.

Still being an addict and needing money for drugs, Mariusz discovered that theft was more profitable than work. However, in his case the institutional intervention (drug therapy) proved to be effective to the point that Mariusz also wanted to continue his education, go to college and study social rehabilitation, and later to work as a drug addiction specialist. He is aware of the options available on the education market; he knows that he must complete upper secondary school and pass final examination first and plans to enrol at a school for adults. His girlfriend is currently expecting a baby and he is again the sole breadwinner, but Mariusz believes he will be able to deal with all the challenges and achieve his plans: "If I got out of drugs, I can do anything."

Conclusion

Because of the strong legal and cultural pressure on completing secondary education in Poland, school disengagement seldom ends in early school leaving (Kaye et al., 2017; Tomaszewska-Pękała, Wrona, & Marchlik, 2017). Usually leaving school early occurs when a young person is challenged by a set of risk factors, often present since early childhood. Reading the stories of these young people, one can notice striking similarities, especially in terms of socio-cultural characteristics and school experiences, as well as differences in how young people deal with certain situations. The stories show that the youngsters have experienced many obstacles in life, including learning difficulties; for example, disengagement with content often starts with problems with one school subject (usually mathematics). Lack of support in the family, at school, in the peer group, peer persecution, harassment at home, difficult or no relationship with parents, own or parents' substance abuse, low socioeconomic status of the family and the need to undertake paid employment to financially support the parents and/or siblings, stressful living conditions, health problems and suicide attempts are key risk factors for entering a turbulent trajectory. But even sets of seemingly similar risk factors are never identical. In addition, when we analyse their interplay with protective factors at different levels (individual resilience, support from other people or institutions) in different periods of time, the picture becomes even more unclear. It is extremely difficult (if possible at all) to predict the end of a journey even when we know the risk and protective factors on the way, the relationship between them, and the succession of events. In the case of some youngsters, ESL can mean the end of their journey and giving up on their dreams, whereas for others it is just a momentary break or even a chance for a more satisfying career.

We see that the key factors which protect from school disengagement, early school leaving and/or becoming NEET are: an optimistic outlook on life, recognising the value of education, and aspirations and belief in one's own abilities together with readiness to accept the help of supportive adults or significant others. The presence of external support the youngsters can always count on, including the professional support of psychologists, therapists and/or educators is also very important.

Our findings clearly show that both risk and protective factors can be located in the family environment, although we should be cautious about putting the responsibility for the disengagement in the family itself, as the difficulties in family life are often caused by institutional and systemic factors. For this reason, we stress that it is worth investing in the development of early support programmes for disadvantaged families and systemic universal prevention measures provided at school. Working with vulnerable families and empowering their participation in school life is the challenge that educational institutions, specialists, teachers and educational systems in general should focus on when thinking about tackling both school disengagement and early school leaving. Future research is needed to further investigate school disengagement in the context of educational trajectories and the link between school disaffection and ESL.

Notes

1 This scientific paper was financed from the funds for science in the years 2013–2018 allocated for the international co-financed project.
2 For example, Lessard et al. (2008) distinguished three major phases leading to dropout: *setting the stage*, which encompasses various family factors – divorce, parental neglect, abuse or crime, death of a parent, low socioeconomic status, etc.; *teetering* – various strategies of dealing with school problems, and factors pulling youngsters out of education; and the

100 *Paulina Marchlik et al.*

final stage of *ending the journey*, which means pivotal moments or a gradual increase of disengagement that leads to leaving school early.

3 *Voluntary Labour Corps* (Ochotnicze Hufce Pracy) – a state institution providing alternative learning pathways (vocational training) to students at risk of dropping out of school.

4 In Poland, upper secondary schools for adults provide only general education courses.

5 Such benefit is paid until the age of 26, provided a young person remains in education.

6 *Youth sociotherapy centres* are educational institutions for students who cannot cope with the requirements in mainstream schools and who present various challenging behaviours or emotional disorders.

References

Abebe, D. S., Bussi, M., Buttler, D., Hyggen, C., Imdorf, C., Michoń, P., . . . Shi, L. P. (2016). *Explaining consequences of employment insecurity: The dynamics of scarring in the United Kingdom, Poland and Norway.* NEGOTIATE working paper no. 6.2. Retrieved from https://negotiate-research.eu/files/2015/04/NEGOTIATE-working-paper-no-D6.2.pdf

Appleton, J., Christenson, S. L., & Furlong, M. J. (2008). Student engagement with school: Critical conceptual and methodological issues of the construct. *Psychology in the Schools, 45*(5), 369–386.

Bernard, P.-Y., & Michaut, C. (2014). Marre de l'école. Une analyse des motifs de décrochage scolaire. *Note du CREN, 17.*

Breckler, S. J. (1984). Empirical validation of affect, behavior, and cognition as distinct components of attitude. *Journal of Personality and Social Psychology, 47*(6), 1191–1205.

Charmaz, K. (2006). *Constructing grounded theory: A practical guide through qualitative analysis.* Thousand Oaks, CA: Sage.

Connell, J. P., Halpern-Felsher, B. L., Clifford, E., Crichlow, W., & Usinger, P. (1995). Hanging in there: Behavioral, psychological, and contextual factors affecting whether African American adolescents stay in school. *Journal of Adolescent Research, 10,* 41–63.

Connell, J. P., Spencer, M. B., & Aber, J. L. (1994). Educational risk and resilience in African-American youth: Context, self, action, and outcomes in school. *Child Development, 65,* 493–506.

Day, C. (Ed.) (2012). *The Routledge international handbook of teacher and school development.* London: Routledge.

Elzinga, C. H., & Liefbroer, A. C. (2007). De-standardization of family-life trajectories of young adults: A cross-national comparison using sequence analysis. *European Journal of Population/Revue européenne de Démographie, 23*(3–4), 225–250.

Entwisle, D. R., Alexander, K. L., & Olson, L. S. (2004). Temporary as compared to permanent high school dropout. *Social Forces, 82*(3), 1181–1205.

Ferguson, B., Tilleczek, K., Boydell, K., Rummens, J.A., Cote, D., & Roth-Edney, D. (2005). Early school leavers: Understanding the lived reality of student disengagement from secondary school. *Final Report submitted to the Ontario Ministry of Education.*

Finn, J. (1989). Withdrawing from school. *Review of Educational Research, 59*(2), 117–142.

Finn, J. (1993). *School engagement and students at risk.* National Center for Education Statistics Research and Development Reports.

Fredricks, J. A., Blumenfeld, F. C., & Paris, A. H. (2004). School engagement: Potential of the concept, state of the evidence. *Review of Educational Research, 74*(1), 59–109. doi:http://dx.doi.org/10.3102/00346543074001059

Glaser, B. G., & Strauss, A. (1967). *The discovery of grounded theory.* New York: Alpine.

Hancock, K. J., & Zubrick, S. R. (2015). *Children and young people at risk of disengagement from school.* Commissioner for Children and Young People, Western Australia.

Johnson, M. K., Crosnoe, R., & Elder, G. H. (2001). Students' attachment and academic engagement: The role of race and ethnicity. *Sociology of Education*, *74*, 318–340.

Kaye, N., D'Angelo, A., Ryan, L., & Lőrinc, M. (2017). *Early school leaving: Risk and protective factors: Findings from the RESL.eu international survey*. London: Middlesex University.

Kluge, S. (2000). Empirically grounded construction of types and typologies in qualitative social research. *Forum Qualitative Sozialforschung/Forum: Qualitative Social Research*, *1*(1). Retrieved from http://nbn-resolving.de/urn:nbn:de:0114-fqs0001145

Lakoff, G., & Johnson, M. (2008). *Metaphors we live by*. Chicago: University of Chicago Press.

Lamb, S., Markussen, E., Teese, R., Sandberg, N., & Polesel, J. (Eds.) (2011). *School dropout and completion: International comparative studies in theory and policy*. Dordrecht, Heidelberg, London & New York: Springer.

Lessard, A., Butler-Kisber, L., Fortin, L., & Marcotte, D. (2014). Analyzing the discourse of dropouts and resilient students. *The Journal of Educational Research*, *107*(2), 103–110.

Lessard, A., Butler-Kisber, L., Fortin, L., Marcotte, D., Potvin, P., & Royer, E. (2008). Shades of disengagement: High school dropouts speak out. *Social Psychology of Education*, *11*(1), 25–42.

Marchlik, P., & Tomaszewska-Pękała, H. (2016). Importance and dimensions of ESL in Poland – school staff's perception. *Kwartalnik Pedagogiczny*, *242*(4), 156–169.

OECD. (2003). *Student engagement at school: A sense of belonging and participation: Results from PISA 2000*, PISA, OECD Publishing. doi:http://dx.doi.org/10.1787/9789264018938-en

OECD. (2013). *PISA 2012 results: Ready to learn: Students' engagement, drive and self-beliefs* (Volume III). Paris: PISA, OECD Publishing. Retrieved from http://dx.doi.org/10.1787/9789264201170-en

Reschly, A. L., & Christenson, S. L. (2012). Jingle, jangle, and conceptual haziness: Evolution and future directions of the engagement construct. In Christenson, S. L., Reschly, A. L., & Wylie, C. (Eds.), *Handbook of research on student engagement* (pp. 3–19). New York: Springer.

Ripple, C. H., & Luthar, S. S. (2000). Academic risk among inner-city adolescents: The role of personal attributes. *Journal of School Psychology*, *38*(3), 277–298.

Schapendonk, J. (2012). Turbulent trajectories: African migrants on their way to the European Union. *Societies*, *2*(2), 27–41.

Skinner, E. A., Furrer, C., Marchand, G., & Kinderman, T. A. (2008). Engagement and disaffection in the classroom: Part of a larger motivational dynamic? *Journal of Educational Psychology*, *100*, 765–781.

Skinner, E. A., Kindermann, T. A., Connell, J. P., & Wellborn, J. G. (2009). Engagement and disaffection as organizational constructs in the dynamics of motivational development. In Wentzel, K. R. & Miele, D. B. (Eds.), *Handbook of motivation at school* (pp. 223–245). London: Routledge.

Tomaszewska-Pękała, H., Wrona, A., & Marchlik, P. (2017). Nauczyciele wobec problemu przedwczesnego kończenia nauki szkolnej. In Madalińska-Michalak, J. (Ed.), *O nową jakość edukacji nauczycieli*. Warszawa: Wydawnictwa Uniwersytetu Warszawskiego.

Van Caudenberg, R., Van Praag, L., Nouwen, W., Clycq, N., & Timmerman, C. (2017). *A longitudinal study of educational trajectories of youth at risk of early school leaving*. Antwerp: Centre for Migration and Intercultural Studies, University of Antwerp.

Van Houtte, M. (2004). Tracking effects on school achievement: A quantitative explanation in terms of the academic culture of school staff. *American Journal of Education*, *110*(4), 354–388.

Zorc, C. S., O'Reilly, A. L., Matone, M., Long, J., Watts, C. L., & Rubin, D. (2013). The relationship of placement experience to school absenteeism and changing schools in young, school-aged children in foster care. *Children and Youth Services Review*, *35*(5), 826–833.

7 The social relations and educational expectations of young people in marginalised areas

Evidence from Sweden

Alireza Behtoui, Marie Björklöf and Isabella Strömberg

"I think students from this school don't get the same educational prerequisites as kids in other schools. We have nothing! Nothing!" Fifteen-year-old Abed stretches his hands in the air as he talks, as if to underline the importance of his words. Anem, sitting next to him, nods her head and says that she is confident that she "will not be able to succeed or do really well [in upper-secondary school], especially in the beginning". "But", she adds, "I still have to. I have dreams that I have to reach!" During an hour-long interview, the two ninth-grade students, together with three classmates, described their educational aspirations, hopes for the future and experiences of their present school environment. Their school is rowdy, they say, and there's a lack of both computers and necessary school supplies. New teachers rarely stay for very long, and the classes are often led by substitutes. Their school is poor – why else would they be denied things that other students get, such as bus passes? However, the five youths also describe how some adults in the school try to inspire them, teachers who strive to encourage them in their school work. They talk about how their friends are helping and supporting one another and about the homework-help group that one of the parents arranges at home in the evenings. The five students are all determined to continue to higher education but are also aware of the obstacles they may encounter on the road.

When young individuals decide to drop out of school and interrupt their educational trajectory, it is seldom a decision made hastily. Such a conclusion is, rather, the end point in a chain of events and part of a troublesome process – a dynamic, multidimensional and cumulative course of disengagement from education and schooling. To study early school leaving (ESL) as dichotomous (a student drops out or does not) means focusing mainly on the individual characteristics of young people and neglecting the social relations that cause them to drop out. Even though we know from earlier studies that "being a member of a low-socioeconomic-status family" is "one of the primary determinants in the likelihood that a student will leave school" (Bradley & Renzulli, 2011), there are obviously many students with the same background who perform well or even excel in their studies. De Witte, Cabus, Thyssen, Groot, and van den Brink

Social relations and educational expectations 103

(2013, p. 17), for example, maintain that, although the most often school-related problems are revealed as the main determinants of dropout, "a large part of the literature is still focused on factors not related to the school, but to pupils themselves and their families".

We would not be able to obtain a profound understanding of this complex process by focusing exclusively on the *micro level* of the characteristics of pupils. Other explanations for students' early departure from school should also be taken into consideration. The *macro level* of the educational system and school politics and the *meso level* of social institutions – for example, relationships within the family, the school, the neighbourhood and the community – have a great impact on pupils' decisions concerning ESL. The meso-level factors, that is, their relations with their parents, teachers and peers, are the immediate social contexts in which education occurs. This chapter highlights the importance of and the way in which the meso level of social relationships can affect the complex process of ESL of young people attending schools in marginalised urban areas of Sweden. One basic assumption of this study, based on previous research (e.g. Rumberger, 1983), is that the educational expectations of young people are a crucial predicator of ESL (failure, frustration and, ultimately, disengagement and dropout). In other words, having fewer educational expectations predicts a higher risk of ESL and explains a substantial portion of the variation in the future educational achievements of individuals (Rumberger, 1983).

Researchers in the field of education studies distinguish between students' educational *expectations* – their realistic goals – and *aspirations* – their ideal goals. As Brookover, Erickson, and Joiner (1967, p. 393) suggest, aspiration is about a wish or "desire to excel", while expectation is about a realistic plan/goal for the future, a "perceived likelihood of success". In other words, while "aspirations" reflect what pupils would hope to achieve through their study, "expectations" are grounded in, firstly, relatively clear valuations of the students' intended educational outcome and, secondly, an awareness of their personal and structural constraints. Many studies in this field acknowledge that "idealistic" aspirations and "realistic" expectations "are highly correlated and yield similar results" and explain a substantial portion of the variation in the future educational achievements of individuals (Buchmann & Dalton, 2002, p. 101). The educational expectations of young people, as we have used the concept in this chapter, refer to "subjective assessments of how far in school they reasonably expect to go" (Reynolds & Burge, 2008, p. 486).

The data used in this study were collected during the period 2014–2016 as a part of the RESL.eu project in Sweden. Inspired by research which links economic and cultural capital with social capital (Bourdieu & Passeron, 1977; Coleman, 1988), we study the impact of the different forms of social capital – the resources in young people's social networks and generated by the different forms of their social relations – on students' educational expectations (Behtoui, 2017a). By using a mixed-methods approach with both survey material, in-depth interviews and participant observation in a selected group of schools, we have tried to highlight these complex relationships.

In the next section, after a short depiction of the Swedish context, the theoretical approach of the study is described. The subsequent section briefly presents the results of our survey in Sweden and the findings from our interviews. In the final section we summarise the chapter.

Context of the study

Until the end of 1990, Swedish schools provided relatively equal educational opportunities for all students. The right to an equal education during this period was a breeding ground for Swedish educational politics (Bunar & Sernhede, 2013). However, school outcomes in the post-1990 period demonstrated a constant decline in Swedish students' performances – mainly as a consequence of a deterioration in equal educational opportunities over the previous two decades (Bunar & Sernhede, 2013). Such a trend is indeed the outcome of different alternations – above all, the widening achievement gap and polarisation between school educational standards in privileged compared with marginalised neighbourhoods. Accordingly, if children from middle-class families with well-educated parents had, in earlier decades, attended the same schools as children from working-class families, there would, today, not be such of a mixture of backgrounds (wealth and ethnicity) neither in schools nor in neighbourhoods.

The rising income inequality of the past four decades, together with changes in housing policy during the 1990s – with priority given to private housing and fewer rental apartments – eventually led to widespread housing segregation. Additionally, around the same time, Sweden experienced a change in orientation within its school politics: first, the responsibility for schooling shifted from central government to the municipalities. Thereafter occurred two additional consequential reforms – free school choice and the privatisation of schools. In combination with extended segregation on the housing market, these reforms led to further school segregation. In such a situation, increasing numbers of quality-education-conscious middle-class parents withdrew their children from schools that they considered to have deteriorated. With this "exit" of middle-class students, the schools lost those parents who would have been the most motivated and determined to put up a fight against the deterioration in standards (Hirschman, 2004). Those parents who had no choice but to stay lacked the resources of the former group (time, knowledge, skill and self-confidence) to "voice" any attempt to change and strive to improve the school situation. Consequently, schools in poor neighbourhoods did not have the same resources as those with middle-class students (Sernhede & Tallberg Broman, 2014). Swedish early school leavers are mainly the products of the first group of schools.

Theoretical framework

According to Feliciano and Rumbaut (2005, p. 1089), the concept of educational expectation has been explained in different ways in the literature. First,

Social relations and educational expectations 105

based on methodological individualism and rational choice, the educational intentions of individuals would necessitate assessing the probable 'costs and benefits' of alternative decisions (see e.g. Breen & Goldthorpe, 1997). On this methodological individualism, which considers a human as having a responsible, thinking mind and being self-reliant on his/her own judgment, Charles Taylor (1997, p. 169) writes that this ideal (however admirable in some respects) tends to "blind us to important facets of the human condition", since, according to this perspective, "We explicitly formulate what our world is like, what we aim at, what we are doing" (Taylor, 1997, p. 170). In this view, the human agent is a *monological* one with a mind which, like a computer, takes information from its surroundings, processes it and then acts on the basis of this information to fulfil his or her goals through a "calculus of means and ends" (Taylor, 1997, p. 63). Such an "I", independent of *body* and *others*, is "a centre of monological consciousness" (Taylor, 1997, p. 169). However, in Taylor's view, "Much of our intelligent action in the world . . . is carried on unformulated. It flows from an understanding which is largely inarticulate" (Taylor, 1997, p. 170). In contrast to these "monological acts", Taylor proposes the "dialogical act" as an adequate way of understanding the real variety of human actions and ways of being. According to the latter approach, like the sawing of a log, ballroom dancing or a conversation, the crucial feature of human actions is their *rhythmising* – that is, when a person places him/herself in a common rhythm with others. Thus our identities, ambitions and expectations are never defined solely in terms of our individual characteristics and "choice". Our embodied understanding exists in us more as the co-agent of common actions rather than individual rational agents.

In line with this approach to explaining young peoples' educational expectations, proponents of "status attainment theories" indicate that such expectations are shaped through interaction with *significant others* (parents, teachers and peers) and conditioned on their perception of the opportunity structure (Sewell, Haller, & Portes, 1969). Significant others serve as role models or a source of information in the young person's learning journey. Educational expectations, accordingly, should be viewed as the product of socialisation processes, conditioned by a person's class background, gender and ethnicity. At the same time, such an expectation "affects subsequent levels of educational attainment" and students' actual school outcomes (Sewell et al., 1969, p. 83). In a further development of this explanation, Bourdieu and Passeron (1977) state that we cannot isolate young people's educational expectations (their disposition towards education), from the social conditions of production of these expectations. We should not isolate young people's dispositions towards education from the objective conditions that determine them. Thus, educational expectations should be understood as the operation of "practical sense", an individual's mental structure and dispositional properties (Ball, 2003) which, in their turn, are affected by the influence of significant others (parents, peers, teachers and other reference groups) as well as an individual's educational and life experiences. Accordingly, the children of parents at the bottom of the social hierarchy are less inclined to have high educational expectations because "[t]hey have internalized and resigned themselves to the limited opportunities for school success that exist" for people like them (Swartz, 1997, p. 197). Several of them accept their lot in life and withdraw from education, which is such an important arena for competition and social stratification.

However, as Swartz (1997) mentions, Bourdieu's explanation of educational expectations determined by objective possibilities is insightful but not always conclusive. One obvious example is the higher educational expectations of the children of immigrants relative to their native peers with the same class background (despite their awareness of the limited career opportunities in the labour market), as numerous studies have demonstrated (Feliciano & Rumbaut, 2005). How, then, can we shed light on this variation? One explanation is the desire and expectations of immigrant parents who have not been able to attain a social position in the new country which would be consistent with their qualifications because of their downward social mobility. Thus they encourage their children to ensure a better life for themselves in the host country through education and to achieve what the parents could not accomplish. Another explanation, the "blocked opportunities" approach, suggests that, since immigrants experience labour market discrimination, they should try to devote more energy to the education of their offspring in order to compensate for these restrictions (Sue & Okazaki, 1990). The final explanation emphasises transnational contacts and the less-salient impact of class position on shaping the networks of immigrant parents in the new country (Behtoui & Neergaard, 2016). These social networks, as a source of social capital, may compensate for immigrant families' economic and educational disadvantages, provide valuable information and promote higher educational goals (Behtoui, 2017a).

Results based on qualitative and quantitative data

In this section we present the main results of the data collected in Sweden. Our focus is on the impact of the different forms of social relations that are involved in shaping pupils' educational aspirations.

Students in 50 schools located in marginalised areas of Swedish main cities participated in the survey on which our quantitative material is based. The final number of respondents, all aged between 15 and 17 years old, was 2,033 students (for detailed information about data and results see Behtoui, 2017b). Our qualitative material was collected during the period 2014–2016 through in-depth and focus-group interviews with young people, their parents and their teachers and through minor fieldwork in four of the schools participating in the survey. To obtain a longitudinal perspective, follow-up interviews were carried out about one year after the first interview with our young respondents. Added to this, two types of focus groups were conducted in each of the four schools – one with students and their peers and one with teachers and other employees. The young informants were selected from the following categories: 1) those who were still attending school but who were considered to be at risk of ESL, 2) those who were already early school leavers and were now studying

Social relations and educational expectations   107

in alternative learning pathways, and 3) those who were early school leavers at the time of the first interview and were not enrolled in education, employment or training (NEET).

As the main subject for this study was students' "*educational expectations*" we constructed, for the quantitative results, an index with nine values based on answers to the survey questions. The lowest value was assigned to those who answered "I don't know" and the highest to those who were determined to continue their education up to university level. The results of a series of linear regressions, with the educational expectations of the respondents as the outcome variable, are presented in Table 7.1.

Individual characteristics

As our results demonstrate, respondents' class backgrounds (indicated by the education and job status of parents) and their family's living standards have a positive and significant impact on a respondent's educational expectations. Those with greater resources in the family tend to have higher educational expectations. Conversely, there is a negative and significant association between having health problems and the educational expectations of young people. Some of our informants who had left mainstream education told us that their physical illness or psychological problems had strongly contributed to ESL. The survey results further show that boys have significantly lower expectations than girls and there is a negative association between being older and educational aim (older respondents have repeated one year or more at school).

After controlling for class background, gender, health problems and age, the majority of the children of immigrants reported higher educational expectations compared with students with a native background (for an explanation of these higher expectations of descendants of immigrants see Behtoui & Neergaard, 2016).

In our interview material, 16-year-old Christina, whose parents struggled hard to establish themselves on the labour market when they migrated to Sweden, told us that part of her motivation to do well at school, after a period of dropout, was due to a sense of obligation towards her family and a way to respect the sacrifices made by them: "I would like to show my family that I can do this. I can study and then get a diploma for university and such". Joseph, 16 years old, who came from a low-income immigrant family, had a similar opinion on the importance of education. However, whereas Christina's parents had a lower level of education, both of Joseph's parents had attained university degrees in their country of origin and undergone downward social mobility after migrating to Sweden. In the interviews, Joseph expressed his wish to acquire a university degree in order to secure his own as well as his parents' future:

> I also want to give my parents money and such, that's the case as well. And I also want to have everything to be as good as possible. . . . I always think in advance, like if they lose their job or become poor.

Table 7.1 Determinants of educational expectation, ordinary least squares (OLS) regression, partial (and standardised) coefficients

	Model 1	Model 2	Model 3	Model 4	Model 5	Model 6	Model 7	Model 8
Class background	.43*** (.20)	.43*** (.20)	.50*** (.24)	.34*** (.16)	.26*** (.12)	.24*** (.11)	.25*** (.12)	.22*** (.11)
Prosperity	.25*** (.12)	.20*** (.09)	.21*** (.10)	.05 (.02)	.01 (.00)	.00 (.00)	-.03 (-.02)	-.04 (-.02)
Health problems	-.33*** (-.15)	-.30** (-.14*)	-.28*** (-.13)	-.17*** (-.08)	-.11*** (-.05)	-.13*** (-.06)	-.13*** (-.06)	-.12*** (-.06)
Boys		-.70*** (-.17)	-.68*** (-.16)	-.53*** (-.13)	-.33*** (-.08)	-.31*** (-.07)	-.26*** (-.06)	-.25*** (-.06)
Age		-.60*** (-.23)	-.56*** (-.22)	-.51*** (-.20)	-.45*** (-.18)	-.44*** (-.17)	-.43*** (-.17)	-.42*** (-.16)
North-Western Europe and North America or Global North			-.14 (-.01)	-.02 (.00)	-.08 (-.01)	-.10 (-.01)	-.10 (-.01)	-.09 (-.01)
Rest of Europe			.55*** (.06)	.15 (.02)	.07 (.01)	.05 (.01)	.01 (.00)	.07 (.01)
Asia			.64*** (.10)	.21 (.03)	.15 (.02)	.08 (.01)	.09 (.01)	.10 (.02)
Africa			.09 (.01)	-.39 (-.03)	-.38 (-.03)	-.39 (-.03)	-.32 (-.03)	-.29 (-.02)
South America			.61 (.03)	.26 (.01)	.42 (.02)	.33 (.02)	.38 (.02)	.35 (.02)
Rest of Europe 2			.20*** (.02)	-.09 (-.01)	-.17 (-.02)	-.22 (-.03)	-.21 (-.02)	-.22 (-.02)
Asia 2			.53*** (.09)	-.03 (.00)	-.05 (-.01)	-.10 (-.02)	-.10 (-.02)	-.06 (-.01)
Africa 2			.46*** (.05)	.02 (.00)	.14 (.02)	.09 (.01)	.13 (.01)	.20 (.02)
Citizenship			.47*** (.07)	.39** (.06)	.46*** (.06)	.44*** (.06)	.43*** (.06)	.47*** (.07)
Parents' expectations				.62*** (.40)	.44*** (.29)	.42*** (.27)	.41*** (.26)	.41*** (.26)
Parents' support				.06* (.03)	.05 (.03)	.04 (.02)	.03 (.01)	.04 (.02)
Two biological parents				.26*** (.06)	.18** (.04)	.16** (.04)	.17*** (.04)	.18** (.04)
Teacher support					.10*** (.05)	.10** (.05)	.13*** (.06)	.12*** (.06)
Teacher judgement					.22*** (.10)	.23*** (.11)	.23*** (.11)	.22*** (.10)
Teacher expectations					.74*** (.30)	.72*** (.29)	.64*** (.26)	.63*** (.25)
Family social capital						.19*** (.09)	.20*** (.09)	.20*** (.10)
Friends							.21*** (.10)	.20*** (.10)

Sport								.01	(.01)
Cultural								**.08*****	(.05)
Religious								−.03	(−.01)
Political								−.07	(−.02)
Social								.04	(.01)
Pupils' council								**.13**★★	(.04)
Scouts								−.01	(.00)
Local association								**−.12**★★	(−.04)
Recreation centre								−.04	(−.02)
Meet friends								**−.06**★★	(−.04)
Social media								.02	(.01)
R^2 adj.	*.086*	*.173*	*.185*	*.331*	*.409*	*.417*	*.424*	*.428*	

Note: ★★★ denotes significance at 1%, ★★ at 5% and ★ at 10% levels.
For each immigrant group, suffix 2 denotes second generation.

110   *Alireza Behtoui et al.*

Within-family social capital

Considering the social relations that students are involved in, we primarily examined "within-family" social capital (Coleman, 1988) consisting of two main determinants:

- whether the parents have been supportive; and
- the expectation they had for their children's educational attainment, potential answers to which ranged from "Not studying further than primary school" (Grade 9) to "Continue on to college or university".

As the results in Model 3 of Table 7.1 demonstrate, the variables indicating within-family social capital have a significant and positive impact on the students' educational expectations.

Our qualitative material, moreover, demonstrates that young students who experienced their parents' support and higher educational expectations had a greater likelihood of returning to education after a temporary ESL. Alexandra, aged 22, one of our informants who we interviewed twice, had left upper secondary school the first time due to illness. She was, at the time of the second interview, enrolled in courses on an alternative learning pathway. Alexandra emphasised the importance of the support that her family had provided her with both during her illness, when she left school, as well as when she later decided to follow an alternative learning pathway. Alexandra's well-educated parents supported her both emotionally and economically during the time she was unable to study and she was thus able to receive quick and efficient medical treatment as well as the financial means to cover her living expenses. This, in turn, gave her the prerequisites and tools with which to focus on her recovery. Hence, support from the family was a crucial factor in her returning to school, not only because of the economic and informational support it provided her with, but also because of the emotional support that contributed to Alexandra regaining confidence in her abilities. Nadia, aged 16, had also received extensive support from her mother. Nadia had a neuropsychiatric diagnosis that caused her to experience difficulties at school. She had also been bullied by other students for this diagnosis throughout elementary school. During an interview she told us, "I think my role model is my mum because she has always, like, supported me all these years that I have had a tough time. Came to school, talked with my teachers and defended me".

Support from parents can be helpful not only for the individual students but also for their friends and classmates. Most of the students did turn to their own family members, such as parents and older siblings, for help with schoolwork but, in some cases, the parents of friends were the first port of call. Safwan, the father of 16-year-old Anem, who is a taxi-driver now, arranged help with homework for his daughter and her friends several times a month in their home. With his background as a university lecturer in mathematics he could offer them valuable support. As Safwan told us, not all students had parents

Social relations and educational expectations   111

who could help them with schoolwork and, since he felt that the school did not provide students with sufficient support in this, he tried to compensate as much as he could.

There are several cases in our qualitative material which indicate a strong link between our respondents' own educational aspirations and the expectations of their parents. These latter could, however, sometimes feel like a burden for young people, who then felt pressure to perform well at school. Carlos, 24 years old, who had family members both in Sweden and in his mother's country of birth, told us about the high expectations that he felt they had:

> It is a lot . . . my mum has three qualifications. She works as a nursing assistant here in Sweden; in Ecuador she was a teacher and then here she studied to become a hairdresser as well. My dad has two qualifications . . . agronomist, I think it's called, and then electrician as well. . . . And then my cousins over there in Ecuador, who are studying at university level. So I am really like in the middle . . . of course I should think about what I want really, but I feel like I don't want to like lag behind and that's why I feel pressure.

Another informant, 22-year-old Johanna, had also been greatly affected by other people's opinions about her educational trajectory. Unlike Carlos, whose family expected him to do well at school and who spurred him to study hard, Johanna's family had affected her educational expectations in a negative way. Johanna explained that she had failed to obtain an upper-secondary school diploma because of her psychological illness and, because of this failure, her family and friends now questioned her plans to go back to school. This also made her doubt herself and her abilities:

> Every time I tell people that I want to study at Komvux (municipal education for adults) they say, "No, you shouldn't, because you wouldn't make it", like. So I don't know if I should do it or not.

School-based social capital

Next we investigated the impact of pupils' relationships with their teachers in the schools. From questions in the survey, we constructed different indicators for teachers' support, teachers' judgements and teachers' expectations for pupils' education. As expected (see Table 7.1, Model 4), good relationships and higher expectations of teachers have a positive and significant effect on young peoples' educational expectations. While those with a higher class background (compared with those from a lower SES) reported more teacher support, both boys and pupils with an immigrant background stated that they experienced less support from their teachers.

A number of interview respondents recalled how teacher support had been of crucial importance to their educational careers. A "good teacher", according

112 *Alireza Behtoui et al.*

to them, was someone who provided emotional, educational and informational support – someone who could see and acknowledge each individual student's potential, a role model who inspired and motivated them. Lisa, 22 years old, illustrates these emotions about the teacher who had meant a lot for her in this way: "She inspired me. She was really kind and helpful; she made me feel like I wanted to impress her. Therefore I never wanted to risk disappointing her". Similarly, Najma, aged 20, assured us that it was because of the headmaster on the alternative learning pathway that she was attending that she wanted to continue her education at that particular school:

> I think it is as good as it can be in my mind. The headmaster here is damn good, listens actually. I think that he listens and takes in what you say. . . . Yes, that is actually the reason why I want to stay at this school, because of [name of headmaster].

Lucas, 21, remembered how the help he had received from the different school staff had enabled him to find an educational and occupational path that suited him perfectly. After trying a couple of different schools and never experiencing the feeling of belonging, Lucas received help from a study counsellor in applying to a school offering alternative learning pathways and signed up for an apprenticeship. While attending the course, he formed a strong bond with one of the teachers whom Lucas felt understood him and his way of learning. This teacher not only provided him with emotional support but also shared advice that was decisive for Lucas's entrance into the labour market after finishing the apprenticeship training course. He stated that this teacher "has helped me SO MUCH that I can even say that he is now a good friend of mine". Lucas told us that, even though his mother was also very supportive and encouraging, she herself had migrated to Sweden as an adult and did not have sufficient knowledge of the Swedish school system. Hence the school staff became an even more important source of information and support for him.

One interesting result when we added together in our regression models pupils' relationships with their parents and their teachers' support was that the negative impact of health problems on educational expectations decreases considerably (by more than 60 per cent). This means that those young people who have health problems but who received help and support from adults at home and in school report higher educational expectations than others with health problems (see the coefficient of health variable in Table 7.1, which decreases from –.33 in Model 1 to –.13 in Model 6).

Alex, 22 years old, described the support he received from school staff during his illness in the following way:

> I got help from the teachers to get in contact with a doctor and a psychologist; it was good in that way anyway. And I got no, they didn't pressure me to, . . . I got, like, to stay at home for them. Until I had sorted it out.

His parents had also been of great help to him, and Alex appreciated the respectful way that the adults around him tried to help him to cope with his illness. Even though he had dropped out of upper secondary school when we met him, he was highly motivated to complete his ISCED 3 qualification and was planning on continuing his studies at university level. Emilia, 20 years old, who is working now and, despite having been at considerable risk of ESL, finished her secondary-school education last year, told us:

> I would not have been able to complete my studies without the love and the massive support and understanding that I got from my parents. I had a diagnosis and problem with concentration. But my mum and dad were always there when I needed them. They sat down with me and helped me with my homework, met my teachers regularly, invited my classmates to our home, and paid for my horse-riding lessons, which I love more than anything else. Without their unbounded care I would not have been able to finish secondary school.

Extra-familial social capital

Analysing our survey results, we find that young people's *family networks* (relationship with their relatives or family friends whom they meet regularly) were an important element in shaping their educational ambition, that is, regular contacts with family friends with higher job status encouraged higher educational expectations (Model 6). Our interview data confirmed these results. Young people with immigrant backgrounds, who met relatives with powerful positions either in Sweden or during visits to their parents' homeland, reported feeling encouraged by these connections. Aspiring to reach high-status occupations later in life, such as those of lawyer, medical doctor or engineer, seems to be a result of personally knowing such role models, according to our respondents. Some of them told us about friends of the family who had given them help in specific subjects such as mathematics or physics when they needed it.

Furthermore, our survey results show that students whose friends had greater academic motivation and ambitious plans for their future education also reported higher educational expectations (Model 7). Abed, 15 years old, for example, described his friends as the first port of call when he needed support with schoolwork: "Half of my grades come from them! Otherwise I would never have made it". Friendship ties with school-motivated individuals also enabled our respondents to gain access to a wider network of people, such as the siblings or parents of friends, who were fruitful social resources. We should not forget that friendships with other young individuals who are not engaged in school work and who demonstrate high rates of disruptive behaviour have the opposite effect on attitudes towards education (the dark side of social capital).

Our survey results indicate that participation in different kinds of extra-curricular social activity (e.g. cultural programmes or involvement in the "pupils' council" in schools) had a significant positive impact on students' future plan for education (Model 8). Amongst the interviewed students, such activities were most commonly related to sports – for example, football and swimming – along with organised cultural activities. Only a small group of the respondents were engaged in other kinds of activity, such as political organisations. Those engaged in athletic and cultural activities told us that their participation enabled them to meet people they otherwise would not have had any contact with, that they learned to cooperate with others and that it strengthened their sense of self. Zeinab, a 16-year-old girl who was the head of her school's pupils' council, reported that the position had allowed her to have an influence over and input into how the school was run. Taking part in decision-making together with school personnel had had an empowering effect on her and further motivated her in her studies: "I want to become a leader! A person who helps others". Maria, 17, described herself as very shy when she was younger, and how she had trouble making friends in compulsory school. She had, however, found a social platform outside school through playing basketball. Since the basketball team consisted of young adults aged between 15 and 25, she came in contact with a group of girls a little older than herself: "They looked after me . . . like I'm their little sister. It was wonderful". She described her friends from the basketball team as providing her with emotional and social support as well as assisting her with her school work.

On the other hand, hanging out with friends and engagement in less-organised leisure activities (at, for instance, youth recreation centres, or YRCs) showed negative associations with young people's educational expectations in our survey. However, the qualitative fieldwork reveals a more complex picture, because of the vast variations between YRCs in different neighbourhoods. For example, one YRC, which was located near the school in which we undertook fieldwork, had problems with the deviant activities of some participants. Through receiving extra resources from the municipality, they were able to recruit additional personnel and arrange leisure activities, such as football, to engage young adults during their after-school hours. On summer holidays, they arranged internships to strengthen these young adults' future employment possibilities.

Students who visited YRCs in other neighbourhoods expressed a strong desire to engage in organised leisure activities. However, a lack of resources prevented these centres from arranging them. Nevertheless, as one of our informants who attended an YRC, said, "Going to the centre was like doing something, rather than nothing" (for more information on the extracurricular activities of pupils in Sweden, see Behtoui, 2017b).

Summary and discussion

The results of this study draw attention to the fact that young people and their families are not isolated islands, but are deeply embedded in a nexus of various kinds of social networks. These networks include kinship members of the extended family, friends of the family and friends of the children. The young

Social relations and educational expectations 115

people also have regular interactions with school personnel, and other adults and adolescents active in different kinds of mainstream and local organisations. These relationships and the social capital they provide, as demonstrated by our results, play an important role in forming the educational expectations of young people. To put it in another way, it is in dialogue and interaction with these "significant others" that the individual students' educational expectations and aspirations are shaped rather than being results of an individual decision based on the assessment of the probable 'costs and benefits' of alternative decisions.

In every dimension of social capital, the lower-class background of young people was associated with less access to networks with valuable resources which, in turn, led to lower educational expectations. These young students are those who, more than any other, are at significant risk of ESL and who undoubtedly need the emotional, personal and informational support of their extra-familial networks.

Hence, it should be emphasised that the environment of neighbourhoods where young people live and the schools they attend strongly shape their social relations and affect their educational expectations. The unequal opportunities of young people in marginalised areas, caused by their social origins, have been intensified by the now extremely segregated school system in Sweden. Without considering the failure of segregated schools in marginalised areas to attain their educational goals, it is impossible to solve the problem of growing ESL in Sweden. External interventions (e.g. attempts by public authorities or civil society organisations) designed to enhance access to social capital for young people from less-privileged families have proven effective when it comes to the extra-familial forms of social relationships. Relationships that are formed in schools and in activities organised by different kinds of organisations (in schools and in the pupils' leisure time) are the spheres of such interventions. These relations can help young people in these areas to gain access to important sources of information and to come into contact with adults who can act as inspirational mentors and role models.

Activities which aim to empower these young people, as Stanton-Salazar puts it (2011, p. 1097), should embed them in resource-rich social networks, enhance their access to resource-generating relationships and connect them to informal mentors and pro-academic friends. Such contacts are fruitful in orienting young people towards this empowerment and thus raising their educational expectations.

References

Ball, S. (2003). *Class strategies and the education market: The middle classes and social advantage.* London: Routledge & Falmer.

Behtoui, A. (2017a). Social capital and the educational expectations of young people. *European Educational Research Journal, 16*(4), 487–503. doi:10.1177/1474904116682248

Behtoui, A. (2017b, August–September). *Swedish young people's after-school extra-curricular activities: Attendance, opportunities, and consequences.* Paper presented at the 13th Conference of the European Sociological Association, Athens, Greece.

116 *Alireza Behtoui et al.*

Behtoui, A., & Neergaard, A. (2016). Social capital and the educational achievement of young people in Sweden. *British Journal of Sociology of Education, 37*(7), 947–969. doi:10.1 080/01425692.2015.1013086

Bourdieu, P., & Passeron, J-C. (1977). *Reproduction in education, society and culture.* London: Sage.

Bradley, C. L., & Renzulli, L. A. (2011). The complexity of non-completion: Being pushed or pulled to drop out of high school. *Social Forces, 90*(2), 521–545. doi:10.1093/sf/sor003

Breen, R., & Goldthorpe, J. H. (1997). Explaining educational differentials. Towards a formal rational action theory. *Rationality and Society, 9*(3), 275–305. doi:10.1177/1043 46397009003002

Brookover, W., Erickson, E., & Joiner, L. (1967). Educational aspirations and educational plans in relation to academic achievement and socioeconomic status. *The School Review, 75*(4), 392–400.

Buchmann, C., & Dalton, B. (2002). Interpersonal influences and educational aspirations in 12 countries: The importance of institutional context. *Sociology of Education, 72*(2), 99–122.

Bunar, N., & Sernhede, O. (2013). *Skolan Och Ojämlikhetens Urbana Geografi: Om Skolan, Staden Och Valfriheten.* Göteborg: Daidalos.

Coleman, J. S. (1988). Social capital in the creation of human capital. *American Journal of Sociology, 94*(supplement), 95–120.

De Witte, K., Cabus, S., Thyssen, G., Groot, W., & van den Brink, H. M. (2013). A critical review of the literature on school dropout. *Educational Research Review, 10*, 13–28. doi:10.1016/j.edurev.2013.05.002

Feliciano, C., & Rumbaut, R. G. (2005). Gendered paths: Educational and occupational expectations and outcomes among adult children of immigrants. *Ethnic and Racial Studies, 28*(6), 1087–1118. doi:10.1080/01419870500224406

Hirschman, A. O. (2004). *Exit, voice, and loyalty: Responses to decline in firms, organizations, and states.* Cambridge, MA: Harvard University Press.

Reynolds, J. R., & Burge, S. W. (2008). Educational expectations and the rise in women's post-secondary attainments. *Social Science Research, 37*, 485–499. doi:10.1080/0141 9870500224406

Rumberger, R. W. (1983). Dropping out of high school: The influence of race, sex, and family background. *American Educational Research Journal, 20*(2), 199–220. doi:10.3102/ 00028312020002199

Sernhede, O., & Broman, I. T. (2014). *Segregation, utbildning Och Ovanliga Lärprocesser.* Stockholm: Liber.

Sewell, W. H., Haller, A. O., & Portes, A. (1969). The educational and early occupational attainment process. *American Sociological Review, 34*(1), 82–92. doi:10.2307/2092789

Stanton-Salazar, R. D. (2011). A social capital framework for the study of institutional agents and their role in the empowerment of low-status students and youth. *Youth & Society, 43*(3), 1066–1109. doi:10.1177/0044118X10382877

Sue, S., & Okazaki, S. (1990). Asian-American educational achievements: A phenomenon in search of an explanation. *American Psychologist, 45*(8), 913–920. doi: 10.1037/ 1948-1985.S.1.45

Swartz, D. (1997). *Culture and power: The sociology of Pierre Bourdieu.* Chicago: University of Chicago Press.

Taylor, C. (1997). *Philosophical arguments.* Cambridge, MA: Harvard University Press.

8 What's school got to do with it?

Comparing educational aspirations of Dutch and English ethnic white girls from lower socioeconomic backgrounds

Talitha Stam and Maurice Crul

Introduction

Each educational system is unique in the many ways it reflects both the context and historical development of a given country (Braster & Theisens, 2016, p. 37). Within an educational system, institutional arrangements are important as they determine further educational and occupational opportunities (Crul, 2015; Van Praag, Boone, Stevens, & Van Houtte, 2015). In the Netherlands, secondary education is organised through tracking where from age 12 pupils are selected into three tracks: an academic, a general-level or a vocational track. These tracks are hierarchically ordered and they prepare students for different future occupations. Amongst the tracks, the vocational track is perceived as the lowest in status. Moreover, it accommodates the highest number of students from families with a low socioeconomic status (SES). Although most Dutch schools or schooling groups offer all pathways, vocational tracks are often segregated in another building than the main school building. This contrasts with England where there are no formal tracks, only within-school tracks. This means that students of all abilities are housed in the same school building (Van Houtte & Stevens, 2015). Over the years, the Netherlands has received criticism on this policy of early selection into different tracks which results in highly segregated schools. In this context, Dutch educational experts have suggested alternative institutional arrangements. The VO-raad, which is the Dutch council for secondary education for instance, suggested implementing the British secondary education model in which high school exams (GCSE) can be done at different levels for each school subject, instead of taking the exams for all subjects at one level as in the case in the Netherlands (Dutch council for secondary education, 2015). The Dutch and English school systems differ from each other in important ways that could potentially influence both the aspirations and the resources to realise pupils' aspirations. In the Dutch school system, because of early selection, pupils are forced to think about their school and job aspirations at an early age. This can potentially have both positive and negative effects. It can be positive because pupils start to think about these issues early and therefore perhaps make more informed choices. It can also be negative because when they make misaligned choices they could be stuck in tracks without possibilities to repair their choices. The English school system with its late formal selection does not ask pupils to make choices early in relation to future professions. This, on the one hand, gives pupils more time to think about their aspirations, but on the other hand, it also perhaps postpones thinking and talking about the matter until it is too late.

We present the narratives of two 15-years-old ethnic white girls from a lower socioeconomic class who attend schools in these two contrasting educational systems. These girls have in common that they both aspire to become game developers. Their stories in pursuit of these aspirations reveal complex issues of power relations between teachers and students, the cultural capital or the lack thereof in their families and the challenges their SES offers (cf. Jonker, 2006). In the in-depth interviews and ethnographic data, we see the interplay between the micro level (individual aspirations), the meso level (school and family context) and the macro (national educational institutional arrangements). The main research question we formulated for our case studies is: "In what ways do Dutch and English girls voice their comparable aspirations, and how do institutional arrangements in education influence their resources and the development and realisation of their aspirations?"

Theoretical framework

In the sociology of education, aspirations are often used as an explanatory factor for school attainment and school achievement, because aspirations can motivate or demotivate pupils to continue with their education. Therefore, much of the existing data on pupils' aspirations actually measures educational intentions or expectations (Baillergeau, Duyvendak, & Abdallah, 2015). An important factor shaping pupils' aspirations is the school type and school context (Archer, DeWitt, & Wong, 2014). The type of school pupils can choose or are allowed to choose, which, amongst other things, relates to the study programme and the subjects offered, is influenced by options presented by the school officials, pupils' competencies and aspirations, and the interactions pupils have with peers, parents and school staff. Pupils' school choice decisions and their aspirations are highly intertwined; hence we investigate in detail how their aspirations are formed and realised over time. Moreover, the messages pupils receive within their specific school context reflect upon and stand in relation to the broader social and cultural context, which students evaluate in relation to their potential abilities and likelihood of success (Fuller, 2009, p. 159). Anyon's (1980) work on 'hidden curriculum' analyses pupil-teacher interactions in American elementary schools, in communities with varying levels of SES; he revealed how the expectations of teachers help to shape what and how schoolchildren learn and what future work they are being prepared for. In a more recent study where power relations in an everyday secondary school context have been studied in relation to the development and realisation of pupils' aspirations, Stam (2017) shows how difficult it still is for pupils in the lowest school levels

What's school got to do with it? 119

to openly express high ambitions in school and, in return, for the teachers to take those ambitions seriously, given both the low level of their school track and their often disruptive behaviour in class. To better understand the development and realisation of pupils' aspirations in lower secondary education, Stam (2017) introduced the concepts 'reasons' and 'resources', in which 'reasons' refers to the explanations behind their aspirations; and 'resources' describes what is needed to achieve aspirations. By linking the study of pupils' aspirations to the literature on the effects of institutional arrangements, we explore how institutional arrangements in education influence both pupils' resources and the development and realisation of pupils' aspirations.

Institutional arrangements characterise an educational system, and shape the opportunities and constraints faced by students and their parents in schools (Erikson & Jonsson, 1996). In a comparative study, Crul, Schneider, and Lelie (2012) found that second-generation Turks across several European countries show very different outcomes, which they explain by differences in institutional arrangements in each country (see also Crul, 2015; Schnell, 201). Based on their results, Crul and Schneider have developed the comparative integration context theory which argues that the success of the second generation across countries depends on opportunities offered by the school systems in place and the way labour market institutions function in the different countries (Crul & Schneider, 2010). Hence, in general, this theory shows the mechanisms between students' agencies and the structures of the school and labour market. According to the comparative integration context theory, the most influential factors within the institutional arrangements in education are the starting age of school, the age of selection and tracking. Tracking, in addition to other forms of ability grouping such as streaming or setting of pupils, is a general feature of institutional arrangements in education in Europe (Van Houtte & Stevens, 2015). The central argument behind tracking is that homogeneous classrooms permit a focused curriculum and appropriately paced instruction that leads to the most productive learning environment for all students (Hanushek & Wößmann, 2006, p. C63). According to Buchmann and Dalton (2002, p. 99), in countries with relatively open, undifferentiated secondary schooling, like England, peers' and parents' attitudes towards academic performance significantly influence pupils' attitudes and aspirations, because most occupational trajectories are still open to all students until late in the game. In the Netherlands, on the other hand, where pupils are sorted into different educational trajectories at an early age, Buchmann and Dalton (2002, p. 102) argue that students' aspirations are already largely determined by the type of school they have been tracked into. Interestingly, empirical results, however, show that the aspirations of Dutch students in lower vocational tracks are not limited to low-level professions (Elffers, 2011; Traag, 2012). This can be explained in part by the fact that it is possible to move from a lower vocational track to a middle vocational track all the way up to higher education. This possibility potentially leaves options open for students.

Study

This chapter is based on an international research project on early school leaving in nine European countries. This collaboration provided the opportunity to make an in-depth comparison between a school in the UK and a school in the Netherlands. The English-Dutch comparison is especially illuminating as the stratified character of the Dutch educational system contrasts with the comprehensive nature of the English educational system.

Research context

The English school is a large, state-funded comprehensive secondary school offering vocational courses and has been ranked as an Ofsted[1] outstanding provider. This school is located in a deprived area in the northeast of England, which has the highest youth unemployment rates in England (Ryan & Lőrinc, 2015; Gregory, 2016). Most of the pupils at this school have an ethnic white English background. The Dutch counterpart is a public school in an inner-city in the Randstad[2] the Netherlands. This school is part of a broader secondary school group, offering all pathways from pre-vocational to pre-academic education. The comprehensive school has approximately 2,000 pupils spread over several buildings in and around a large city in the Randstad. For this chapter, we focussed on one school location, which offers basic and advanced pre-vocational secondary education programmes. This school location has approximately 500 pupils from predominately lower-class backgrounds.

Schools

In Table 8.1 we give a brief overview of both schools under study and also show how to progress to the study of game design within the Dutch and English school systems.

Table 8.1 Differences in school characteristics and tracking differences between two target schools in England and the Netherlands

	Dutch secondary school	English secondary school
Number of pupils	500 (mixed)	1,500 (mixed)
Age	12–16 (years 1–4)	11–16/18 (years 7–11/13)
Class size	18 pupils	22 pupils
Special needs	70% (LWOO[1])	20% (SEND[2])
National school inspection	Satisfactory 2016	Outstanding (Ofsted 2013)
Between-school tracking	End of primary school (age 12), pupils are divided into three tracks: vocational, general and academic	Up to the end of year 9 (age 14), all pupils follow the same curriculum

	Dutch secondary school	English secondary school
Ability grouping	Within the vocational track there are four ability levels	Each year pupils are set in groups 1–6 for English, Mathematics and Science
Choosing subject options	Vocational pathway in year 2 (ages 13/14) for years 3 and 4	End of year 9 (age 14) for years 10 and 11
National curriculum assessments	Year 4 (ages 15/16)	Year 9 (age 14) Key Stage 3 SATs
		Year 11 (age 16) GCSE[3]
School results	100% of the pupils received a vocational diploma	30% Level 1 (D–G levels); 70% Level 2 (C, B, A and A+ levels)
Progression to study of game design		
Preparatory training	MBO Level 2 Creative Production course	BTEC Level 2 Media Production course
Entry level for preparatory training	Basic vocational programme diploma plus successful interview and ability test	4 GCSE at grades D–E, including Mathematics and English; possibility to retake English and Mathematics GCSEs plus successful interview and visual work
Duration preparatory training	1–2 years full-time	1 year full-time
Game design course	MBO Level 3 game design	BTEC Level 3 game design
Entry-level game design	Middle-management vocational programme diploma or equivalent MBO Level 2 qualification plus portfolio of work and successful interview	Four GCSEs at grades A+–C/9–4, including English or Mathematics or equivalent BTEC Level 2 qualification; portfolio of work; successful interview and satisfactory reference
Duration game design study	2–3 years full-time	2 years full-time
Progression after Level 3 game design study	MBO Level 4	BTEC Level 3, the Extended Diploma
Duration	2–3 years full-time	1 year full-time
Progression to university degree	University of Applied Sciences BA Creative Media and Game Technologies in Game Design	University BA Digital Arts
Duration university degree	4 years full-time	3 years full-time

Notes:

1 Learning support (LWOO) is available for pupils who need extra support in obtaining their lower secondary vocational diploma and is usually provided by the schools in the form of extra lessons or homework assistance (source: www.government.nl/topics/secondary-education/contents/pre-vocational-secondary-education-vmbo).

2 Special educational needs and disabilities (SEND) can affect a child or young person's ability to learn (source: www.gov.uk/children-with-special-educational-needs/overview).

3 The General Certificate of Secondary Education (GCSE) is the principal means of assessment for 16-year-olds.

Data collection

During the school year 2014–2015 a school ethnography and biographical interviews were conducted in both schools; Stam spent three months in the English school and ten months in the Dutch school. The core respondents were 20 ethnic white working-class girls between 15 and 17 years old. The ten racially white girls of Dutch descent were in their final year of lower secondary vocational education and had diverse backgrounds in terms of their parents' educations and occupations. However, none of their parents had a university degree. All ten racially white girls of English descent received the Free School Meal, which is based on the low incomes and the education levels of their parents. They were in Key Stage 4, Year 10, and age 15, with various educational levels. Two years later, a second round of interviews took place with the Dutch girls. Through the official local authorities and school records we were informed about the educational position of the English girls two years later in school year 2016–2017.

Analysis

The aim of this chapter is to explore how institutional arrangements in education influence pupils' aspirations. Our data provided a unique opportunity to analyse a Dutch and an English girl who had a similar aspiration of becoming a professional game maker; on top of this both girls lived in single-parent homes. Hence, the respondents were very similar, which allowed us to explore the importance of differences within the schools embedded in two different national school systems. The data of the two girls were systematically compared and analysed through the concepts of 'reasons' and 'resources' of pupils' aspirations as explained in the theoretical framework paragraph.

Meet the girls

Let us first introduce the two girls, fictively named Melanie and Mandy, both 15-year-old ethnically white working-class girls who are being raised in a single-parent home where both their mothers left school without a secondary school diploma. During the first round of interviews, Melanie attended a Dutch lower secondary vocational school and Mandy an English comprehensive state-funded secondary school.

Dutch girl: Melanie

Every spare moment of the day Melanie plays video games on her PC or the Xbox that was given to her for free by a family member. She has eye-catching brightly coloured hair that changes from time to time to green, purple, red or black. Her coloured hair contrasts with her pale face, and she wears dark, alternative-styled clothes. Melanie went for the first time to an Animae[3] event with her friends when she heard that it would take place in her own city. Melanie and her friends saved money to go fully dressed up to the event where people of all ages come together to enjoy Animae, video games, Manga[4] and other popular modern Asian videos and games. "At this event it suddenly occurred to me. I love Animae. Wouldn't it be supercool to design my own video game, where strong, beautiful and smart girls with normal (not half naked) clothes play the leading roles?!" Although she had no idea how much the job of game maker would pay or whether there were actual jobs in this sector, it nevertheless seemed great to her to become a game maker. Melanie lives with her mother in a suburb where they rent a three-bedroom apartment in a large apartment building in front of the metro station, which is a few stops away from the school. Her father is unknown to her as he left when she was 2 years old. She has no siblings. Her mother works in the care work sector as a cleaning lady. Sometimes Melanie helps her mother make extra money, in addition to her student job as a cashier at a local supermarket. She uses that money for her personal expenses. In appearance Melanie resembles her mother and vice versa; both wear alternative dark clothes and both dye their hair. From the very start of secondary school, Melanie has dyed her hair various colours. Her friends also have coloured hair, but at the secondary school she attends she is one of the few pupils who look like that. Melanie is attending this secondary vocational school because it was the closest lower secondary vocational school to her home. She works on her Manga drawings whenever she is not in class.

English girl: Mandy

Mandy is a 15-year-old petite, ethnically white English girl with a pale face and dyed dark red hair. She wears the standard dark blue school uniform with pants and a polo shirt, all a size too big for her. Mandy has been drawing Manga cartoons since primary school age. "I really got into it and started to improve more and I really like it." After school, she plays free online video games and listens to Japanese rock music. "I love the Japanese culture and all that." Mandy lives with her mother in a small three-bedroom apartment in a deprived neighbourhood in the northeast of England. Her father is unknown to Mandy. Her mother was 17 years old when she had Mandy, a year after having "failed her final examinations (GCSE[5])", which resulted in her mother becoming a NEET.[6] Mandy explains: "Without good GCSE grades, you have huge difficulties to find good jobs. Me mum [my mother] never found a steady job." A similar thing happened to the grandmother of Mandy. "Even me nanna [my grandmother] had to go to work at the age of fifteen, when she got me mum [my mother]. She was smart, but she never got the opportunity." Trying to prevent the same fate for Mandy, she and her mother decided to go to the best school in the area. Hence, Mandy takes a 30-minute bus ride every day to come to this school. "This school gets really good Ofsted rates and so me mum [my mother], we both decided on this school." Her favourite school subject is Mathematics, because she is very good at that. Mandy has heard that you must be good at Mathematics to become a game developer. Her teacher told her that it pays very well and that it provides many job opportunities. Mandy said she needed to ask her teacher twice about the job opportunities and salary just to be sure, because she says; "I don't want to end up like me mum [my mother]."

Aspirations analysed

There is much research about how specific features of educational systems influence the educational trajectories of young people (Van de Werfhorst & Mijs, 2010; Crul & Schneider, 2010; Crul, Schneider, & Lelie, 2012; Van Praag et al., 2015; Van Houtte & Stevens, 2015). This study combines the literature on the effects of institutional arrangements with studies on pupils' aspirations. For this, we elaborate on the concepts 'reasons' and 'resources' (Stam, 2017) in which 'reasons' refers to the explanations why pupils have certain aspirations; and the 'resources' that are needed to achieve these aspirations. The stories of Melanie and Mandy are analysed through the concepts 'reasons' and 'resources' to unravel how specific features of educational systems influence the distinctive ways of shaping similar aspirations.

Melanie's reasons

"I love Animae. Wouldn't it be supercool to design my own game?"

The Dutch girl Melanie developed her aspiration of becoming a game developer primarily based on what she likes doing, independent from the study programme she was following in secondary vocational education. In the Netherlands, at age 14, vocational students are already required to select a vocational programme that prepares them for a specific profession. However, many of these vocational students experience difficulties in selecting a programme that suits their interests and abilities (Elffers, 2011). Melanie chose the study programme Health Care, because that was the only available programme where Mathematics was not compulsory. However, later Melanie developed an interest to design her own video games. Via the Internet Melanie figures out which senior vocational college offers a study programme to become a professional game developer. Together with her mother she visits the college on introduction day. At this college, and in contrast to her secondary vocational school, she meets other girls who are also into gaming. She immediately feels at home in the new school and makes many new friends. "There was this girl there, also with coloured hair, and I thought that she must have had the same interests as me and I was right, so we became friends."

Melanie's resources

Family and school

Buchmann and Dalton (2002, p. 104) stated that in a differentiated secondary school system, like in the Netherlands, students may feel that the opinions of parents do not matter much, because trajectories are pretty much determined at an early stage. Although the vocational education trajectory of Melanie seemed rather fixed in secondary vocational education already, Melanie could still switch to a study where she could learn to become a game developer. Melanie pursues her aspirations with the support of her mother. In her choice to become a game developer, making money is not an important motivation, even when her own mother tries to make ends meet every month. Her mother is also happy with everything Melanie desires to become: "if it is something she loves doing, it is fine with me", says Melanie's mother. Melanie's mother is not pushing her daughter to aim for a job with a particular high salary either, but supports what Melanie wants to do. This is in line with what teachers in the Netherlands advocate for vocational education students from a young age onwards. Because pupils must make choices at a very young age, within the limits of the school track they attend, the emphasis is on choosing programmes that speak to the aspirations of children. Parents seem to follow the approach of the school in supporting what their children like to do.

School and classroom climate

Melanie described her secondary vocational school as being "large and loud". Melanie talks about her classmates as "disrespectful to the teachers". This resonates with our ethnographic observations during classes and is in line with the OECD findings that the Netherlands has one of the lowest indexes of disciplinary classroom climate (OECD, 2013, 2016). Stam in a previous publication (2017) demonstrated how disruptive classroom behaviour indirectly impedes the realisation of pupils' aspirations. "In the context of both the low educational level of the school and disruptive class behaviour, it is difficult for teachers to take pupils' high aspirations seriously and, therefore, assist them accurately in the realisation of their dreams" (Stam, 2017, p. 267). The problematic disciplinary class climate meant for Melanie that her teachers were often too occupied with controlling the classroom situation and unintendedly overlooked her needs. Less attention of teachers meant more dependency on her mother and significant others to develop and realise her aspirations. Because of Melanie's strong desire to become a game developer, she figured out by herself what was needed to realise her aspiration.

School system

At first glance, the Dutch education system seemed to be restrictive for Melanie because she needed to select one of the four vocational programmes offered by her secondary school that prepare pupils for a specific job or job sector. But, none of the offered pathways appealed to Melanie. Her eventual choice for the health care programme was simply because that was the only one in which Mathematics was not a compulsory course. When the final year of secondary vocational education arrived (at age 16), she needed to sign up for senior vocational education (SVE). The Dutch vocational education system has a high degree of flexibility even when choices for specific programmes are made earlier. This allows students to change the direction of their studies. Thus, Melanie had the opportunity to pursue her aspirations even though she had earlier chosen a very different study programme. After obtaining her secondary vocational school diploma, Melanie took a preparatory training course that she needed to finish first in order to enter her gaming study. For Melanie, the transition to SVE is an opportunity to make a new start in her educational career and realise her aspiration. However, the flexibility of the Dutch educational system is for many pupils more disadvantageous.

Mandy's reasons

Mandy's reasons for wanting to become a game developer form an interesting combination of aspirations and skills and an assessment of job opportunities. Since primary school, she has enjoyed drawing Manga cartoons, and she regularly plays online free video games. At the same time, a subject she likes and performs above average in is Mathematics, a crucial subject for becoming a game developer. She is also concerned with the job opportunities, because she does not want to end up like her mother, who was a NEET when she left secondary school. Given the current educational level and working-class family background, Mandy's aspirations could be considered to be relatively high. British studies have so far largely been unable to adequately explain the high aspirations of working-class students (Fuller, 2009, p. 160). Freie (2007, p. 4) argues that, in the changing economy and job market, the traditional expectations of a working-class man earning money while a woman stays at home with the children is no longer economically feasible for most working-class families. Therefore, achieving advanced education and finding employment for women are increasingly viewed as necessary steps to obtain financial stability (Freie, 2007, p. 110).

Mandy's resources

Family and school

In an open, comprehensive schooling system, such as that in England, parents and significant others tend to largely influence pupils' educational choices, because their trajectories are more open and decisions on further education are only made at the end of secondary school (Buchmann & Dalton, 2002, p. 99). In this context, both Mandy and her mother view the current position of Mandy, being in a low ability class, as temporary and they still both aim for the highest possible educational level, with the specific aim of getting the best job opportunities. Mandy said about her mother: "When I get like Es, she [mother] tends to say, 'You need to revise more. You need to try better.' She [mother] wants us to revise and get good grades and get a good job." The expectation of Mandy's mother for her daughter to succeed is high, and corresponds with the general finding that overall parents' expectations in the United Kingdom are high (OECD, 2012). Mandy continues: "The pressure is on me, just to achieve these things, because they [mother and grandmother] couldn't when they were younger." Mandy noticeably discusses her future plans in the light of the educational and occupational experiences, failures and struggles of her mother by stating, "I don't want to end up like me mum [my mother]." Several other studies likewise showed how daughters both identify and empathise with the struggles of their mothers and translate these experiences into a need for financial independence (Freie, 2007; Hubbard, 2005). Luckily for Mandy the occupation of game developer offers, according to her teachers, "good job opportunities" and therefore Mandy's mother supports Mandy in her aspirations.

School

At secondary school, Mandy worried about getting the highest grades possible. She believed that, if she failed, her future options would be drastically limited just as had previously happened with her mother and grandmother. Mandy: "It just affects your whole future." This focus seems in part to take pupils away from developing their aspirations to achieving the best possible GCSE results. The English teachers interviewed for the research seem to follow a similar approach: "You are just trying to get the kids the best possible grades for that particular course so that's more our focus." Even in Mandy's low-ability class, pupils work hard to get the best possible grades for their GCSEs. Most of her classmates openly express their hopes and dreams of going to university. However, in private, teachers communicate that university is unreachable for most of the low-ability learners, and say, "If they [pupils] are more motivated by the idea of going to uni [university], well . . ." An OECD (2012) report showed that teachers' expectations of students in the UK are well below average, which could result in teacher attitudes that may negatively influence pupils' learning environments. Fuller (2009, p. 140) argues that there is a circular element in this environment: "The messages students receive within school are a response to an individualised defeatist sense of their own abilities that then impacts on attitudes to education." Mandy's motivation, however, is largely external; she concentrates on her favourite and best school subject, Mathematics, because she has understood that one must be good at Mathematics to become a game developer.

School system

In the English educational system, the General Certificate of Secondary Education (GCSE) test takes place at the end of compulsory secondary education, at age 16. For that reason, secondary education is predominantly focused on preparations for this national curriculum assessment. Although Mandy knew from an early age onwards that she was interested in game developing, her GCSE results were not sufficient to enter the BTEC Level 3 study Game Design, where the benchmark of satisfactory achievement is 5+ GCSEs at grades A+ to C, including English and Mathematics (Ryan & Lőrinc, 2016). Although repeating years in English secondary schooling is not possible, Further Education (FE) colleges do now offer GCSE re-sits. This was not the case when Mandy's mother and grandmother went to school. This meant that, although Mandy first got stuck in the system with her strong aspirations, she found a loophole by doing the BTEC Level 2 preparatory training course, while also taking extra courses at the FE College to re-sit the GCSE test scores. In this way, she still hopes to progress to the BTEC Level 3 Game Design, which can be a route into higher education.

Discussion

Various studies have shown how institutional arrangements in education determine further educational and occupational opportunities (Van de Werfhorst & Mijs, 2010; Crul & Schneider, 2010; Crul et al., 2012; Van Praag et al., 2015). By combining the bigger literature on the effects of institutional arrangements with studies on pupils' aspirations, this chapter explored how institutional arrangements in education have influenced the development and realisation of pupils' aspirations. For this, we have used our ethnographic and longitudinal data that provided a unique opportunity to analyse similar aspirations amongst two ethnic white Dutch and English 15-year-old girls who happened to have been involved in the same Japanese Manga sub-cultures and had a comparable SES. We explored their stories and how specific features in the Dutch and English educational systems influenced the development and realisations of their aspirations through the concepts 'reasons' and 'resources' (Stam, 2017). 'Reasons' referred to why pupils have certain aspirations and contributes to the development of pupils' aspirations, and 'resources' described which elements, both positive and negative, in terms of family support, the school environment and national school system, influence these aspirations and contribute to the realisation of pupils' aspirations. The 'reasons' we identified for both girls seeking to become game developers are very similar and are largely shaped by the global culture around gaming. However, their 'resources' are different and are formed partly by differences in the two school systems. The Dutch school system with its early tracking closes off many options at a young age. Moreover, it negatively influences the school climate for students who are grouped together in the lowest tracks. Besides this negative aspect of the school system, however, is also a more positive element to early tracking. Students at a very early age need to start thinking about future career options. This creates feelings of great uncertainty for those who are unsure about what path to choose, but for those who have a clear idea about what they want to become, it creates the opportunity to explore early on what they need to study and at what school level and direction they need to finish to fulfil their dreams. Early tracking in the Netherlands also comes with second chances to repair mistakes in choices made previously by providing the possibility to switch while entering senior vocational education (SVE). The case study from the Netherlands shows that such loopholes, especially for motivated students, offer chances to realise their aspirations. The much more open comprehensive school system in England offers the illusion of providing chances for all, but through informal ability tracking many pupils will not be able to pursue higher educational opportunities. This system also offers loopholes for the most motivated lower-educated students. The two school systems seem to restrict opportunities for children from disadvantaged backgrounds in different ways but with very similar results. To overcome the hindrances of both systems, both students profiled in this chapter had to carve out alternative routes via preparatory trainings that relied on their own and on family resources. Strong aspirations played an important role in forging these alternative pathways.

Although our results are based on an ethnographic study of ethnic white Dutch and English girls attending two secondary schools, it can be argued that our results could be relevant for other groups as well. For example, research amongst children of immigrants has shown that the use of alternative pathways is very common amongst successful students in this group (Crul et al., 2012; Schnell, 2014). Moreover, our study outcomes may be extended to other comparable countries.

The findings in this chapter help us to refine the mechanisms we described between agency and structure in the integration context theory (Crul & Schneider, 2010; Crul, 2015). Aspirations play a key role in understanding why some groups make use of loopholes and alternative pathways in the educational system. It usually asks for extra resources and motivation to find and make use of these loopholes. Both individual motivations of self-fulfilment and family support and pressure play a role in explaining this further.

Notes

1 Ofsted is the Office for Standards in Education, Children's Services and Skills. They inspect and regulate services that care for children and young people, and services that provide education and skills for learners of all ages.
2 The Randstad is a conurbation in the Netherlands and consists of the four largest Dutch cities (Amsterdam, Rotterdam, The Hague and Utrecht) and the surrounding areas. It has a population of more than seven million people.
3 Animae are Japanese animated cartoon videos.
4 Manga are Japanese comics.
5 General Certificate of Secondary Education (GCSE).
6 Young people (aged 16 to 24) who are not in education, employment or training.

References

Anyon, J. (1980). Social class and the hidden curriculum of work. *Journal of Education*, 67–92.
Archer, L., DeWitt, J., & Wong, B. (2014). Spheres of influence: What shapes young people's aspirations at age 12/13 and what are the implications for education policy? *Journal of Education Policy, 29*(1), 58–85.

Baillergeau, E., Duyvendak, J. W., & Abdallah, S. (2015). Heading towards a desirable future: Aspirations, commitments and the capability to aspire of young Europeans. *Open Citizenship*, *6*(1), 12–23.

Braster, S., & Theisens, H. (2016). Het onderwijs in de Lage Landen in historisch en internationaal perspectief. In Eidhof, B., Van Houtte, M., & Vermeulen, M. (Eds.), *Sociologen over onderwijs. Inzichten, praktijken en kritieken* (pp. 37–61). Antwerpen, Apeldoorn: Garant.

Buchmann, C., & Dalton, B. (2002). Interpersonal influences and educational aspirations in 12 countries: The importance of institutional context. *Sociology of Education*, 99–122.

Crul, M. (2015). Is education the pathway to success? A comparison of second generation Turkish professionals in Sweden, France, Germany and the Netherlands. *European Journal of Education*, *50*(3), 325–339.

Crul, M., & Schneider, J. (2010). Comparative integration context theory: Participation and belonging in new diverse European cities. *Ethnic and Racial Studies*, *33*(7), 1249–1268.

Crul, M., Schneider, J., & Lelie, F. (Eds.) (2012). *The European second generation compared: Does the integration context matter?* Amsterdam: Amsterdam University Press.

Dutch council for secondary education. (2015). Diploma op maat; Ruimte voor talent in het voortgezet onderwijs. *Report*.

Elffers, L. (2011). *The transition to post-secondary vocational education: Students' entrance*. Ph.D. Dissertation, University of Amsterdam, The Netherlands.

Erikson, R., & Jonsson, J. O. (Eds.) (1996). *Can education be equalized? The Swedish case in comparative perspective*. Boulder, CO: Westview Press.

Freie, C. (2007). *Class construction: White working-class student identity in the new millennium*. Lanham, MD: Lexington Books.

Fuller, C. (2009). *Sociology, gender and educational aspirations: Girls and their ambitions*. London: A&C Black.

Gregory, M. (2016). The employment landscape for young people in the UK. Challenges and opportunities. *Report EY Foundation*.

Hanushek, E. A., & Wößmann, L. (2006). Does educational tracking affect performance and inequality? Differences-in-differences evidence across countries. *The Economic Journal*, *116*(510), C63–C76.

Hubbard, L. (2005). The role of gender in academic achievement. *International Journal of Qualitative Studies in Education*, *18*(5), 605–623.

Jonker, E. (2006). School hurts: Refrains of hurt and hopelessness in stories about dropping out at a vocational school for care work. *Journal of Education and Work*, *19*(2), 121–140.

OECD. (2012). United Kingdom. In *Education at a glance 2012: OECD indicators*. Paris: OECD Publishing.

OECD. (2013). Netherlands. In *Education at a glance 2013: OECD indicators*. Paris: OECD Publishing.

OECD. (2016). Netherlands. In *Education at a glance 2016: OECD indicators*. Paris: OECD Publishing.

Ryan, L., & Lőrinc, M. (2015). Interrogating early school leaving, youth unemployment and NEETs: Understanding local contexts in two English regions. *Educação, Sociedade & Culturas*, *45*.

Ryan, L., & Lőrinc, M. (2016). 'Getting your foot in the door': The role of serendipity, heightened sensitivity and social networks in recruiting education research participants. *CIAIQ2016*, *5*.

Schnell, P. (2014). *Educational Mobility of Second-Generation Turks*. Amsterdam: Amsterdam University Press.

Stam, T. (2017). Reasons and resources: Understanding pupils' aspirations in lower vocational Dutch education. *Ethnography and Education, 12*(3), 259–270.

Traag, T. (2012). *Early school leaving in the Netherlands: A multidisciplinary study of risk and protective factors explaining early school-leaving.* Ph.D. Dissertation, Maastricht University.

Van de Werfhorst, H. G., & Mijs, J. J. (2010). Achievement inequality and the institutional structure of educational systems: A comparative perspective. *Annual Review of Sociology, 36*, 407–428.

Van Houtte, M., & Stevens, P. A. (2015). Tracking and sense of futility: The impact of between-school tracking versus within-school tracking in secondary education in Flanders (Belgium). *British Educational Research Journal, 41*(5), 782–800.

Van Praag, L., Boone, S., Stevens, P. A., & Van Houtte, M. (2015). How tracking structures attitudes towards ethnic out-groups and interethnic interactions in the classroom: An ethnographic study in Belgium. *Social Psychology of Education, 18*(1), 165–184.

Part III

Educational trajectories of youth (at risk of) leaving school early

9 Switching practices in vocational education

A comparative case study in Flanders (Belgium) and the Netherlands

Lore Van Praag, Elif Keskiner, Rut Van Caudenberg, Ward Nouwen, Talitha Stam, Noel Clycq, Mariana Orozco, Christiane Timmerman and Maurice Crul

Introduction

Across educational systems, ethnic and social inequality processes take place in various ways (Stevens & Dworkin, 2014). Structural characteristics of educational systems are often more influential than we realise, as they can strengthen or weaken existing social and ethnic inequalities in education as well as later on in life (Crul et al., 2012). In this chapter, we focus on one particular aspect that shapes the educational routes of young people to acquire an educational qualification in two different yet comparable educational systems (Braster & Theisens, 2016): the main aim of this study is to shed light on and compare the switching practices between fields of study/tracks during one's educational trajectory – in- and outside mainstream vocational secondary education in Flanders (northern part of Belgium) and the Netherlands. The study of switching practices is relevant as these practices are used in most educational systems to adjust and/or specify one's educational choices over the course of one's educational career, to align these choices with students' abilities, interests and aspirations, and to allow some kind of specialisation towards the end of secondary education. However, less attention has been paid to how these practices are put into use and the side effects associated with them, such as feelings of demotion, school disengagement and/or early school leaving (Kalmijn & Graaykamp; Kloosterman & De Graaf, 2009, 2010; Spruyt, Van Droogenbroeck, & Kavadias, 2015; Van Praag, Boone, Stevens, & Van Houtte, 2015).

This chapter aims, firstly, to understand how switching practices takes place in urban contexts in Flanders and the Netherlands, considering how their respective educational systems influence the institutionalised and individual switching practices of students between fields of study and tracks. Secondly, we focus on how youngsters' switching practices towards and within vocational education is considered as being less prestigious in both systems (Clycq, Timmerman, Van Avermaet, Wets, & Herman, 2014; Rezai, Crul, Severiens, & Keskiner, 2015; Van Praag et al., 2015). In previous studies, we already found that youngsters in vocational education tracks change between fields of study/tracks more frequently over the course of their career and also do this more often at other moments than the foreseen transitional moments, compared with youngsters in other educational tracks (Van Praag et al., 2015; Lamote et al., 2013; Dronker & Korthals, 2016; Clycq et al., 2014). Previous research on educational trajectories studied the interplay between individual, institutional and systemic features that characterise the routes of youngsters through education, such as truancy (e.g., Attwood & Croll, 2006), track placement and choices (e.g., Dauber, Alexander, & Entwistle, 1996), the timing and process of labour market entry (e.g., Saar, Unt, & Kogan, 2008) and potential enrolment in higher education (e.g., Turner, 2004). However, less attention has been paid to the actual features of educational systems that influence how young people navigate within these systems and change between distinct fields of study or tracks. The focus on switching practices within vocational tracks provides an important starting point to reflect upon students' trajectories within the Dutch and the Flemish systems, which are often only briefly touched upon in research and/or policy papers and difficult to grasp for people not familiar with these systems. Gaining a deeper understanding of these switching practices within different educational systems is important, as it could shed light on how these practices may hinder learning and teaching practices, disturb the alignment between students' aspirations and opportunities, and complicate the restructuring of educational systems (Van Praag et al., 2015). Furthermore, insights into practices of students changing fields of study and tracks shed an interesting light on the functioning of and the ways to navigate through educational systems, showing that youngsters increasingly use their agency during their educational trajectories.

The Dutch and the Flemish educational systems compared: switching practices

Both the Flemish and the Dutch educational systems are situated in similar contexts vis-à-vis education and migration. They have a comparable hierarchical structure between more academically and more vocationally oriented study tracks in secondary education and share a similar history in the development of their respective educational systems (Braster & Theisens, 2016). What becomes apparent in comparative literature on both educational systems is that the different opportunity structures in both educational systems lead to different educational pathways in terms of length, transitions and outcomes amongst socially disadvantaged ethnic minority students (Crul & Schneider, 2010; Crul et al., 2012). However, the two systems are different with regard to the structuring within educational tracks and fields of study, as well as track allocation (i.e., the use of standardised tests and certificates to pass to the next year), and the thresholds for entering higher education (Stevens & Dworkin, 2014). Nevertheless, despite the differences, both possess an implicit – not formally

Switching practices in vocational education 137

acknowledged – hierarchy in terms of the more academically oriented and the more vocationally oriented study tracks, which deeply affects students' opportunities with respect to their futures. We briefly sketch some of the main differences between the two systems that are relevant for this chapter (for more information, see Eurydice, 2015; Stevens & Dworkin, 2014).

In Flemish regular full-time education, students can – next to the academic track (ASO) and arts track (KSO) – choose between (or are oriented to) the technical track (TSO), which offers more theoretical courses and is meant to orient students to both the labour market and professional higher education, and the more practically oriented vocation track (BSO), which includes fewer theoretical courses and more directly prepares its students for labour market entry. While students in academic, arts and technical tracks get automatic access to higher education, students in vocational tracks first need to follow a specialist ('seventh') year. Besides these tracks, youngsters from the age of 15 or 16 onwards (depending on having finished lower secondary education) also have the possibility to enrol in so-called alternative learning arenas that offer part-time work-based learning. Within the broadly categorised field of 'vocational education', students have to opt for very specialised fields of study, such as hairdressing, woodwork, care or mechanics. Students' educational trajectories are steered by the certificate they receive from their teachers at the end of each school year. There are three types of certificates (A, B and C) that indicate in respective order whether students A) can pass to the next year in the same track/field of study, B) can choose between either passing to the next year provided they change track/field of study or repeat their year in the same track/field of study, or finally, C) have to repeat their year. This results in a lot of potential transition moments that include educational choices between fields of study and tracks. Students have to consider these certificates and – given the fact that changing from more vocational tracks (back) to academic tracks is very unlikely – these transitions are almost always one-way: from more academically or theoretically oriented to more vocationally and practically oriented tracks. In theory, from the start of secondary education students enjoy a lot of freedom to change between fields of study, tracks and schools (Van Praag, Stevens, & Van Houtte, 2014). At the same time, the certification process in Flanders – and the high level of freedom teachers and schools have in evaluating their students and deciding on the certificate they will receive – is not uncontested, as it is found to advantage some social groups over others as a result of teacher bias (Clycq et al., 2014; Spruyt, Laurijssen, & Van Dorsselaer, 2009).

In this particular element of the use of certificates based on teacher evaluation, the Flemish system differs fundamentally from the Dutch one, where students are directed to either lower secondary vocational education (VMBO), general secondary education (HAVO) or pre-university secondary education (VWO) based on the test results (called the "CITO" test) and the teachers' advice. The certification procedure and the tracking of students have crucial implications for students' upper secondary education options (Keskiner, 2015).

138 *Lore Van Praag et al.*

Similar to Flanders, the vocational track in the Netherlands prepares students for senior vocational education (SVE), while the general and academic tracks prepare them for higher education. Students also have the opportunity to leave their study over the course of their educational career and enrol in a different school, programme or location, yet the implications of switching clearly vary. In the Netherlands, students always need to wait for the next semester or sometimes year, depending on the programme, to start a new study. If a student wants to change her study to a different topic covered within the same department within the same location and school, the transition is smoother. They can transfer their points from the previous study and the school is not affected much by this change, whereas if the student goes to a different location or a different school or study programme, then they need to start their course of study over and the school loses its funding for this student. It is important to note that switching between Dutch SVE programmes is accompanied by financial consequences for both the students and the educational institutions. SVE institutions receive a certain amount of money from the Dutch government, amongst other things, based on the number of students and the number of degrees obtained within these institutions. For this calculation, the duration of a student's attendance of SVE is also taken into consideration – SVE institutions receive an increasingly smaller sum each year for a student. Switching is thus not fiscally prudent and not promoted by SVE institutions, because it often will take more time for these students to obtain a degree.

In the following sections we illustrate the impact of distinct switching practices, possibly leading to early school leaving, by comparing the educational trajectories and experiences of four youngsters within these systems.

Methods

Data were collected in two large, multi-ethnic cities with a relatively high percentage of early school leavers in Flanders, the northern part of Belgium, and in the Netherlands. Students were asked to participate in two semi-structured interviews, with a minimum of six months in between each interview. For this case study, we selected four youngsters to illustrate the various impacts of switching in two comparable but distinct educational systems. To grasp the reasons, ways and consequences of switching practices in these two educational systems, we first examined youngsters' entire educational trajectories. We selected youngsters who have switched between fields of study during their school career (Table 9.1).

We used the institutional arrangements of the educational systems as a starting point for comparison. Questions of the semi-structured interviews focused on nine themes: 'Aspirations and motivations', 'Educational trajectories', 'School-related and study behaviour', 'Connectedness to school and education', 'School-related and study behaviour', 'Employment experiences', 'Perceived challenges and resilience', 'Identity', and 'Social (support) networks'. These themes formed the starting point for more in-depth analyses that focused upon the educational

Switching practices in vocational education 139

Table 9.1 Background and educational features of the selected youngsters

	Hamza	*Sarah*	*Karima*	*Manu*
Gender	Male	Female	Female	Male
Ethnic descent	Moroccan descent	Angolan descent	Moroccan descent	Belgian descent
Educational system	Flemish	Dutch	Dutch	Flemish
Field of study enrolled in during the first interview	Car mechanics	Health and care	Cooking	Woodwork
Educational status at time of the second interview	Enrolled in regular secondary education (seventh specialization year)	Enrolled in regular SVE, school-based learning, Level 4)	Enrolled in regular SVE, school-based learning, Level 2	Enrolled in part-time work-based vocational track

trajectories of the youngsters. In each of these themes, the impact on the decision-making processes of the youngsters were discussed. All citations are translated from Dutch and edited by the authors to facilitate legibility.

Results

This case study shows how similar youngsters 'at risk' of early school leaving navigate their respective educational systems, and how switching practices within these systems manifest. While many more, varying trajectories can be noted, these cases are highly illustrative of the ways particular features of educational systems (in this case, switching between fields of study) affect the decision-making processes and aspirations of youngsters.

Hamza

Hamza, a Belgian boy of Moroccan descent, describes himself as a 'mediocre' student, as '*you can always achieve better*' and was attending the final and specialist year of vocational education, in the field of Car Mechanics, by the time of the second interview. When students are enrolled in this (seventh) specialist year, they are considered to be successfully finishing their educational career, and almost ready for labour market entry. However, when looking at Hamza's educational trajectory, it is less straightforward than would appear at first sight:

INTERVIEWER: "Have you even been to other schools or have you just been to this one here?"
HAMZA: "No, I've also been to other schools."

140 *Lore Van Praag et al.*

INTERVIEWER: "And which fields of study have you been enrolled in?"

HAMZA: "My first year of secondary school, I went to School A in City Z; there, I was enrolled in ASO [the academic track]. I immediately discovered that it didn't suit me. We had too much course material, and the teacher also told me that I was actually a lot better in working with my hands and stuff and that you can also study something technical. So, then I got a B-certificate [at the end of the school year], then I, myself, decided to just go to BSO [vocational track]."

Like many other students in Flanders, Hamza started his school career in the academic track, but changed to the vocational track (Van Praag et al., 2017). The quote shows how early on in his school career both school-driven and individual decision-making processes resulted in the youngster's enrolment in the vocational track. When he received a B-certificate at the end of his first school year in secondary education, it made him feel obliged to change tracks if he did not want to repeat his year. He then decided not to go to a technical track, but enrol immediately in a vocational track as his teacher suggested he would achieve better "when working with his hands". Although it remains unclear whether this teacher got actual information about his manual skills (as in academic tracks, teachers only see students' performances in academic, theoretical courses), he decided to follow this advice. What followed, however, was a trajectory of switching fields of studies and schools:

HAMZA: "In the second year, I actually changed school; I went to School B and attended a second year of 'office and retail'. I was still young. I had no sense then of a diploma or anything so I didn't actually know why I actually went to school. I played too much. I also did my second, and my third year and then I went to School C and there. . . . No, I did my second year in School C. And then, I went to School B in my third year and there it ended really badly."

INTERVIEWER: "You did not have a good experience?"

HAMZA: "That wasn't a good experience. I had good grades, but there were few. . . . There were teachers whom I couldn't stand. No, they couldn't stand me actually. . . . And yes, they gave me a C-certificate at the end of the school year, while I didn't actually *deserve* a C-certificate. I wanted actually, I wanted to take further action [to protest against it], but then I actually just went on a journey and I changed my mind a bit. And I really searched for a good school and I know many students – you know my neighbourhood boys who actually have all gone to school here [School D] – and they have always said that it's a really good school here and it is also near where I live. So it is actually not far. And then I came here, I did my third year again, 'Basic Mechanics', and it proceeded actually pretty good, so I did my third year and then I did my fourth year again here, 'Basic Mechanics'. Then we were allowed to choose whether we wanted a mechanical direction. 'Car Mechanics' or 'Bodywork (Cars)'. I already made up my mind to do 'Bodywork'. I did my fifth year here and also did my sixth year, and now

Switching practices in vocational education 141

I'm in my seventh year and I actually think this is actually the best school I've been in so far."

These interview extracts indicate that Hamza encountered difficulties when searching for a (vocational) career he would like to pursue later on. These difficulties were related to his relationships with teachers, perceived fairness of evaluation and the content of the courses he was enrolled in. However, in contrast with his bumpy start in secondary education, once he found a school where he felt he belonged and where he could study a career he appears to like, his educational trajectory took a more 'stable' turn. After finishing year 6 of vocational education, he even decided to continue studying and enrol in a seventh, specialist year, which allowed him to obtain an upper secondary education diploma, and in theory improve his labour market opportunities.

Sarah

Sarah is an Angolan-Dutch girl who arrived in the Netherlands at the age of 10. She started in SVE (senior vocational education) as Hairdresser in Level 2, a field of study she really enjoyed. Moreover, as her aunt owned a black hair studio, she could easily find an internship and get access to useful resources. She attended this programme for its entire two-year duration; however, she could not graduate with a diploma, because she was not able to complete her final assignment. This assignment was to find a male model with 'European hair', but that proved very difficult for her. She was really disappointed about not finishing her degree in Hairdressing. To be able to obtain a SVE diploma, she continued into Tourism. She chose this profession because since elementary school she had always wanted to become a flight attendant. However, Tourism turned out to be a more challenging programme for her than Hairdressing:

SARAH: "It [Tourism] was so high-paced. The Hairdressing training was so easy in terms of assignments, so to speak. But in Tourism, we had to hand in a lot of portfolios, assignments, while in Hairdressing, I could do everything in the end; I planned in the last minute. . . . So that wasn't very good of me of doing that. So that's why I didn't make it."
INTERVIEWER: "What do you think when you look back?"
SARAH: "When I think about Tourism, the job, with Tourism you just can't get a job easily. There's not much demand. Yet Care is in higher demand."

As becomes evident from this quote, after failing Tourism, she switched to Health and Care. When asked about her motivation to enrol in Care, she mentioned that her mother had been working in care for about 13 years, and directly encouraged her to choose this profession:

SARAH: "And she [mother] always said 'enrol in Care'. I didn't want that due to [working with] old people. It just didn't seem like something for me. Then she said like [motivated her to choose Health and Care], last year, I said well

142 *Lore Van Praag et al.*

OK then I will try Care and see what it's like. OK, now I'm doing that, and it's actually not for me either, but I have to push through to . . . now, I want to become a midwife."

After having tried two different vocational trajectories, Sarah began to study the Health and Care profession, which she was not very enthusiastic about. The care training required internships including eldercare and she was not fond of the idea of helping elderly people bathe, etc. She wanted to study to become a midwife, which is a vocational tertiary education study, and to do that, she had to first finish her degree in Care in Level 4. Hence, as she puts it, she had to 'push through' to get her diploma. She feels she has to complete her internship and educational programme, as this is her 'last chance':

INTERVIEWER: "They told you this is your last chance? [agrees] How did they tell you?"
SARAH: "Intake. Like, prior to this I did two other fields of study and they won't take me seriously any longer if I stop this one and start a different one again. They [employers] won't take me in anymore, since I'm not being serious."
INTERVIEWER: "And you have done all trainings at Institution A?"
SARAH: "Yes, it won't work either at Institution B [the only other SVE-institution in City X]; they sort of work together."

Sarah talks about how after switching three times, she needs to stick to her training to be taken seriously by potential employers. This case demonstrates how switching between different topics and levels forced Sarah to stay enrolled in the last programme. This case is interesting in that – despite the fact that she was not fond of the Care programme – this youngster found it acceptable to enrol in Care in order to realise a future goal, namely becoming a midwife. She got this idea from her cousin who works as a midwife; after talking to her, Sarah wanted to be a midwife, too. In her second interview after a year, she was no longer considering switching between fields of study, as she had firmly decided to become a midwife.

Karima

Karima is a Dutch girl of Moroccan descent who is enrolled in the cooking track in upper secondary vocational education (SVE) in the Netherlands. Already during our first interview, she was planning to study baking after this study. When asked about her reasons for studying cooking, she first said that she did not want to do this study at all and that her previous study was specialised pedagogical worker training (PWT); however, she failed her internship assignments and because of low grades she had to quit that career:

INTERVIEWER: "Did you complete your degree?"
KARIMA: "No, unfortunately not, because of my internship assignments, which was with those competencies – that was very hard. I've done the assignments

Switching practices in vocational education   143

like five times. Every time, it was not good enough. After the fourth time, they were done with me, yeah 'this is not working out'. I was in my second year, almost going to the third . . . yeah that really sucks but there are actually no prospects for work so then I think yes, it's for the better that I didn't continue my education, yes otherwise nice bonus. I had to . . . in February I was signed out, February, start of February, I was signed out of school."

Yet, this was not the first time Karima had changed her field of study. In fact, she began her SVE in Health and Care. She finished this SVE at Level 2 (minimum qualification) and continued her pedagogical degree at Level 3, because she decided she did not want to work in eldercare. Yet, she was not able to finish that level because of her assignments, and thus changed to cooking:

KARIMA: "The teacher said, you know, take it easy . . ., start a new course of study in the next semester. And then I was thinking like this is not what I want; I want to start right now. [They told me:] '*No, that's not possible, because all schools have already started*'. What I did is . . . I went to School X by myself. I signed up for the cooking course, but that woman told me that it was impossible because the schools had already started. I said, '*Please, I really want to*'; I almost cried. Because that woman felt sorry for me, in the end, she said, 'Well, I'm going to check if School Y is available', then she made a phone call to School Y. Then that man said, '*Come by*'; two days later I had to come by and that week I was allowed to start immediately and that's how I ended up at the cooking school."

We see that Karima managed to circumvent the strict starting date and, without losing a semester, started with a new programme. However, things did not turn out as expected in this new school Y: she changed back to her previous school Z because she could not really connect to her classmates, who were (except for one Moroccan boy) of Dutch descent. She felt like she was the only one who had a distinct ethnic descent and who was considerably older. School Z was also more comfortable for her since she did her previous two studies in that school. When asked about her choice of cooking study, she said:

INTERVIEWER: "But how did you know that the cooking school was . . ."
KARIMA: "Because I always wanted to cook: cooking has always been my passion since high school. Since high school I always had a passion for cooking so . . . it's not really my . . . because I also did PWT [pedagogical worker training], I thought maybe later . . . but then I quit that training and went to the cooking school. Anyhow, I was thinking what would be my options in other fields of study? There wasn't really any other field of study I liked. I wanted to enrol in bakery school but they said that there were no internships for that [field of study] and that it would be hard to find an internship."

What is interesting is that even though she has finished Level 2 in Care, Karima was also following the cooking training in Level 2 and after two years, by the second interview, she was still not finished. Furthermore, in the second interview a year after the first, she mentioned that she wanted to go back to her pedagogical training study. The case of Karima is interesting as it shows that switching between fields of study could be related to failure in one field of study, lack of interest in pursuing a profession – even after receiving a diploma – and also feelings of not being accepted in the educational institution. Unfortunately, in the end, even though she enjoyed the school experience in general, Karima did not seem to like the cooking training and her internship experiences were not very positive either.

Manu

During the first interview, Manu, a boy of Belgian origin, was enrolled in part-time vocational education and training, specialised in Woodwork, and was combining an educational training with workplace learning. Throughout his educational trajectory, he followed several fields of study, all in the vocational track, in various schools and institutions. Throughout the interview, he mentioned that he had already obtained professional qualifications in forklifting, cooking, truck driving and hairdressing, showing that he had frequently changed fields of study. Changing fields of study became a habit, as also shown by the following quote: "*Most of the time, you already try to see like, 'What am I going to do next year?'*" These changes can be better understood when looking at his lack of motivation to study in the past. Although he seemed to understand the value of education, along the road, Manu frequently questioned the importance of getting an educational qualification; in the end, however, he decided to 'go for it':

MANU: "I really first want to get a degree before I moved on with my life. That [a degree] is then at least something I can have in my hands, and then you have a degree and that's certainly not nothing. So, yes, I have achieved that, in my head, I think I want to go for a degree *after all*. Because there were moments, when I was fifteen, sixteen years old, that I thought: '*Screw that degree!*' and then just wait and finally go to work when I turn eighteen."

As shown in this citation, the long route and the time spent at school ultimately made this youngster want to obtain his degree. Nevertheless, Manu seemed to have experienced school fatigue at several moments during his school career, which did not help him when making a study choice. This resulted in frequent switching between fields of study within the vocational track, without obtaining any particular qualification. He states, "*So the practical courses indeed do not appeal to me. It's really mostly for my degree that I want to go [to school], but it's indeed because you **have** to choose a career.*" Later, he refers to the fact that his choice for a future professional career will be guided by the professional careers or sectors that have the most work opportunities. Manu's reasons for choosing so many different fields of study during his career varied but overall, it was

Switching practices in vocational education   145

because he was indecisive about his career plans and he perceived obtaining an educational qualification merely as an 'additional' asset:

MANU: "I chose Woodwork, because I had already followed that and I'd better finish that. Well, that's how I see it. If I am able to still 'get' [obtain the certificate of] Woodwork, that would be nice but it's not my biggest concern to get it anyhow."

INTERVIEWER: "You would not want it per se, but if you are able, you could use it as a competitive asset to get a job?"

MANU: "Yes, and I also do not really know what I really am going to want later on. But, it is indeed a nice 'extra' [asset] for the future."

Policy makers aim to give young people the option to change fields or study/tracks, even within the same semester, if they decide another line of study is better suited to them. This could help students who regret their previous educational choices to reorient themselves. These switching practices are allowed because they are believed to increase students' motivation. However, as depicted in Manu's case, this did not result in an educational career inspired by his aspirations. Rather, the option to switch resulted in an educational trajectory filled with various distinct fields of study that did not necessarily prepare Manu for a particular future career and resulted in him repeatedly questioning the importance of education.

Discussion

In this chapter, we examined and compared how differences in features of educational systems ultimately shape youngsters' educational pathways and careers. By looking into the switching practices within vocational education of four youngsters (two in the Flemish and two in the Dutch educational systems), we illustrated how comparable but distinct institutional arrangements subtly but significantly affect youngsters' educational careers. The importance of these institutional arrangements are frequently neglected in research and when considering changes in educational structures. When contrasting the trajectory of Hamza in Flanders with Sarah in the Netherlands, we see some similarities with regard to switching; however, when these youngsters make educational decisions, they followed the possibilities they had within their educational system. Sarah switched three times between distinct fields of study before settling with her final choice in which she plans to obtain her degree. This trajectory shows that switching practices in SVE in the Netherlands *forced* the student to stick to her final programme, fearing she would otherwise drop out without a chance for a diploma. However, Hamza in Flanders appeared to be *lucky* to have finally found a field of study that matched his interest and that was given in a school in which he felt at home, and where he decided to continue on to do a specialist year so that he could obtain his diploma. Furthermore, the trajectories of Karima and Manu illustrate how switching in both educational systems needs to be accompanied by a considerable amount of guidance and/ or clear aspirations if one wants to prevent turbulent educational trajectories (see also Stam, 2017). The limited number of opportunities to switch between fields of study during one's educational career in the Netherlands seemed to work counterproductively for Karima, as her choices did not lead to any degree. By contrast, for Manu in Flanders, the higher extent of freedom of choosing between distinct fields of study resulted in a rather long and complex educational trajectory – also not necessarily adding to more positive school experiences or more informed choices. This youngster was, however, aware of the importance of an educational qualification on the labour market and wanted to have at least that qualification because it would make all his efforts worthwhile.

In both systems, there seem to be distinct opportunities and limitations with respect to switching between fields of study within vocational tracks. In general, the Dutch system is less likely to allow students to switch between fields of study at any given moment compared with the Flemish educational system. Our results illustrate how youngsters at risk of early school leaving seem to lack the resources to realise their aspirations (Stam, 2017; see also Chapter 8 in this book). When looking at the switching practices embedded in these systems, in theory, the opportunities to change fields of study or tracks are meant to assist students to find the most suitable training. Yet, we see that in practice these opportunities do not always seem to help youngsters figure out what they want to study. In both systems, youngsters had distinct institutionalised opportunities to change tracks/fields of study during their educational career. Whereas in the Dutch educational system young people are more institutionally supported when changing from more vocational to more academic tracks or fields of study (in hierarchical terms: 'upward' track mobility), this was not the case in Flanders (which is characterised by the – in practice – lack of upward track mobility). Conversely, in Flanders, young people could more easily change between fields of study within the vocational track during the academic year, which could help them to more efficiently discover a field of study that matches their interests and abilities, but could also lead to more confusion, random changes and a lack of direction. The latter is especially the case as these practices are not institutionally foreseen, hardly supported by student counsellors and often insufficiently recognised by policy makers. Hence, while these cases illustrate that in both systems young people appear to adapt to them easily, more attention could be paid to the guidance of students when they are making choices, also across educational programmes, institutions and schools. In both systems, young people would benefit from more information about fields of study or more practical experience before or when making choices, in order to sort out what particular careers one can actually pursue and how one goes about realising those respective career goals. To conclude, the findings of this chapter add to a better understanding of the functioning of educational systems and the consequences for youngsters' educational pathways – particularly the consequences that could lead to early school leaving.

References

Attwood, G., & Croll, P. (2006). Truancy in secondary school pupils: Prevalence, trajectories and pupil perspectives. *Research Papers in Education*, *21*(4), 467–484.

Braster, S., & Theisens, H. (2016). Het onderwijs in de Lage Landen in historisch en internationaal perspectief. In Eidhof, B., Van Houtte, M., & Vermeulen, M. (Eds.), *Sociologen over onderwijs. Inzichten, praktijken en kritieken* (pp. 37–61). Antwerpen, Apeldoorn: Garant.

Clycq, N., Timmerman, C., Van Avermaet, P., Wets, J., & Herman, P. (2014). *Oprit 14: Naar een schooltraject zonder snelheidsbeperkingen*. Gent: Academia Press, 255.

Crul, M., & Schneider, J. (2010). Comparative integration context theory: Participation and belonging in new diverse European cities. *Ethnic and Racial Studies*, *33*(7), 1249–1268.

Crul, M., Schnell, P., Herzog-Punzenberger, B., Wilmes, M., Slootman, M., & Aparicio Gómez, R. (2012). School careers of second-generation youth in Europe: Which education systems provide the best chances for success? In Crul, M., Schneider, J., & Lelie, F. (Eds.), *The European second generation compared: Does the integration context matter?* (pp. 101–164). Amsterdam: Amsterdam University Press.

Dauber, S. L., Alexander, K. L., & Entwistle, D. R. (1996). Tracking and transitions through the middle grades: Channeling educational trajectories. *Sociology of Education*, *69*(4), 290–307.

Dronkers, J., & Korthals, R. A. (2016). Tracking, school entrance requirements and the educational performance of migrant students. In Hadjar, A. & Gross, C. (Eds.), *Education systems and inequalities: International comparisons* (pp. 185–205). Bristol, UK: Policy Press.

Eurydice. (2015). The structure of the European education systems 2015/16: Schematic diagrams. *Eurydice facts and figures*. Luxembourg: Publications Office of the European Union. Retrieved from https://webgate.ec.europa.eu/fpfis/mwikis/eurydice/images/0/05/192EN.pdf

Keskiner, E. (2015). 'Is it Merit or Cultural Capital?' The role of parents during early tracking in Amsterdam and Strasbourg among descendants of immigrants from Turkey. *Comparative Migration Studies*, *3*(9), doi:10.1186/s40878-015-0014-7

Kloosterman, R., & De Graaf, P. M. (2009). Zittenblijven of afstromen? De relatie tussen sociaal milieu en keuzes in het voortgezet onderwijs voor drie cohorten leerlingen. *Mens en Maatschappij*, *84*(1), 5–28.

Kloosterman, R., & De Graaf, P. M. (2010). Non-promotion or enrolment in a lower track? The influence of social background on choices in secondary education for three cohorts of Dutch pupils. *Oxford Review of Education*, *36*, 363–384.

Lamote, C., Van Landeghem, G., Blommaert, M., Nicaise, I., De Fraine, B., & Van Damme, J. (2013). Voortijdig schoolverlaten in Vlaanderen: een stand van zaken en een voorstel tot aanpak. In Callens, M., Noppe, J., & Vanderleyden, L. (Eds.), *De Sociale Staat van Vlaanderen* (pp. 13–60), Brussel: Studiedienst van de Vlaamse Regering.

Rezai, S., Crul, M., Severiens, S. E., & Keskiner, E. (2015). Passing the torch to a new generation: Educational support types and the second generation in the Netherlands. *Comparative Migration Studies*, *3*(12), 1–17.

Saar, E., Unt, M., & Kogan, I. (2008). Transition from educational system to labour market in the European Union: A comparison between new and old members. *International Journal of Comparative Sociology*, *49*(1), 31–59.

Spruyt, B., Laurijssen, I., & Van Dorsselaer, Y. (2009). Kiezen en verliezen-Een analyse van de keuze na het krijgen van een B-attest in het Vlaams secundair onderwijs als een replicatie van Kloosterman en De Graaf (2009). *Mens en maatschappij*, *84*(3), 279–299.

Spruyt, B., Van Droogenbroeck, F., & Kavadias, D. (2015). Educational tracking and sense of futility: A matter of stigma consciousness? *Oxford Review of Education*, *41*(6), 747–765.

148   *Lore Van Praag et al.*

Stam, T. (2017). Reasons and resources: Understanding pupils' aspirations in lower vocational Dutch education. *Ethnography and Education, 12*(3), 259–270. doi:10.1080/17457823. 2016.1237880

Stevens, P. A. J., & Dworkin, G. A. (2014). *The Palgrave handbook of race and ethnic inequalities in education.* London: Palgrave Macmillan.

Turner, S. (2004). Going to college and finishing college: Explaining different educational outcomes. In Hoxby, C. (Ed.), *College decisions: How students actually make them and how they could.* Chicago: University of Chicago Press.

Van Praag, L., Boone, S., Stevens, P., & Van Houtte, M. (2015). De paradox van het watervalsysteem: wanneer het groeperen van studenten in homogene groepen tot meer heterogeniteit leidt in het beroepsonderwijs. *Sociologos. Tijdschrift voor Sociologie, 36,* 2.

Van Praag, L., Demanet, J., Stevens, P., & Van Houtte, M. (2017). Everyone has their own qualities': Tracking and academic self-appraisal in Flemish secondary education. *Social Psychology of Education, 20*(3), 601–618. doi:10.1007/s11218-017-9371-4

Van Praag, L., Stevens, P., & Van Houtte, M. (2014). Ethnicity and educational inequality in Belgium. In Stevens, P. A. J., & Dworkin, G. A. (Eds.), *The Palgrave Handbook of Race and Ethnic Inequalities in Education.* London: Palgrave.

10 Educational trajectories of early school leavers in Portugal

Processes and conditions of (in)equality

Sofia A. Santos, Eunice Macedo and Helena C. Araújo

Introduction

Concerned about the intersectionality of social and educational conditions of disadvantage inherent to early school leaving (ESL), this chapter brings to the fore processes of inequality affecting young adults who left mainstream school without a certificate of upper secondary school or its equivalent (ISCED 3). Taking the views of Portuguese early school leavers into account, we highlight the challenges faced by young men and women to fit into an increasingly competitive school and labour market. Our analysis identifies, on the one hand, the institutional, social and educational conditions associated with ESL, and on the other, the choices, challenges and resources involved in young people's decisions, given the likelihood of exclusion and the lack of alternatives. This discussion takes place at a time when ESL is an increasing concern (Araújo, Magalhães, Rocha, & Macedo, 2014; Magalhães, Araújo, Macedo, & Rocha, 2015). The growing set of educational policies and measures to promote new conditions support young people facing school disaffection evidence this (Macedo, Araújo, Magalhães, & Rocha, 2015). Therefore, what is at stake here is how the lack of conditions in young adults' trajectories affects their learning and working contexts.

With this in mind, ESL must be understood as a question of social inequality conditioned by people's "cultural and social capital" but also by the individual's changing and changeable locations of power. This chapter starts from the concept of *habitus* (Bourdieu, 1972) and its possibilities of encompassing the *genesis of new creative responses* (Reay, 2004) in the light of a *new equality agenda* (Baker, Lynch, Cantillon, & Walsh, 2006, 2004; Lynch, 2009). Early school leavers' views on their own trajectories are read under this lens, including the analysis of processes of (in)equality that inform the lack of conditions and their related decisions to leave school.

Habitus and the generation of creative responses

The notion of *habitus* (Bourdieu, 1972) is still extremely influential in sociological research, even if it has been an object of criticism. Bourdieu himself seems to have updated the meaning of the concept over time. As a system of embodied dispositions that organises the ways in which individuals perceive the social world and react to it, *habitus* concerns the individual experience in relation to objective opportunities. In a deterministic fashion, *habitus* represents the way group culture shapes the body and mind, through a process of socialisation, within which people adjust spontaneously to the constraints imposed on them – the reproduction of the social structure (Bourdieu & Passeron, 1970). Hence, certain individuals belong to the same social category/group because they experience similar conditions and build similar behaviours and views of the world (Bourdieu, 1972). In this vein, the *habitus* is both structured by the objective past position in the social structure and has strong impact on the future life trajectory.

In our research, if we kept to this deterministic view of the *habitus*, we would expect all participants at risk in schools to present shared paths and views. However, the analysis has shown different possibilities. The work of Reay (2004) is useful for our purposes as it challenges the determinism of Bourdieu's concept of *habitus*. As she sees it, the *habitus* also "carries within it the genesis of new creative responses that are capable of transcending the social conditions in which it was produced" (Reay, 2004, p. 435). More recently, Croce (2016) also tackles some major criticisms addressed to the *habitus* by emphasising it as guidance on how people renegotiate practices.

To develop a framework that helps us find *if* and *how* early school leavers build *creative responses* to face their challenges, we look into the *agenda of equality of condition* as a means to achieve social justice. The concept of equality has been a cornerstone in educational theories that attempt to extend educational rights to all individuals and groups. The works of Lynch and Baker (2005) and Baker et al. (2004, 2006), in which *equality of condition* shifts away from *equality of opportunity* are interesting to explore the agendas of equality by considering that social inequalities and collective choices are informed by changing and changeable social structures that may be deconstructed/questioned by an *agenda of equality of condition*.

This agenda comes to reconfigure a set of key dimensions of equality, as follows:

- *Respect and recognition* – celebration of diversity
- *Redistribution of resources* – satisfaction of basic needs and provision of a human and material safety net
- *Love, care and solidarity* – promotion of "circumstances in which everyone has ample scope for forming valuable human attachments", feeling some sense of affiliation and concern for others (Baker et al., 2004, p. 34)
- *Power* – enabling "each person to influence the decisions that affect their lives" and as result, to challenge power in other areas (family, economy, education, religion, etc.)
- *Working and learning* – "ensuring that everyone is enabled to develop their talents and abilities, and (. . .) has a real choice among occupations that they find satisfying and fulfilling; occupational equal opportunity" (Baker et al., 2004, p. 34)

Trajectories of ESL students in Portugal   151

This agenda pays attention to power relations and emphasises the influence of social factors on people's choices, actions and behaviours. Such a discussion is essential to rethink *if* and *how* societies are empowering "people to exercise (...) real choices among real options" beyond the simple access to opportunities (Baker et al., 2004, p. 34). The matching up of *equality of condition* and the *habitus* are relevant to understand the processes leading to ESL and the post-ESL trajectories in a search for *creative responses*.

Methodological notes

Standing for the acknowledgement of young adults' capacity to discuss and build knowledge about their own lives and school experiences, this chapter builds on data from 11 biographical interviews with seven young adults, aged 19 to 23, who left school without an upper secondary education diploma. These early school leavers were studying in Porto (our main research area) and were identified as early school leavers through the follow-up of an extensive survey[1] within the RESL.eu project. However, given the impossibility of reaching all of them for a second interview, just four young adults of the eight listed in Table 10.1 were willing to be interviewed twice. Indeed, contacting these young adults was quite challenging. Strenuous attempts to find them were wide-ranging: several contact attempts via telephone, *Facebook* and *WhatsApp*, calls to the schools where they had studied, going to their houses and asking former colleagues to find them.

The interviews were conducted and recorded in public spaces (parks, gardens, train stations, etc.). Confidentiality and anonymity were ensured to participants by using pseudonyms. Data were analysed by making use of *NVivo* with some socio-demographic and educational career categories that focused on educational trajectory, employment experience and social support networks.

Transitions, advances and setbacks of early school leavers

This section highlights the educational trajectories of young adults that led to ESL, what early school leavers did after leaving school and the influence of their social networks in these processes. Oscillations, nuances and changes are identified (Van Caudenberg, Van Praag, Nouwen, Clycq, & Timmerman, 2017). Table 10.1 gives an overview of early school leavers' characteristics and trajectories between interviews, bringing to evidence the diversity of young adult lives in this sample.

Allowing deeper detail on the data presented in Table 10.1, we present a summary narrative of the trajectories of early school leavers who were willing to be interviewed twice, highlights the transitions, advances and setbacks affecting their experiences before and after ESL. Moreover, this emphasizes that there is no such thing as a typical early school leaver but diverse combinations of difficult conditions that impact this process.

It is worth noticing that Elvira's interview was not considered in the analysis. Her case is interesting to mention because it illustrates the difficulties young

152   *Sofia A. Santos et al.*

Table 10.1 Characteristics and trajectories of early school leavers

Early school leavers	Sex	Age at first interview	Educational attainment at first interview	Educational/work status at first interview	Educational/work status at second interview
Rafaela	F	19	12°	ESL/work	ESL/new work
Rodrigo	M	20	12°	ESL/work	Concluded ISCED 3★
Filipe	M	20	10°	ESL/NEET★★	–
Pedro	M	20	11°	ESL/work	ESL/NEET
Sara	F	19	11°	ESL/NEET	–
Sónia	F	21	11°	ESL/NEET	ESL/work
Elsa	F	21	11°	ESL/NEET	–
Elvira	F	20	12°	–	–

Notes: F – female; M – male
★ ISCED 3: International Standard Classification of Education and Level 3 corresponds to upper secondary education.
★★ NEET: Not in Education, Employment or Training.

adults have in defining themselves as early school leavers. At the first contact she considered herself an early school leaver because she had left mainstream education; however, she attained grade 12 via a vocational track.

"I gave up!"

Rafaela failed twice in grade 12 before leaving school because of problems in mathematics. She was not expecting it and felt frustrated. School was "satisfactory" and "good for students" and she never had conflicts. She always saw herself as a "good student" seeking improvement, although difficulties and failure remained. She found a job while studying. Insecurity and lack of self-confidence led her to give up the idea of concluding upper secondary. At the second interview, she had moved to another job via her boyfriend. She plans to return to evening school mainly to please her parents, as long as she is able to reconcile the demands of job and school.

"The school moved very slowly for me"

Rodrigo left regular school in grade 12 without completing two subjects and after three grade repetitions. Despite the fact that he jumped between four different state schools hoping for enthusiasm and saw himself as the best student until grade 10, he always felt disconnected from school. He had problems with peers and family problems (parents' drug addiction) that led him to live with his aunt for some years. As an early school leaver, he found odd jobs for two years, to feel useful and not for financial reasons. In the second interview, he had finished school as a result of his mother's pressure. He was waiting for a reply from university.

Trajectories of ESL students in Portugal   153

*"I had to work to survive, to sustain a house,
to have something to eat"*

Pedro lived in a youth shelter beginning at age 6. He considered himself a good student and in grade 6 he was on the honour roll. He loves drawing. When the school put all boarding school students in the same class, he became a bully and started having conflicts with peers and teachers. In grade 10 he moved to an artistic school but felt disappointed with school organisation, practices and competitiveness. He left both institutions and found a job in a supermarket to be independent and help his unemployed mother. He had held two jobs in the intervening time but was unemployed at the second interview. He enrolled in the army academy and is planning to return to mainstream school. He aims to open his own tattoo business.

"I never liked school"

Sónia is from a small village near Porto. She considered herself to be shy, to not have many friends and felt disconnected from education. She failed twice because of health and family problems. After losing her father, her loss of interest in school increased with the experiences of failure. She felt left behind by the school. She moved to a vocational school, which she left because of problems with teachers. As an early school leaver, she got pregnant and was unemployed. At the second interview, she had found a job via her boyfriend. Completing grade 12 at a vocational school is a possibility but only if she can reconcile school and employment. She would like to have her own business.

As demonstrated by these narratives, the different conditions affecting young adults' trajectories included giving up school, the perception of the maladjustment of the school to the expectations of the student, financial needs and disengagement from school.

Taking the group of seven early school leavers as a whole, including the ones that were interviewed once and twice, one may say that in their educational trajectories they went through frequent transitions amongst schools and educational tracks. Three enrolled in vocational lower secondary education on the advice of their schools when problems began (e.g., grade repetition); the rest refused to do so, because of the stigma that surrounds vocational courses. All of them failed at a certain point (curiously, confirming gender stereotypes, most young women in mathematics and most young men in Portuguese). For some, grade retentions came as unforeseen. They felt frustrated when their friends moved forward while they stayed behind, opening the path for school disengagement.

Of the seven early school leavers, two left school in grade 12, four in grade 11 and one in grade 10. Amongst the main factors for ESL, young adults referred

154 *Sofia A. Santos et al.*

to family financial and health problems (depression, addictions) and domestic violence, bullying amongst students, student disconnection with curricula, lack of motivation and a wish for more practical approaches.

Interestingly, after leaving school, their diverse paths are marked by gender. All the young women seemed focused on initiating family life and remained as caretakers. Sónia and Elsa got pregnant; Sara looked after her ill mother and grandmother; and Rafaela went to work and live with her boyfriend. As for the boys, their trajectories were more unstable and job-oriented. Rodrigo spent two years figuring out what he wanted to do and had some odd jobs. Filipe and Pedro tried to get into the labour market because of financial needs. The first never succeeded; the latter had two jobs after leaving school (supermarket/café) but became unemployed.

Similarly, all early school leavers tried to get into the labour market after leaving school. Four found jobs via personal contacts while three faced great difficulties. Most went through situations of hard work and precarious contracts, mainly because they were underage and had not attained grade 12. Some had even started their professional experiences while still in school through temporary, part-time or full-time jobs (at restaurants, call centres and cafés). As the interviewees stressed, none of the parents pressured them to work but they felt responsible to help the household. Also, the difficulty in reconciling work and school compelled some to give up school. This suggests that the educational system may need to rethink options for student workers.

The influence of social networks on ESL is quite relevant. All the young adults but two – those who were raised in social protection institutions – had family support before and after leaving school. Their parents' qualifications are below the secondary level, and one is illiterate. Most of the parents have low-profile and unstable jobs. Despite their situations, some parents tried to provide educational support (e.g. tutorials, sports, talking to teachers at school, looking for information online).

If the financial difficulties of families, peers' influence and problems at school (e.g. bad grades and disinterest) appear to be the main reasons to leave school, high expectations about school from some families along with labour market demands were the major drivers to return to education/training. Only one interviewee had completed school, but they all said they planned to do so. As we develop later in the chapter, friend networks are changeable and tend to become more fragile after ESL, despite their key role towards influencing students' leaving or staying in school. Hence, some young adults said at the second interview that they felt lonely. The following section discusses these ESL trajectories in the light of *equality of condition* (Baker et al., 2004).

Conditions of (in)equality surrounding trajectories of ESL

The analysis that follows allows identifying the impacts of certain conditions on early school leavers' trajectories and highlights young adults' attempts to make sense of their lives concerning four dimensions of *equality of condition*:

"resources", "love, care and solidarity", "power", and "working and learning burdens and benefits" (Baker et al., 2004; see also Lynch & Lodge, 2002), some of which are explored herein. "Respect and recognition" is an umbrella dimension in these young adult lives. This is why it is seen as inherent to the analysis of the other four. Whereas the authors make a macro-analysis of *equality of condition*, we turn to their milestone work at the micro level, in search for young adults' *creative responses* (Reay, 2004) to facing difficulties.

(In)equality of resources: beyond the limits of social status

The lack of financial resources to stay in school affects the trajectories of all these early school leavers but one. Most wanted to help their families and stop being a burden. For instance, those in art schools could not afford the expensive materials. Mainly young men perceive earning money as the door to the real world. The difficulty in accessing goods and the will to do so were key reasons to opt for the labour market or vocational schools, where they receive small subsidies. Financial pressure triggered ESL:

> I wouldn't mind trying to make school again. But, in the economy we are in, the bills don't pay themselves. I've got to help.
>
> (Pedro)

Returning to school also deserves second thoughts because it means costs. Earning or paying money was one of the main factors that influenced young adults' decisions to go or to prevent them from returning to school. Time spent in school meant less time to work, another cost:

> To finish the course I will have to pay (. . .) to re-enrol. I have to pay each module.
>
> (Sónia)

> I went to the course because there I earned some money (. . .). I was there for four months.
>
> (Filipe)

These comments show the link between lack of economic resources and educational inequality, contributing to the reproduction of the social capital. Despite poverty, some students paid private tutors to improve their marks, showing how the access to resources is not always enough to prevent school disengagement. After ESL, some young adults also challenged the constraining dimension of the *habitus* by finding *creative responses* to improve their lives beyond the family condition, such as having their own businesses (a tattoo shop, making jam).

Looking at these young adults, one might think that they do not have the *cultural and social capital* to support them in their lives. However, outside school,

156 *Sofia A. Santos et al.*

early school leavers' peer networks – their social capital – also seem crucial as the main resources to find jobs. Despite seemingly mitigated bonds of friendship and limited access to powerful networks, young adults felt supported and guided by peer networks with similar experiences of precariousness:

> My boyfriend's sister works there (. . .) we e-mailed her and she sent it (. . .), it was easy.
>
> (Rafaela)

Hence, young adults' resourceful use of their networks helps them access resources (financial and non-financial). The tension between the presence and lack of these safety networks defines the contours of post-ESL experience, as some manage to face ESL and reconfigure the *habitus*. This analysis aims at identifying the diversity of networks of resources and its relevance in young early school leavers' trajectories, going in line with the Baker et al. (2004, p. 36) proposal, supported by Bourdieu's concept of *social capital*:

> [E]quality of condition accepts the urgency of satisfying basic needs and providing a safety net against poverty. But its wider understanding of resources helps us to recognise a wider range of needs (. . .) and to take a less market-oriented view of how these needs should be satisfied.

(In)equality of love, care and solidarity: the school as a place for teasing or not so much?

Besides constituting resources for the access to goods, in the case of early school leavers, human attachments in school (teachers and peers) are extremely relevant. As mentioned, their absence may lead to ESL. In the case of early school leavers, peers are key in the emotional decision to leave or stay in school:

> I had my friends and I just wanted them (. . .). I started failing because of friends. I started doing more stupid things, missing classes.
>
> (Filipe)

In Sónia's trajectory, clashes with peers led her to ESL but in the second interview she highlighted that their presence was decisive to re-enroll in school:

> Nothing else interests me at school because also all my colleagues are working and not in the course.
>
> (Sónia)

Bullying and conflicts amongst peers were a constant in these young people's lives, either as bullies (Pedro, Filipe and Elsa) or victims (Sónia, Sara and

Rodrigo). These conflicts made them dislike school and feel unattached, with impact on their well-being and success as students, both as a victim –

> I was [a] victim of bullying more than once in all schools. (. . .) They've even beaten me.
>
> (Sara)

– and as a bully –

> I was suspended because of a boy (. . .), he took my hat off, I was pissed, went after him, threw a stone at him, broke a glass. (. . .) I've always had a temper.
>
> (Pedro)

Feeling pressured and bullied at school revealed a fundamental condition of inequality, which caused difficulty both in building a sense of belonging and concern for others and in fostering a capacity to form bonds of solidarity and kinship – inhibiting the possibilities for a successful school trajectory.

Differentiated teacher support based on power relations of social status within the classroom emphasises the impact of lack of affection on students' learning and will to stay in school:

> I shouldn't have dropped out. I should have overcome the fact that the teacher only gave attention to that girl and not to me. (. . .) I think I missed that push to wake me up. (. . .) We can't all be geniuses.
>
> (Sónia)

> I didn't identify much with my class because for teachers there were the good boys (. . .) those who were born with a silver spoon in their mouths, thought they were better than everyone else. (. . .) They were really competitive.
>
> (Pedro)

For most youngsters, teachers did not pay attention to their learning difficulties and interests. They were not heard or taken into account, although most felt emotionally supported by one or two teachers, school principals or a school psychologist. Early school leavers who attended a vocational track or the artistic specialisation reported a closer teacher-student relation mainly because of the smaller number of students in the classroom, which meant a more familiar and closer environment, and more flexibility and opportunity to be with teachers in informal situations.

To rethink ESL in light of equality of condition implies valuing emotional and affective bonds in school, where care, solidarity and love must find room to be revealed and reinforced. In line with Baker et al. (2004, p. 37), solidarity

158 *Sofia A. Santos et al.*

and bonds of friendship "as active support for others, not just passive empathy", bring meaning to school life, and can work as a tool for success as well as provide a sense of fulfilment and belonging.

(In)equality of power: claiming autonomy in decision making and learning

Concerning the conditions that enable each person to influence the decisions that affect his or her life (Baker et al., 2004), it is interesting to see how they challenge power in areas such as school and the labour market. Early school leavers emphasised the lack of tools and conditions that would allow them to be autonomous learners in the classroom:

> Teachers tried to solve the exercises on their own, didn't give us time (. . .). If we do it by ourselves we manage to get to the parts we want, but if they do it, it doesn't work.
>
> (Rafaela)

> I have big problems with Portuguese tests, such as the way they ask questions and what they want me to answer (. . .). Teachers say, "Interpret this text", and I have no room to interpret the text; what I have to do is answer what teachers have indicated (. . .) what the teacher told you about it or how you've been taught, not "interpret".
>
> (Rodrigo)

Early school leavers criticise the emphasis on theoretical knowledge to the detriment of the practical:

> The theoretical part helps but the most important is the practice because you go to a company, if you don't have the practice, you may have [a] lot of theory but it will do you no good. That was the problem at school.
>
> (Pedro)

Studying has to make sense, to be about a subject they like. As an example, all early school leavers stated they had good grades in subjects they enjoyed and where teachers engaged them.

In the labour market, the same young adults experienced opportunities to learn with apparently greater autonomy, increasing their success as workers and their personal fulfilment. Learning by doing provides empowerment:

> Having someone not in charge, but that gives us some support while we work, that tells us: "No, you can't do it this way, you have to do it that way", you start learning more than you can do and more than the skills you have (. . .) you learn many things you've never imagined (. . .). I felt a big

difference. I was more willing to work than to go to school. I paid more attention to work.

(Rafaela)

As they see it, the lack of relationship between school and work was one of the major reasons for disempowerment: school does not prepare them for the labour market, where they are challenged and taught to develop useful skills.

The greater sense of power and autonomy that the access to goods gives was mainly evident in the second interview. As stressed by Sónia, she already had a car and was planning to get a driver's license. From a different angle, Pedro also felt empowered to decide about his future by himself:

I have not told my mother yet that I am going to the army. (. . .) Sometimes family is not everything. I have to move on with my things.

(Pedro)

Despite the increasing autonomy that a salary allows – still far from equality of power – early school leavers report precariousness and abuses in the labour market:

They always found a way to complain (. . .) they gave me the contract with a different date and did not even pay for my food allowance.

(Pedro)

In the call centre we have clients who get to the point of insulting us and we cannot do anything.

(Rafaela)

They didn't allow us to study because we work every day and they'd lose money.

(Elsa)

After early school leavers' difficult labour experiences, parents are able to highly motivate their children to return to school as a way to have more power and opportunities, opening room to reduce the burden of *social and cultural reproduction*. Under their parents' influence, early school leavers became more aware of the value of grade 12 to find jobs and ameliorate their status within society; they recognised the hindrances and consequences of not completing compulsory schooling and looked at school differently.

Autonomy and power ought to be relevant conditions in early school leavers' search for *creative responses*, which seem to be lacking here. As highlighted by Baker et al. (2004, p. 39), equality of condition "supports a stronger, more participatory form of politics in which ordinary citizens, and particularly groups who have been excluded from power altogether, can have more control of decision-making".

Working and learning: great expectations, great disappointments

As mentioned, inequality of work opportunities was evidenced by early school leavers' trajectories because they were young, inexperienced, unqualified and socially unprotected by law. Most were disappointed with the lack of choice, opportunities and types of work. As a central aim of *equality of condition*, the promotion of prospects and satisfying work for everyone (not only with regard to wage conditions) would imply a real possibility to choose a satisfying occupation. However, the burdens and benefits of work are unequally distributed, and "privileged groups have better working conditions, better opportunities for successful and satisfying work, and better chances of worthwhile learning" (Baker et al., 2006, p. 414).

It is worth emphasising both the unpaid (and often unrecognised) work developed by most of these young adults and the volunteering – the second as a "real choice" of satisfying work – which accompanied their trajectories before and after ESL. This is the case for an early school leaver who never liked studying and school but became a tutor of disadvantaged students after ESL. His choice echoes his will to be useful and to conduct his own learning-teaching practice:

> I don't know if volunteering changed me a lot because I always dealt a lot with children. (. . .) I am not paid but (. . .) I did something.
>
> (Rodrigo)

The benefits of volunteering and learning while still in school are also stressed:

> I loved doing volunteer work in the Multi-disabilities Unit. We get to learn a lot of things. I saw that many of those who were there had skills. (. . .) I like helping and seeing them evolve (. . .); it is very good for a person who is volunteering.
>
> (Rafaela)

Alongside these positive experiences, it seems that being a caretaker became a "natural" path for early school leavers, particularly women, doing work frequently neglected by society. Whereas motherhood was seen by the young people as a rewarding experience, the work of care for relatives was seen as a burden because it implied engagement, time, energy and emotional challenges. This was revealed by a student with no opportunity to look for a job after leaving school:

> Unfortunately, I haven't had any work experience. Maybe people think "you're at home, doing nothing", that's a total lie. (. . .) I've been out of work to accompany my grandmothers, who are ill, to do things at home because my grandfather is also in bed. I spent the day there keeping company and helping. (. . .) I'm not walking around. I'm doing things that are also important.
>
> (Sara)

The burden of lack of solidarity on young adults' choices leads to consideration of the social distribution of voluntary and unpaid work and its impact on young adults' trajectories. Is it choice or *habitus*? Equality of condition requires the recognition of care work, implying that the educational system provides opportunities for diversified forms of learning, personal relationships, engagement and participation in society. However, it seems that after not having satisfying experiences at school, some early school leavers found *creative responses* to develop their skills through volunteering.

Final remarks

As shown by these young adults' trajectories, ESL is influenced by individual, meso and macro factors that schools do not seem to tackle. As these young people see it, school is not playing its role in their training. It is too focused on grades, assessment and national goals and not so much on meaningful and diversified learning that takes students' voices into account. Youngsters complain about the lack of time to assimilate useful information and to discuss doubts about their learning progress with teachers. For some, the provision of relevant knowledge and student-teacher relations are highlighted as good aspects of school life. When compared with teachers, peers are pointed out as the main influence to stay or leave school, even if conflicts and bullying are significant detrimental factors.

This chapter focused on matching up the influence of diverse conditions in young adult lives and creative responses. In the cases discussed, education and school emerge as "instrumental" after early school leavers realise that without compulsory education they face many more difficulties. It seems that reengaging – and having success – in school depends on greater awareness about the difficulties inherent in the labour market. It also depends on the possibility of reconciling schoolwork and jobs. School education becomes an added value associated with work and social status.

The tensions early school leavers experience between the desire to go back to school – only one young man returned – and the financial constraints to do so reinforce the links between low social status and the processes of inequality, in which dimensions of *equality of condition* seem to be inhibited. According to our findings, young adults' trajectories may be interpreted in the light of the presence/absence of processes of equality, in what concerns the access to equal "resources", "love, care and solidarity", "power", and "working and learning". In the first dimension, low resources are a common feature amongst early school leavers, expressing their lack of social capital. However, even if some young adults are disaffected from school and education, it became clear that families with low socioeconomic status do invest in their children's education, as both parents and young adults still believe it promotes social mobility – a belief that needs to be questioned because of persistent high rates of youth unemployment. Moreover, young adults have managed to develop peer networks that act as resources in their search for a position, even if volatile and low, in the labour market. The relevance of love, care and solidarity in young adults' educational trajectories, in their learning and work processes, in the relationships with teachers and peers, highlights the need to rethink the roles of schools and the workplace to provide emotional and affective bonds as tools for young adults' fulfilment and achievement.

Autonomy and power in learning, in the construction of meaningful knowledge, and a better balance between theory and practice – factors which were identified by young adults – allow rethinking the learning-teaching models that prevail in our educational system in order to make it more interactive. Moreover, even if young adults perceived they had greater autonomy in the labour market, their experience of lack of power shows the need to rethink – or introduce – strategies of youth protection that lead to greater professional and human dignity and prevent abuse. The analysis also highlights both the need for social recognition of unpaid work and volunteering as important contributions to society, as well as the limits to the dimension of working and learning in young adults' lives, as they do not have the opportunity to choose amongst equally valued occupations. Revaluing vocational education and training by ameliorating its social status might be of interest, such as to provide work-based learning to students, who then might become more skilled and have greater opportunities to secure skilled labour positions as a result.

Finally, the lack of supportive conditions may lead to the need to find *creative responses* in the search for educational and work trajectories that break the constraints of the *habitus*. This was the case of early school leavers' plans to conciliate work and school in order to complete studies, create their own job/business or build a family as a life project. This approach positions young adults as *sophisticated thinkers* (Elley, 2013) whose voices contribute to better understanding the contours of ESL, and suggests rethinking the possibilities of a young adults–friendly school and labour market as contexts that must take their diversity of conditions, needs and expectations into account.

Note

1 The survey A1 was applied at the beginning of the project to 2,223 students from grades 10 and 12 in 22 schools from two research areas (Porto and Amadora). Then, shorter versions of the survey were repeated twice, allowing tracking of students' trajectories.

References

Araújo, H. C., Magalhães, A., Rocha, C., & Macedo, E. (2014). *Policies on early school leaving in nine European countries: A comparative analysis.* Antwerp: University of Antwerp.

Baker, J., Lynch, K., Cantillon, S., & Walsh, J. (2004). *Equality: From theory to action.* Basingstoke: Palgrave Macmillan.

Baker, J., Lynch, K., Cantillon, S., & Walsh, J. (2006). Equality: Putting the theory into practice. *Res Publica, 12*, 411–433.

Bourdieu, P. (1972). *Esquisse d'une théorie de la pratique: Précédé de 'Trois études d'ethnologie kabyle'.* Genève: Librairie Droz.

Bourdieu, P., & Passeron, J. (1970). *La reproduction: Éléments d'une théorie du système d'enseignement*. Paris: Editions de Minuit.

Croce, M. (2016). The habitus and the critique of the present: A Wittgensteinian reading of Bourdieu's social theory. *Sociological Theory, 33*(4), 327–346.

Elley, S. (2013). *Understanding sex and relationship education, youth and class: A youth work-led approach*. London: Palgrave Macmillan.

Lynch, K. (2009). Affective equality: Who cares? *Development, 52*(3), 410–415.

Lynch, K., & Baker, J. (2005). Equality in education: An equality of condition perspectives. *Theory and Research in Education, 3*(2), 131–163.

Lynch, K., & Lodge, A. (2002). *Equality and power in schools: Redistribution, recognition, and representation*. London: Routledge & Falmer Press.

Macedo, E., Araújo, H. C., Magalhães, A., & Rocha, C. (2015). La construcción del abandono temprano de la escuela como concepto político: Un análisis en la sociología de la educación. *Profesorado: Revista de Curriculum y Formación del Profesorado, 19*(3), 28–42.

Magalhães, A., Araújo, H. C., Macedo, E., & Rocha, C. (2015). Early school leaving in Portugal: Policies and actors' interpretation. *Educação, Sociedade & Culturas, 45*, 97–119.

Reay, D. (2004). 'It's all becoming a habitus': Beyond the habitual use of habitus in educational research. *British Journal of Sociology of Education, 25*(4), 431–444.

Van Caudenberg, R., Van Praag, L., Nouwen, W., Clycq, N., & Timmerman, C. (2017). *A longitudinal study of educational trajectories of youth at risk of early school leaving*. Retrieved from www.uantwerpen.be/images/uantwerpen/container23160/files/RESL%20eu%20 Publication%205%20FINAL.pdf

11 Neglected aspirations

Academic trajectories and the risk of early school leaving amongst immigrant and Roma youth in Spain

Silvia Carrasco, Laia Narciso and Marta Bertran-Tarrés

Introduction

Reducing early school leaving (ESL) has been one of the most compelling challenges in the EU in the past decade as a key indicator of social inequalities experienced by the most vulnerable youth. The rate of non–EU-born early leavers in 2015 at the EU level is almost twice that of the native-born (19.8% vs 10.1%), and the estimated prevalence of ESL amongst Roma youth is by far the highest (OCDE/European Union, 2015). The picture is worse for Spain, still with the highest ESL rate in the EU, although it has declined from 28.4% in 2010 to 20.3% in 2015 (Eurostat, 2016). The highest proportions of foreign-born early leavers from education and training are found in Spain (33.3%), where the ESL rate amongst foreign-born early leavers is 16 points higher than their native-born peers (Eurostat, 2016). Finally, more than 93% of Roma youth are early school leavers in Spain, the EU country with the third largest Roma population (OCDE/European Union, 2015).

The composition by origin of Spanish youth has radically changed in the past 20 years. One in four young people aged 15 to 29 have a foreign-born parent today. These youngsters are the first generation of children of immigrants predominantly educated in Spain, and their education was one of the major indicators of success of their parents' migration projects. These millennial youngsters of the early twenty-first century, who are the children of new and intensive immigration flows to Spain, find themselves less equipped than their native-born peers for a labour market in a production structure that has undergone deep transformations following their families' migration and settlement processes and the economic crisis. Jobs in a knowledge-based economy require better education credentials, which may also help to cope with the risk of unemployment, legal insecurity and the effects of austerity policies. This socio-historical context calls for a generational approach to students' itineraries (Garcia, Casal, Merino, & Sánchez-Gelabert, 2013) and makes a strong case for a perspective based on integration context theory (Crul & Schneider, 2010) to understand the rapid shift in the conditions of integration experienced by immigrant parents and their children. In parallel, the Spanish Roma have intensely experienced the hardship of the economic crisis and advances in

Neglected aspirations   165

education and labour market integration for Roma youth have slowed down. Therefore, preventing ESL amongst youngsters most at risk of social exclusion becomes essential.

Drawing on preliminary results of the RESL.eu project, Nouwen, Clycq, and Ulicna (2015) have called for educational interventions that raise the aspirations of disadvantaged students while ensuring additional resources and advice. In effect, previous research has broadly put into context the assumption that immigrant/minority students' educational aspirations are high (Kao & Tienda, 1995; Strand & Winston, 2008) and may have positive effects on their attainment (Portes, Aparicio, Haller, & Vickstrom, 2010; Timmerman, 2000) although schools' capacity to build on them remains uncertain, while the aspiration paradox in students with migrant and minority backgrounds between high aspirations and low attainment persists. Qualitative research has shown how similar welcoming discourses and exclusionary practices coexist in different educational systems and national contexts, where the effects of inadequate pedagogical practices and internal school organization, as well as teachers' limited notions of minority and working-class academic success, remain hidden or naturalized under culturalist explanations despite students' aspirations (Carrasco, Pàmies, & Ponferrada, 2011; Gibson, Carrasco, Pàmies, Ponferrada, & Rios, 2013). Although schools with lower levels of segregation, higher resources and a better climate can make a difference (Suarez-Orozco, Suarez-Orozco, & Todorova, 2008), the effect of schools in promoting immigrant students' aspirations has been described as low compared with individual and family factors (Cebolla-Boado & Martínez, 2015; Bertran, Ponferrada, & Pàmies, 2016). This is also the case amongst Roma students with high aspirations, for whom even the benefits of targeted policies such as the EU Decade for Roma inclusion remain vague at the school level (Bereményi & Carrasco, 2015).

All this suggests it is important to further explore whether and how aspirations can become protective factors for disadvantaged youngsters to reduce the risk of ESL, in combination with supportive families and teachers, flexible, proactive and caring schools as well as in processes of self-determination as identified by Tilleczek and colleagues (2011). The aim of this chapter is to reconstruct and understand the processes experienced by a group of students who were considered at risk of ESL because of immigrant and minority backgrounds, all of whom expressed clear aspirations in contradiction to the assumption of "aspiring poor" as related to ESL. We focus on the relationship amongst students' aspirations, families' support and schools' support mediated and delivered by teacher practices, as perceived by the youngsters themselves. Regardless of their diversity, all the youngsters' initial aspirations were relatively high, although in some cases they were equal to those attained by other family members (a parent before migration, relatives in other countries) and in others they would be considered low or limited (e.g., completing compulsory lower secondary education) but were higher than the average attainment in their families and communities. That is to say, all of them had some kind of aspirational capital (Yosso, 2005), but following Archer, DeWitt, and Wong

166 *Silvia Carrasco et al.*

(2013) we intend to "move away from the focus on 'high' aspirations towards an emphasis on 'diversifying' and 'informing' aspirations, with appropriate support, to ensure that all young people can find routes to achieve interesting and fulfilling, well-paid jobs" (Archer et al., 2013, p. 77). Therefore, we explore and analyse what kind of support they received from families and teachers to fulfil their aspirations and, eventually, to cope with the risk of ESL between lower secondary education and further educational itineraries.

Methods and description of cases

The RESL.eu study in Spain was carried out in two densely populated and economically dynamic areas north of Barcelona (one coastal, one inland), with the participation of 3,646 students from 35 schools. The qualitative work was conducted in the area of Vallès Occidental (inland) and focused on 32 youngsters theoretically at risk of ESL and the schools and training centres they attended (16 in four schools; eight in four out-of-school compensatory programmes; eight not in education, employment or training [NEET]). The selection of youngsters still in school was based on perceived school engagement and social support in Survey A1 (Kaye, D'Angelo, Ryan, & Lőrinc, 2015) and complemented with relevant context-specific socio-demographic factors drawing on previous research on achievement inequality and ESL. In our study, this purposive sampling strategy added gender, immigrant and Roma background, parents' education and home language(s) other than the language of tuition (Catalan), and the same criteria were applied in the selection of the other two subsets of youngsters (in alternative learning arenas and NEETs). The analysis developed in this chapter is based on the ten youngsters with immigrant and Roma backgrounds included in the 32 case-study youngsters.

This sub-sample (Table 11.1) comprises four girls and six boys, eight from working-class families and two from families with some academic capital in the countries of origin; eight were first-generation immigrants from five different countries and two were Spanish Roma (Gitano) youngsters. All the youngsters were interviewed twice within a period of six months to one year, and participated in focus group discussions. All the transcriptions were coded and analysed with NVivo10 software (Carrasco, Narciso, Ruiz, Reyes, & Berémenyi, 2016).

Findings

Aspirations: as high as the highest

One surprising survey finding in the Spanish sample was that all youngsters, regardless of their backgrounds, showed the highest level of aspirations of the 19,631 youngsters in the dataset, in contrast to the highest rate of ESL of Spain:[1] 90.7% of the students surveyed in Spain aspired to some form of post-secondary education, well above the average 61.4% (Kaye, D'Angelo, Ryan, & Lőrinc, 2015). Further, 80.9% of the youngsters born outside the EU in the Spanish sample also had these high aspirations.

Table 11.1 Brief description of cases

Pseudonym	Gender	Migrant/minority background	Parents' education	Parents' occupation	Languages at home
Mohamed	Male	Moroccan origin, first-generation immigrant, arrived at the age of 8	Mother primary education; father none	Unemployed	Arabic, in addition to Catalan and Spanish
Najim	Male	Moroccan origin, first-generation immigrant, arrived at the age of 8	None (both)	Mother housewife; father construction worker (unemployed)	Amazigh (Berber)
Andrei	Male	Romanian origin, first-generation immigrant, arrived at the age of 3	Tertiary (both)	Mother waitress; father light and sound technician	Romanian, in addition to Catalan and Spanish
Juan	Male	Roma minority	None (both)	Mother and father unskilled self-employed (street market)	Spanish
Ionela	Female	Romanian origin, first-generation immigrant, arrived at the age of 9	Lower secondary (both)	Mother domestic cleaner; father security guard	Romanian
Carlos	Male	Bolivian origin, first-generation immigrant, arrived at the age of 9	Father upper secondary (general)	Father chef in restaurant	Spanish
Samira	Female	Pakistani origin, first-generation immigrant, arrived at the age of 11	Unknown (both)	Mother housewife; father mobile phone shop owner	Urdu, English as second language
Asma	Female	Moroccan origin, first-generation immigrant, arrived at the age of 13	Unknown (both)	Husband construction worker (unemployed)	Amazigh (Berber)
Marcelo	Male	Ecuadorian origin, first-generation immigrant, arrived at the age of 7	Unknown (both)	Mother geriatric assistant; father unemployed	Spanish
Pilar	Female	Roma minority	Unknown (both)	Mother and father unskilled, formerly self-employed (street market), currently unemployed	Spanish

168 *Silvia Carrasco et al.*

Our qualitative data confirm these results. All the youngsters who were still in school or in out-of-school training programmes aspired to attain a post-compulsory level (ISCED 3) or higher qualification, although not all of them had a clear idea of what specific tracks to opt for or what paths had to be followed to achieve them. Even Juan, a Roma youngster, who aspired to complete only lower secondary education (Educación Secundaria Obligatoria, ESO: ISCED 2), had a relatively ambitious goal compared with the average attainment of Roma students, which is still the lowest. Even the youngsters with NEET status during fieldwork expressed aspirations in education or training, however vague as "to do something at least", including Samira, from a Pakistani immigrant family, who planned to pursue higher education despite having left an initial vocational education and training (VET) track and lacking all orientation.

Differences by class previous to migration as well as gender seemed to shape these youngsters' aspirations. Working-class youngsters expressed their educational aspirations in relation to better opportunities in the job market, while middle- or lower-middle-class youth thought about achieving advanced stages of education as a goal in itself, often as maintaining the continuity of previously attained levels of education within their families. Eight of the ten youngsters aspired to intermediate or higher post-compulsory education (including one Roma and two immigrant females), the level identified by the Horizon 2020 strategy as the minimum level for participating in the knowledge economy. Only two youngsters aspired to obtain a graduation certificate from lower secondary education (including one Roma male and one immigrant female), still the only compulsory secondary level in the Spanish education system. This would include them in the future numbers of early school leavers at age 18.

Three dominant narratives of aspirations were identified, closer to work-oriented or to education-oriented goals:

Obtaining a diploma as a way to find a job

Juan, the Roma youngster, was repeating the last year of lower secondary schooling (ESO), and Asma, a Moroccan-born, young, married woman who arrived at the age of 13, did not work or study and was at home taking care of her children. Both from working-class families (Juan's parents were unemployed after working in street markets; Asma's husband was unemployed after working in the building sector), they wanted to get a job as soon as possible but they believed that they needed a minimum diploma to do so (ISCED 2), which neither of them had yet obtained:

> ESO is important, to do anything or to be anything. That is, to work in anything.
>
> (Juan)

A similar logic drove Pilar's and Marcelo's reasoning, although they had left lower secondary education (in year 2 in her case, and after repeating year 4 in his) and deeply regretted it:

Nowadays they ask you [to have] ESO for everything, to work and everything, even to get your driving license[2] and like . . . you need it for everything.

(Pilar)

Both Pilar's parents and Marcelo's father were unemployed, and both youngsters intended to obtain education certificates through training courses. At the time of the first interview, they were in training and insertion programmes (Programas de Formación e Inserción). These experiences encouraged them to develop new aspirations oriented to pursuing initial VET options (Ciclos Formativos de Grado Medio, ISCED 3) as a means of "being qualified in a trade", although none of them could specify any concrete desire as to what to study or in which area to work, with changing ideas about it:

I'd like to be able to do something, like have a qualification that is worth more than ESO, or at least be more prepared for the entrance exam. (. . .) If I pass I'll get into VET and if not, I'll finish the PTT and then get into VET later.

(Marcelo)

Enrolling in VET tracks to become qualified professionals in a competitive labour market

The idea expressed in the heading above was sustained by Najim, a Moroccan immigrant reunited by his father with his mother and other siblings at the age of 8, who was in his last year of lower secondary education in an adapted grade-level group, and by Carlos, a Bolivian immigrant reunited with his father at the age of 9, who was in his first year of a post-compulsory VET course in Business and Finance. They were both aware of their families' work experiences and developed a rational analysis of the Spanish recession and the new requirements of the changing labour market. It was their wish to move beyond their parents' negative experiences of job insecurity, in the case of Carlos, and of unemployment, in the case of Najim, which explained their plans:

You see the scenario and you want to study to avoid a bad situation, you know? (. . .) I want to do more because, I don't know, lots of people have a mid-level diploma.

(Carlos)

They both intended to complete an Intermediate VET course (ISCED 3) and continue to Advanced VET studies (ISCED 5B):

Because it's better, right? Intermediate level, to have some certificates to show that you have studied this. And the higher level to do it professionally, right?

(Najim)

170   *Silvia Carrasco et al.*

A similar reasoning was followed by Mohamed, another Moroccan immigrant reunited by his father at the age of 8, who was in his last year of lower secondary in an adapted grade-level group and intended to enrol in an intermediate-level VET course (ISCED 3) but adapted his aspirations under the influence of his brother's knowledge of job sectors with better opportunities:

> First, I wanted to be a car mechanic, but then my brother told me I have to study to be a computer repair technician, and that's it.
>
> (Mohamed)

All these youngsters and their families believed in education as the means to access better job opportunities. Those with an immigrant background were consistent in thinking with their families' migration projects of better life opportunities and social mobility.

Going to university as the continuation of successful education trajectories and/or keeping up with the family's academic capital

A different logic prevails in the group of youngsters oriented towards academic education. Ionela and Andrei were Romanian immigrants from families with middle-class backgrounds in their country of origin. In the first interviews they were in their first year of post-compulsory academic tracks and spoke about going to university afterwards as the next logical step. Ionela intended to study law and Andrei considered a wide range of options, all of them within higher education:

> I would love to become a lawyer, to study at university, if I can get in.
>
> (Ionela)

> Maybe work in law enforcement, or even devote myself to neuroscience. I don't really know. It's quite different, almost opposite. Criminology, or even law. I don't know. Now I'm more into social sciences but I'm not going yet [to university], I'm still not sure about it.
>
> (Andrei)

Samira, the Pakistani immigrant youngster from a family with a middle-class background before migration, held similar views. She was repeating the first year of a post-compulsory intermediate VET course after having lost the previous year because of sickness, but she wanted to go to university although she knew her aspirations in Spain would be a long and difficult path from intermediate VET. She expected to be able to move to the UK later, where the language barrier would disappear – English was one of the languages she spoke and she was fluent in Spanish, but not so much in Catalan, the language of tuition in Catalonia. She specifically wanted to become an officer in international airports:

I think I'll be able to continue studying there [in the UK], at a university there. I think that it will be easier for me, because it's in English. . . . I *only* spoke Urdu, Punjabi and English when I came.

(Samira)

In all these cases, the existence of university graduates in their family networks is apparently more relevant than their parents' actual level of education. These youngsters' families were sending messages promoting their children's high-level involvement in education in Spain as a protection in the face of their own experiences of downward mobility in the labour market or the long hours they had to work regardless of their qualifications in their country of origin.

Harder trajectories and adapted aspirations[3]

The ordinary school trajectory in Spain begins with enrolment in pre-school at the age of 3 (98% of attainment), followed by primary education with additional support if required but no special classes and, when regarded as necessary, the possibility of repeating one year. Transition to lower secondary education (ESO) entails a change of school in the public sector, as primary and secondary education are taught in different schools. The way support is delivered may vary considerably according to each school, especially in the last two years of lower secondary, when dropping out is a higher risk, for example, by placing students in temporary reinforcement groups, in permanent ability groups or in student-focused measures, or making the students repeat a year. Lower secondary education (ESO) graduation rates for native-born students at 16 are high (90% in 2016), and families usually expect their children to enrol in post-compulsory academic tracks, with a wide range on offer and non-competitive entry. However, there is a reduced and locally dispersed offer of less prestigious VET tracks after ESO, and access is based on grade point average in ESO or the score obtained in an entry exam. Students who do not graduate with a lower secondary education diploma – those who drop out before completion or do not pass all the final exams – can only try to be selected for out-of-school compensation programmes or try to get a job. Many of these youngsters become NEET, an intermittent status alternating with temporary training in compensatory programmes or unqualified temporary jobs.

However, immigrant and minority students' trajectories are more likely to undergo specific experiences that can limit their academic aspirations. They are more likely to start a little later in primary education, and be placed in reception classes for one or two years on a full-time or part-time basis where the focus is learning Catalan, especially if they arrive after the age of 8. The transition to lower secondary education generally implies a change of school as more than 80% of students with immigrant backgrounds attend public schools (Estadística d'Ensenyament, 2016). In secondary schools they may spend another one or two years in full-time newcomers' classes or part-time reinforcement classes, or may be placed in lower-ability groups in schools that organize them. Dropout

172 *Silvia Carrasco et al.*

amongst immigrant and minority groups (especially Roma or black African youngsters) even in years 1 and 2 of lower secondary is more likely to be naturalized as social or cultural practices of withdrawal from school (Abajo & Carrasco, 2004; Pàmies, 2008; Narciso & Carrasco, 2018). Such youth are also more frequently guided to VET tracks and out-of-school training, although they find themselves competing for a limited number of available places from which they may be excluded because of lower grades or language skills. As a consequence of the combination of systemic and institutional factors, they end up being overrepresented amongst early school leavers and NEETs (Table 11.2).

The second wave of interviews (between six months and one year later) made it possible to reconstruct the trajectories of the case-study youngsters of our sample and compare their initial aspirations with the new aspirations they had adjusted to since the first interview. Although the youngsters' experiences were very diverse even in a small sample, amongst those identified as early school leavers in the second interview four types of trajectories were found.

Progressive absenteeism and disengagement

Juan left school before the end of the academic year when he was repeating ESO year 4, giving up his initial goal of graduating. He mentioned a severe migraine episode coinciding with the final exams as the cause. He then joined his family's street trade. Pilar had already dropped out of ESO in year 2 but after re-enrolling for the second time she was able to complete lower secondary education in a student-focused measure with adapted curriculum. Her trajectory had entered into a loop and, because of mistakes made in her application form to enrol in a VET track, she decided to do another programme of the same level but in a different trade, which she gave up twice because she said she did not like it very much and got easily discouraged.

Sudden absenteeism because of personal or family vicissitudes

Samira dropped out of VET studies in year 1 twice. The first time was due to illness resulting in long-term absence, although she had partially completed the course requirements (one term passed); the second time was due to the mobility of her family for work reasons. In the new town, she was doing a hairdressing training course, encouraged by her family to "do something", and her initial aspiration of going to university seemed to move farther away although she still mentioned it. She concluded that "the academic track (baccalaureate) is very difficult for immigrants".

School failure and the limited effectiveness of compensatory programmes

Marcelo did not graduate from lower secondary education (ESO), nor succeed in the entrance exam for intermediate VET. Then he decided to repeat ESO year 4 and again he failed. He enrolled in a compensatory measure, an initial

Table 11.2 Students' ordinary and possibly specific trajectories in Spain

Ordinary trajectories of mainstream students	98% early childhood education and care	100% pre-school	Regular primary	Regular lower secondary years 1 and 2	Regular lower secondary years 3 and 4	Demanding baccalaureate tracks; competitive access to VET tracks★; out-of-school training programs; work/education-oriented NEET
+ possible:			Additional support; 1-year repetition	Additional segregated measures; 1-year repetition	High risk of dropout; other measures; 1-year repetition	Highest risk of dropout; no retention measures
Students with immigrant or minority background	Lower early childhood education and care	95% pre-school	Arrival after the age of 8; reception class; segregated 1 or 2 years (part time)	Reception class; segregated 1 or 2 years (part time); late arrivals report from primary	Dropout naturalized for some groups (even from year 1 or 2)	Less oriented to baccalaureate tracks; competitive access to VET tracks★; less selected to out-of-school programmes, training programs, work/education-oriented; overrepresented in NEET

Source: Prepared by the authors.

★ Not at risk, highest access.

174   *Silvia Carrasco et al.*

professional qualification programme that initially got him motivated and he tried to get into intermediate VET again. However, as the months passed he changed his mind and planned to look for a job instead. He felt he was growing old and decided to enrol in an adult education centre to try to obtain the graduation certificate of lower secondary education (GESO, ISCED 2). He downgraded his previous aspirations, expecting to juggle work and study: "I want a qualification because I want to be able to say I *finished* this and this and this".

Asma's situation was also highly frustrating for her. She had dropped out before completing compulsory education and enrolled in a compensatory programme to finally find out afterwards that she had wrongly thought it was another way of obtaining the GESO diploma. At the time of the second interview, she had given up and was transferring her aspirations to her children while broadening her goals for them – she wants them to go to university, an aspiration she had never had but was already imagining for her children. This gender pattern had been already identified in previous research with Spanish Roma and Moroccan young women (Abajo & Carrasco, 2004; Bertran, Ponferrada, & Pàmies, 2016).

Unexpected low performance in post-compulsory education

Ionela, with a trajectory of achievement in compulsory education, dropped out of baccalaureate in year 1, disappointed with unexpected poor grades in the first term and was needed to help with her family health problems. However, she did not give up education and later enrolled in a VET track in Business and Finance. She had given up her aspirations of becoming a lawyer but she might still be able to reach university although through a longer and more uncertain itinerary.

More in parallel than in contrast to the outcomes presented up to this point, almost all the youngsters identified as non–early school leavers in our sample adapted their aspirations. Most case-study youngsters had undergone periods of low performance and were still vulnerable to ESL (Table 11.3). Mohamed and Najim had attended student-centred measures in primary and secondary school and they both had repeated one year. By the time of the second interview they were enrolled in the first year of post-compulsory VET tracks, the year and education track with the highest risk of dropout in Spain.

Only Carlos and Andrei followed the standard educational trajectories and were both about to complete ISCED 3 in vocational and academic tracks, respectively, and to obtain their diplomas by the time of the second interview. They were also likely to continue on to higher education (ISCED 5B). Carlos had simply been moving ahead in educational stages without clear plans:

> Well, I'm still not sure what I want to study. . . . I did this just to do something. . . . I'm still not sure at all.

Table 11.3 Trajectories of immigrant and minority case-study youngsters

Cases	Situation at the time of first interview	Initial aspirations	Situation at the time of second interview	Adapted expectations	Early school leavers
Juan	In education; lower secondary (year 4, compulsory education)	Lower secondary education (ISCED 2)	In work; unskilled self-employee (flea market)	In work; unskilled self-employee (flea market)	
Pilar	Compensatory in-school training programme	Lower VET studies (ISCED 3)	Compensatory in-school training programme (at the end of school year)	Compensatory in-school training programme (other trade)	
Samira	NEET	University degree (work in an airport)	Training course for unemployed (hairdressing)	Vague	
Marcelo	Compensatory out-of-school training programme	Lower VET studies (ISCED 3)	Compensatory out-of-school training programme (at the end of school year)	Lower secondary education (ISCED 2)	
Asma	NEET	Lower secondary education (ISCED 2)	NEET	No educational expectations	
Mohamed	In education; lower secondary (year 4)	Intermediate VET (ISCED 3)+; advanced VET (ISCED 5B; computer repair technician)	In education; intermediate VET (ISCED 3, year 1; sales)	Intermediate VET (ISCED 3, year 2; sales)	**No early school leavers**
Najim	In education; lower secondary (year 4)	Intermediate VET (ISCED 3)+ advanced VET (ISCED 5B; electricity and electronics)	In education; intermediate VET (ISCED 3, year 1; electricity and electronics)	Intermediate VET (ISCED 3, year 2; electricity and electronics)	
Carlos	In education; intermediate VET (ISCED 3, year 1)	Intermediate VET (ISCED 3)+; advanced VET (ISCED 5B)	In education; intermediate VET (ISCED 3, year 2)	In education; advanced VET (ISCED 5B)	
Andrei	In education; upper secondary academic track (year 1)	University degree (law enforcement, neuroscience or criminology)	In education; upper secondary academic track (year 2)	Advanced VET (ISCED 5B) +university degree	
Ionela	In education; upper secondary academic track (year 1)	University degree (law)	NEET	In education; intermediate VET (ISCED 3, year 1)	

Source: Prepared by the authors.

176   *Silvia Carrasco et al.*

Andrei, the most successful case amongst the youngsters with immigrant and minority backgrounds and the only one in this sample attending a predominantly middle-class high school, had changed his mind to adapt his expectations:

> When I finish the second year [of baccalaureate], I'm going to do an advanced VET track, although I still want to go to university, of course. But most unis demand quite a high mark, and my average is six, a bad one.

In the following section, we explore the role of different kinds of social support required and received at crucial points of the youngsters' educational trajectories in relation to their aspirations, especially focusing on issues related to their immigrant and minority situations.

Teacher and family support in the youngsters' aspirations and trajectories

RESL survey findings show that school engagement amongst Spanish youngsters was the highest and perceived teacher and social support were also high and above the average despite the prevailing high ESL rates (Kaye, D'Angelo, Ryan, & Lőrinc, 2015). Respondents with immigrant and Roma backgrounds in the sample followed these trends, and qualitative data seemed to confirm these findings.

Families, rather than teachers and schools, were mentioned when the youngsters were asked to identify their main source of support in both interviews. Nine out of ten of the youngsters referred to their families as their first ports of call, providing different kinds of support to make it easy for them to remain in education or training, mostly emotional but also financial, despite their limited resources, for example, by being relieved from work-seeking despite economic difficulties in the household as identified in previous research (Schnell, Keskiner, & Crul, 2013; Bertran et al., 2016; Abajo & Carrasco, 2004). Only one youngster, Mohammed, explicitly made the point of not receiving support from his family but rather an imposition from his older brother to enrol in post-compulsory VET.

The youngsters' descriptions of their families' efforts to support them varied between *unspecific trust* and *active encouragement*: from parents' basic trust in the youngsters' possibilities, as well as in the schools' and teachers' work, to explicit mobilization of resources to prevent dropout and ESL. Support was delivered by various means:

- By counter-examples: "You have to make an effort and go on studying if you do not to want to end up like me" is a narrative of working-class families in our data, especially mothers (such as Andrei's mother after her downward mobility in the labour market experienced with migration)
- By not only allowing, but also pushing their daughter into "doing something else" to prepare her to have a better job, discharging her from domestic duties, if necessary (Pilar's Roma parents' uncommon positive attitudes

Neglected aspirations   177

towards their daughter's education [Abajo & Carrasco, 2004] were not understood as relevant by the school as they were)

- By exploring educational or training opportunities through extended family networks (Samira gets information from her father, her relatives in the UK and international TV channels in English the family watches together; she is also advised by her father not to wear a headscarf as it may limit her opportunities)
- By designing and implementing specific post-compulsory VET plans after gathering information about job opportunities in the area (as Mohammed's brother did, since their parents are illiterate and unfamiliar with the system) or changing schools following the native working-class aspirational pattern of moving from state schools to privately owned, state-funded schools in search of "more discipline and quality" (Carlos's father)

Those with middle- and lower-middle class status in the country of origin or with academic capital in the family (Andrei and Ionela from Romania; Samira from Pakistan; Marcelo from Ecuador) had clear grounds on which to forge their aspirations. However, three of them (Ionela, Samira, Marcelo) experienced the impact of limited expectations from the teachers in the predominantly working-class schools they attended (with virtually no native-born, middle-class students), even after having enrolled in post-compulsory tracks (Ionela and Samira). Following Yosso's framework (2005), these youngsters' aspirational capital was not met by the navigational capital required.

All the youngsters experienced situations of risk in their trajectories that made them vulnerable and would have required targeted support, some of them in common with their working-class, native-born peers but also other specific circumstances related to their immigrant or minority status. Those five youngsters who remained in education after ISCED 2 (Andrei, Carlos, Ionela, Mohammed and Najim) counted on families who encouraged and supported them strongly in different ways. Some had relatives with higher education (Andrei and Ionela) or better local information (Mohammed's older brother), and had benefitted from student-focused measures that had worked (newcomers' class in primary school: Ionela, Mohammed, Najim; one year repetition and classes with adapted curriculum in high school: Mohammed, Najim). At different levels and to a higher extent, those circumstances were *pushing them closer to their native working-class peers' common and fragile ways out of ESL risks*; namely, into the first year of post-compulsory VET tracks:

- Mohammed and Najim were placed in the manual VET tracks where working-class boys are overrepresented
- Andrei was struggling with the overwhelmingly encyclopaedic content of the pre-college year in the academic tracks (baccalaureate) that made him think university was unachievable (Samira and Ionela shared this view); also like many working-class youngsters in the academic tracks, Andrei was considering enrolling instead in any advanced VET track

178 *Silvia Carrasco et al.*

- Ionela experienced the strategy mentioned by teachers of lowering students' results in the first term of the academic tracks "to motivate" and send the message of "major efforts required" that end up pushing working-class students into intermediate VET tracks (Carrasco, Narciso, & Bertran, 2015)
- Carlos was not really motivated but remained engaged for instrumental reasons, closely monitored by his father; still, he felt homesick and also revealed that he felt he did not belong at the school or in the country

Also, the experiences of those five youngsters who did not complete ISCED 2 or left after trying to continue in post-compulsory education or training (Marcelo, Samira, Asma, Juan and Pilar) described the *variety of situations of risk usually undergone* by their working-class peers and *specific additional difficulties resulting from their migration processes/minority status*, despite family support and their own aspirations:

- Marcelo had experienced high emotional stress because of his *process of family reunification*. He was the last child to be *reunited with* his parents and brothers after eight years of separation during which his older sister in Ecuador remained his only close reference. His family pushed him to study and his brothers and sister had completed higher education in Ecuador and in Spain. He was grateful to his last ESO tutor for encouraging him to enrol in a compensatory programme he had not heard of, although in the end it did not work for him (failing the VET entry exam on several attempts).
- Samira's family, especially her father, were her support in life and they encouraged her to remain in education – her older sister and brother had gone to university in Pakistan – but they had *little or no information about the educational system in Spain*. In the second interview (by phone), after having moved to the Basque Country, she sadly remarked *she felt they were unwelcome there* and missed her school friends in Catalonia, with whom she was in daily contact through social media. She resented that *the teachers had just let her go with a certificate and no further remarks or help when informed of her imminent mobility*, as well as having been forced to take all the subjects again in her second attempt in a VET track after recovering from illness.
- Asma's support was her husband. She was a regular recipient of social services as a *poor immigrant young mother*, like many of her friends. Although she had been counselled by a social worker since high school (concerning benefits and the usual free courses for immigrants such as Catalan lessons), she had gotten *wrong information about the professional training* in bakery she had completed, which was not equivalent to the GESO diploma and neither did it improve her employability. She expressed deep frustration about this.
- Juan's aspirations were supported by his Roma family but he was never selected for student-focused support measures, which had undergone severe budget reductions and therefore not all the students in need of the measures could be included. In the first interview, he said his school was like family, but in the second interview he resented not having received

Neglected aspirations 179

"a single phone call from the school" and that *they had just let him go* after having finally had to drop out because of his health problems.

- Pilar lacked proper school guidance despite having the support of her Roma family. She also described her school as a second home, but her *chances depended on relationships with specific teachers.* She explained that because of her counsellor's sick leave, she had no one to help her complete the application form correctly to enrol in a VET track, which she finally did when she happened to come across the counsellor in a corridor the following year.

Teacher support was generally defined as *caring for* students rather than *caring about* their circumstances or needs (McKamy, 2011). In fact, immigrant and minority youngsters spontaneously mentioned *care* ("they care about us") rather than *quality* when referring to teachers and schools, regardless of the educational resources they actually enjoyed. Caring teachers were described as being close, friendly, sharing personal concerns or details about their lives (Andrei); encouraging and helping with administrative procedures (Pilar); providing crucial information (Marcelo: alternatives of compensatory training; Ionela: grants); or simply treating students well, in a caring way, "making them feel at home" (Juan). None of these youngsters defined *quality* in teachers the way middle-class, native-born students did, like being knowledgeable or teaching well, but rather as capable of managing disruption fairly and not giving up on students. Care apparently embedded the notion of quality. For some youngsters, "the school" as a whole was seen as an elusive caring resource (Mohammed played within the school's grounds on weekends; the schools of Juan and Pilar were amongst the only public institutions in their neighbourhoods). But they did not specifically expect teachers to care, and only three youngsters (Juan, after dropping out; Marcelo, referring to the high school previous to the training programme; and Samira, after moving) adhered to the "teachers did not care" explanation (Valenzuela, 1999) when things did not work out for them. They rather tended to produce different versions of the *self-blaming narrative* common amongst youngsters with damaged academic identities without challenging meritocratic beliefs (Pérez-Benavent, 2016): "I lost faith in it", "I could not make it", "I finally gave up".

Conclusion

A huge amount of research has shown the impacts of family reunification processes, poor information about the new educational system, selective and segregating practices, family mobility strategies, poverty and ethnic discrimination on students' trajectories. A longitudinal analysis centred on the youngsters' perceptions and grounded experiences provides insights into how they struggled through their transitions after lower secondary education with additional difficulties. The high overrepresentation of youngsters with immigrant and Roma backgrounds in the numbers of ESL in Spain unfortunately makes more sense and illustrates how immigrant and minority status operate in the increased educational polarization of Spanish youth with high shares of early school leavers and college graduates (Carrasco et al., 2015). Our analysis has unravelled the key importance of teachers' and public schools' support in providing responsive and sufficient, non-selective educational resources as well as sustained care and advice to prevent from uncertainties, barriers and gaps that lead to discouragement and disengagement. Despite their different outcomes, a closer look at the school experiences of the two groups of youngsters – those who left school early and those who did not – reveals that they do not differ that much. This should be a warning to us about the *fragility of the non-leavers' trajectories* amongst vulnerable groups while providing evidence to regard this *dichotomy between early school leavers and those who are not as empirically feeble*. For these immigrant and minority students, the support received from schools and alternative training programmes was not consistent and stable along their trajectories, and thus it did not play a decisive role in reducing their risk of becoming early school leavers by compensating for the effects of systemic inadequacies in unfamiliar contexts. Rather than leaving education early, they were trying to remain in it but their aspirations often ended up being neglected. Having aspirations, in their schools' contexts, was not enough to constitute a strong protective factor. There is no conclusive evidence that raising aspirations per se can improve achievement or prevent ESL. Despite families' diverse types of support, students' aspirations of all kinds can be neglected when counselling and monitoring resources are limited in schools, not enough or inadequate guidance is provided and teachers project limited notions of success on certain groups of students. Higher aspirations may be discarded as unrealistic student self-assessments but also lower aspirations can be overlooked as unsuitable or unworthy. Modest aspirations in the schools' perspectives should also be taken into account as legitimate ambitions to complete education that is reasonably designed to grant access to the labour market or to leave the door open for further educational stages in a time when life-long learning is taken for granted.

The experiences of youth in the present-day world have changed; their transitions are not linear and it is necessary to leave behind neoliberal narratives of choice and individual accountability (McGregor, 2017), especially when analyzing a complex, multifactorial process such as ESL (Rumberger, 2011). But there is room for action within schools and out-of-school programmes to move beyond the risk of ESL by improving and targeting their support to the needs of working-class, immigrant and Roma students based on learning how to draw on their aspirations.

Notes

1 Previous survey research has also reported similarities in aspirations. Similar but "modest" levels of aspirations between native-born and immigrant youth were found in the extension of CILS (Children of Immigrants Longitudinal Study) in Madrid and Barcelona (Portes et al., 2010) and more optimistic ones in the CHANCES project in Madrid (González-Ferrer et al., 2015).
2 Obtaining a basic education diploma became a strong motivation for Roma street traders in the past because it was a compulsory requirement to take the driving license test, although it is no longer necessary.

3 "Adapted aspirations" is used as meaning different from expectations. Case-study youngsters were asked the same questions about aspirations in different interview rounds in time. We are not referring to the questions about aspirations vs expectations in the same interviews.

References

Abajo, J. E., & Carrasco, S. (2004). *Experiencias y trayectorias de éxito escolar de gitanas y gitanos en España*. Colección Mujeres en la Educación, 4. Madrid: CIDE-Instituto de la Mujer.

Archer, L., DeWitt, J., & Wong, B. (2014). Spheres of influence: What shapes young people's aspirations at age 12/13 and what are the implications for education policy? *Journal of Education Policy*, 29(1), 58–85. doi:10.1080/02680939.2013.790079

Bereményi, B-Á., & Carrasco, S. (2015, April). Interrupted aspirations: Research and policy on Gitano education in a time of recession in Spain. *Intercultural Education*, 1–30. doi:10.1080/14675986.2015.1028166

Bertran, M., Ponferrada, M., & Pàmies, J. (2016). Gender, family negotiations and academic success of young Moroccan women in Spain. *Race, Ethnicity and Education*, 19(1), 161–181. doi:10.1080/13613324.2014.946486

Carrasco, S., Narciso, L., & Bertran, M. (2015). ¿Qué pueden hacer los centros públicos ante el abandono escolar prematuro? Explorando las medidas de apoyo al alumnado a través de dos estudios de caso en Cataluña en un contexto de crisis. *Profesorado*, 19(3), 76–92. Retrieved from www.redalyc.org/articulo.oa?id=56743410006

Carrasco, S., Narciso, L., Ruiz, I., Reyes, R., & Berémenyi, B. Á. (2016). *A longitudinal analysis of youth at risk of ESL*. Country Report – Spain. RESL.eu.

Carrasco, S., Pàmies, J., & Ponferrada, M. (2011). Fronteras visibles y barreras ocultas: la experiencia escolar del alumnado marroquí en Cataluña y mexicano en California. *Revista Migraciones*, 29, 31–60. Retrieved from http://revistas.upcomillas.es/index.php/revistamigraciones/article/view/932

Cebolla-Boado, H., & Martínez de Lizarrondo, A. (2015). Las expectativas educativas de la población inmigrante en Navarra. ¿Optimismo inmigrante o efectos de escuela ? *Revista Internacional de Sociología*, 73(1), 1–13. doi:10.3989/ris.2013.02.22

Crul, M., & Schneider, J. (2010). Comparative integration context theory: Participation and belonging in new diverse European cities. *Ethnic and Racial Studies*, 33(7), 1249–1268. doi:10.1080/01419871003624068

Departament d'Ensenyament – GenCat. (2016). *Estadística de l'ensenyament, curs 2016–2017*. Retrieved from http://ensenyament.gencat.cat/ca/departament/estadistiques/

Eurostat. (2016). Europe 2020 indicators – education. *Eurostat Statistics Explained*. Retrieved from http://ec.europa.eu/eurostat/statistics-explained/index.php/Europe_2020_indicators_-_education

Garcia, M., Casal, J., Merino, R., & Sánchez-Gelabert, A. (2013). Itinerarios de abandono escolar y transiciones tras la enseñanza secundaria obligatoria, *Revista de Educación*, 361. doi:10–4438/1988–1592X-RE-2011–2361–2135

Gibson, M., Carrasco, S., Pàmies, J., Ponferrada, M., & Rios, A. (2013). Different systems, similar results: Youth of immigrant origin at school in California and Catalonia. In Alba, R. & Holdaway, J. (Eds.), *The children of immigrants at school, a comparative look at integration in the United States and Western Europe* (pp. 84–119). New York: New York University Press.

González-Ferrer, A., Kraus, E., Fernández, M., Cebolla-Boado, H., Soysal, Y., & Aratani, Y. (2015). Adolescents' life plans in the city of Madrid. Are immigrant origins of any importance? Metamorfosis. *Revista Del Centro Reina Sofía Sobre Adolescencia y Juventud*, (2), 25–49. Retrieved from http://repository.essex.ac.uk/18600/1/Num2-Articulo2.pdf

182 *Silvia Carrasco et al.*

Kao, G., & Tienda, M. (1995). Optimism and achievement: The educational performance of immigrant youth. *Social Science Quarterly*, 76(1), 1–19. Retrieved from http://globalnet work.princeton.edu/piirs/Kao%20and%20Tienda.pdf

Kaye, N., D'Angelo, A., Ryan, L., & Lőrinc, M. (2015). *Student's survey (A1) preliminary analysis*. Project Paper N° 5 RESL.eu.

McGregor, G. (2017). Counter-narratives that challenge neo-liberal discourses of schooling 'disengagement': Youth professionals informing the work of teachers. *British Journal of Sociology of Education*, 38(4), 551–565. doi:10.1080/01425692.2015.1113859

McKamey, C. (2011). Restoring "caring" in education: Students' narratives of caring for and about. *Narrative Works*, 1(1). Retrieved from https://journals.lib.unb.ca/index.php/NW/article/view/18475

Narciso, L., & Carrasco, S. (2018). Movilidad al país de origen familiar: Representaciones distorsionadas de jóvenes y familias de origen negroafricano en los mass-media. In Carrasco, S. & Bereményi, B. Á. (Eds.), *Migraciones, movilidad y educación: Estrategias familiares y respuestas escolares*. Barcelona: Bellaterra (in press).

Nouwen, W., Clycq, N., & Ulicna, D. (2015). *Reducing the risk that youth with a migrant background in Europe will leave school early*. Brussels: Migration Policy Institute Europe and SIRIUS Policy Network on the Education of Children and Youngsters with a Migrant background. Retrieved from www.sirius-migrationeducation.org/

OCDE/European Union. (2015). *Indicators of immigrant integration 2015: Settling in*. Paris: OCDE Publishing. doi:10.1787/9789264234024-en

Pàmies, J. (2008). Identidad, integració i escola: Joves d'origen marroquí a la perifèria de Barcelona. *Colecció Aportacions*, 32. Observatori Català de la Joventut. Generalitat de Catalunya.

Pérez-Benavent, M. J. (2016). From messing about to getting wound up: Metaphor and coherence in the stories of five young people who return to CFGM. *Revista de Educación*, 373, 35–56. doi:10.4438/1988–1592X-RE-2016-373-320

Portes, A., Aparicio, R., Haller, W., & Vickstrom, E. (2010). Moving ahead in Madrid: Aspirations and expectations in the Spanish second generation1. *International Migration Review*, 44, 767–801. doi:10.1111/j.1747-7379.2010.00825.x

Rumberger, R. (2011). *Dropping out: Why students drop out of high school and what can be done about it*. Cambridge, MA: Harvard University Press.

Schnell, P., Keskiner, E., & Crul, M. (2013). Success against the Odds: Educational pathways of disadvantaged second-generation Turks in France and the Netherlands. *Education Inquiry*, 4(1), 125–147. doi:10.3402/edui.v4i1.22065

Strand, S., & Winston, J. (2008). Educational aspirations in inner city schools. *Educational Studies*, 34(4), 249–267. doi:10.1080/03055690802034021

Suárez-Orozco, M., Suárez-Orozco, C., & Todorova, I. (2008). *Learning a new land: Immigrant students in American society*. Cambridge, MA: Harvard University Press.

Tilleczek, K., Ferguson, B., Edney, D. R., Rummens, A., Boydell, K., & Mueller, M. (2011). A contemporary study with early school leavers: Pathways and social processes of leaving high school. *Canadian Journal of Family and Youth*, 3(1), 1–39. Retrieved from www.researchgate.net

Timmerman, C. (2000). Secular and religious nationalism among young Turkish women in Belgium: Education may make the difference. *Anthropology and Education Quarterly*, 31(3), 333–354. ISSN 0161–7761.

Valenzuela, A. (1999). *Subtractive schooling. US.-Mexican youth and the politics of caring*. New York: SUNY Press.

Yosso, T. J. (2005). Whose culture has capital? A critical race theory discussion of community cultural wealth. *Race Ethnicity and Education*, 8(1), 69–91. doi:10.1080/1361332052000341006

Part IV

Strategies to deal with early school leaving

12 No bridges to re-engagement?

Exploring compensatory measures for early school leavers in Catalonia (Spain) from a qualitative approach

Silvia Carrasco, Isidoro Ruiz-Haro and Bálint-Ábel Bereményi

Introduction

Optimistic views about the capacity of the educational system to retain a higher proportion of youngsters at risk of dropping out and early school leaving (ESL) resulting in appalling rates of youth unemployment since 2007 in Spain have proved to be based on weak grounds. Despite recent improvements since 2015, both ESL and youth unemployment rates remain amongst the highest in the European Union[1] and there is no empirical proof for any direct link between declining rates and recent policy reforms. However, most local policies have been focusing on the transition from school-to-work and job-training opportunities (García, 2016; Servei Comarcal de Joventut, 2015) instead of tackling ESL but rather adding as a complementary goal the completion of lower secondary education, the last compulsory stage in Spain. In fact, the lack of awareness about ESL as defined by the EU Commission is still pervasive amongst policy makers, administrators and teachers (Carrasco & Narciso, 2013; Rambla, Tarabini, & Curran, 2013).

As a result of the great recession, significant changes have been introduced in the field of active labour market policies (ALMP), youth employment, education and particularly vocational education and training (VET) policies (González-Menéndez et al., 2015; Hadjivassiliou, Eichhorst, Tassinari, & Wozni, 2016). Most compensatory measures were originally designed under the EU umbrella of the Youth Guarantee Plan as short-term interventions and were disproportionally work-oriented rather than education-oriented. Increased awareness of the incapacity of the educational system to deal with young people who drop out required a shift of perspective by decision makers, to adapt already running programmes to the new aim of struggling against ESL (González-Menéndez et al., 2015). Thus, beyond improving young people's employability and assisting their access to the labour market,[2] the reforms highlighted the potential of those measures to re-engage them in the formal educational system, especially in initial VET tracks.

This chapter focuses on two initially work-first–oriented compensatory measures implemented by the Catalan autonomous government[3] that were reallocated within the Youth Guarantee Plan in 2015: 1) Youth for Employment

Programme (YfE) [*Joves per l'Ocupació*] of the Employment Service and 2) Training and Labour Insertion Programmes (TLIP) [*Programes de Formació i Inserció*] of the Department of Education. According to recent redefinitions, both schemes pursue a twofold objective: to offer basic work-based training in order to improve youth employability and to re-engage those at high risk of becoming early school leavers in the educational system. Previous research in Spain has assessed the design and implementation of similar second-chance programmes, focusing on their effectiveness in improving both labour market access and the return to formal education (Alegre, Casado, Sanz, & Todeschini, 2015). Other authors have focused on young people's own interpretations about their discontinuous transition process from (compulsory) lower secondary education to post-compulsory training or compensatory schemes (Horcas López, Bernad i Garcia, & Martínez Morales, 2015; Olmos & Mas, 2014; Pérez Benavent, 2016). Nevertheless, the role of compensatory schemes in tackling ESL and their impact on young people's experiences remain largely unexplored.

Drawing on qualitative data gathered within the RESL.eu project in these two compensatory measures, this chapter explores the views and experiences of youngsters and staff about their effectiveness in tackling the risk of ESL in relation to their official goals and the participants' expectations after leaving lower secondary education.

Overlapping goals: tackling youth unemployment and early school leaving

Recently, youth unemployment and finishing lower secondary education without a certificate (GESO) have been at the core of social and political debates in Spain. However, education and activation policies that target most directly young people in Spain are still at a very initial stage of development and are less bold than in other EU countries (Hadjivassiliou et al., 2016). In fact, the "activation turn" (Nelson, 2013) generated an increasing volume of research on ALMP assessment focusing on the effectiveness of programmes mostly based on macro data (e.g. see Card, Kluve, & Weber, 2010; Martin & Grubb, 2001; Polidano, Tabasso, & Tseng, 2012).

Most large-scale analyses are based on the OECD labour market policy database. These macro data do not allow us to understand fundamental context-related information such as institutional settings, policy and programme execution (Clasen, Clegg, & Goerne, 2016). Recently, qualitative and mixed-method studies have helped focus on the assessment of particular programme types. Findings of this body of research suggest that classroom and on-the-job training show effectiveness in the long run, usually after two years (Card et al., 2010). Evidence shows that only if youth are involved in the measure long enough do they make a lasting difference and, especially for the most vulnerable youth, programmes should be multifaceted in order to avoid dropout (Bloom, Levy Thompson, & Ivry, 2010). Short-term measures, often designed to ensure attendance, do not produce durable changes (Bloom et al., 2010; Card et al., 2010).

It also seems crucial to define the target beneficiaries with sensitivity, while ensuring that interventions are designed in responsive ways to the constraints of that particular group (Cunningham, Sanchez-Puerta, & Wuermli, 2010). Bloom et al. (2010) also draw attention to the risk that a deficit-focused targeting may negatively fix the social identity of those youth. Therefore, measures should go beyond training and technical support. They should be able to provide experiences in diverse environments and varied activities in different domains in order to build supportive relationships and a positive self-image for young people. Targeting and planning should not point at existing damages (Lindemann Nelson, 2001), and naturalise disengagement or present it as individual deficits, omitting wider underlying social inequalities (Simmons & Thompson, 2011). Finally, time out from school may have positive effects if it allows young early school leavers to mature and develop clearer aspirations (Polidano et al., 2012) in a supportive environment.

Broader institutional organisation of the programmes is essential. Bloom et al. (2010) highlight the need for non-official or compensatory programmes to be tightly linked with regular post-compulsory occupational and academic programmes. Efforts aimed at retaining young people in regular programmes through preventive measures are crucial because the system of second-opportunity programmes is in many countries scarce and complex. It is hard to access and poorly connected with the mainstream educational system, especially for those who drop out at an earlier stage, and for those from families with poorer academic capital (García, Casal, Merino, & Sánchez-Gelabert, 2013).

Several authors suggest that grouping in these measures and programmes should be flexible, creatively adapted to the beneficiaries in order to avoid more traditional classroom dynamics (Bloom et al., 2010; Hutchinson & Kettlewell, 2015). For certain target groups, safe training settings with trusting relationships can be a crucial issue (Cunningham et al., 2010). However, while personal relationships, care and nurture are important for success, practitioners may reproduce simplified views of at-risk students as mostly non-academic, practical and work-oriented, restricting their aspirations (Simmons & Thompson, 2011). Partly in relation to this, receiving post-programme certification is essential (Mattero, 2010), especially if the qualifications provide access to the regular school system, even if second-chance programmes tend to offer low-status certificates (Simmons & Thompson, 2011).

Research on compensatory measures, as part of a more or less homogeneous set of programmes outside the educational system, is relatively scarce in Spain. Most of the programmes and measures that can be currently identified as part of the compensatory strategies to tackle ESL usually overlap with those previously existing measures that targeted youth unemployment. The shifting perspective identified – to re-orientate the aims of the measures to tackle youth unemployment into measures towards combating ESL as well – and the continuous education reforms of the past two decades complicate the present mapping of available options for young people at risk of ESL. These *alternative learning arenas*, defined as "alternative learning schemes aside from mainstream education where young people may have the opportunity to obtain educational qualification" in the RESL.eu project (Van Praag, Van Caudenberg, Nouwen, Clycq, & Timmerman, 2017), have been the subject of only a limited number of studies, mostly carried out by IVÀLUA, a governmental policy assessment institution. In several reports (Alegre et al., 2015; Blasco & Casado, 2013), they conclude that the work-first programmes for NEET youngsters and school-to-work transition measures promoted in recent years have proved to be highly ineffective in improving the employment chances of its participants. Some of these measures, however, were effective in the re-engagement of vulnerable youth into formal education; particularly those implemented within secondary schools that targeted youngsters between 16 through 18 years old, although in the long run, these benefits were not translated into a higher level of achievement in post-compulsory education (Alegre et al., 2015).

Horcas López et al. (2015) explored how youngsters participating in second-chance schemes analysed their educational trajectories and future aspirations. They identified three typical "second-chance trajectories"; they could either end up in low-qualified and precarious jobs, in welfare-protected contexts with high dependency, or in marginal activities within highly vulnerable networks. These different outcomes were interpreted by the authors as tensions between social reproduction and resistance. Similarly, Pérez Benavent (2016) offers an insight into the complex and often discontinuous transition from compulsory education to post-compulsory vocational tracks. Youngsters often coming from the margins of the standard curriculum, that is, from adapted and separate measures, in lower secondary education have to rebuild their identity as students on shaky grounds. Following Jonker (2006) and De Graaf and Van Zenderen (2013), Pérez Benavent (2016) argues that processes of exclusion tend to be perceived by these youngsters as a series of individual decisions through which they accept structural constraints by adapting their personal narratives to them.

These perspectives and findings from previous research inform our analysis of two out-of-school programmes for youth at risk of becoming early school leavers in Spain. By focusing on the participants' experiences and views, we intend to explore their limits and possibilities as compensation measures not only to offer opportunities for training for those who have dropped out but also, more importantly, to positively affect and re-engage them into formal education.

Methods

Data collection was conducted in one of the two research areas of the RESL. eu project in Spain, in the metropolitan region of Barcelona (Vallès Occidental), in four compensatory measures developed in different institutions (two job-training centres, one adult education centre and one high school) designed for dropouts and early school leavers. This chapter focuses on two measures developed in two public out-of-school training centres (A and B) of one local council: Youth for Employment (YfE) and Training and Labour Insertion Programmes (TLIP).

In the spring of 2014, before our longitudinal qualitative fieldwork, an in-person adapted version of RESL.eu Survey A1 was administered to all the 160 early school leavers applying for one of the measures of the research area (Youth for Employment) before it was included within the global Youth Guarantee Plan scheme in 2015. The respondents' profiles were mostly working-class youth (65% males, 35% females), and 10% of them had an immigrant background. Although the results of this survey are not discussed in this chapter, they are part of the contextual background for the analysis and sampling strategy. As in the survey results, the case-study youngsters included in our qualitative approach had two profiles: most of them came from working-class backgrounds, both native and foreign-born, and lived in impoverished neighbourhoods.[4] Both groups of youngsters used Spanish as their primary language, regardless of their origin or nationality, rather than Catalan, which they learnt at school.

The data used in this chapter are drawn from in-depth, semi-structured interviews and focus group discussions (FGDs) with young participants and training staff of the two measures analysed. A total number of 23 young people participated in these interviews and FGDs (16 males and seven females). Two females and one male were Roma, and six males were first-generation immigrants (from Morocco, Bolivia, Ecuador and Colombia). In-depth, semi-structured interviews were also carried out with two supervisors and two implementers of both measures (one of each per measure, three females and one male) in the training centres where they were developed. The youngsters were interviewed twice. In the first period of fieldwork the two compensatory measures selected were in different stages of their implementation: YfE (Training Centre A) was in its final stage and the TLIP courses (Training Centre B) were in the middle of their first term.

Analysing compensatory measures in practice

Limited resources, controversial selection

The two measures analysed (YfE and TLIP) have been recently re-oriented under the umbrella of the Youth Guarantee Plan, as it is implemented in Catalonia, towards a mixed scheme with the dual objective of promoting re-engagement with the educational system, especially towards VET studies, and the improvement of employability and labour market insertion of young early school leavers.

The purpose of YfE is to provide basic vocational training, guidance and support for participants, as well as to assist them in completing an internship with local partner companies, although not all the participants are offered this possibility. YfE is a mainly work-based VET compensatory measure that, according to their official goals and objectives, pursues a double aim: 1) to provide the target group with professional competencies which can facilitate their access to the labour market, with minimal guarantees of stability, and 2) to

190   *Silvia Carrasco et al.*

engage participants in the educational system again. The second aim is adapted to the two educational situations of youngsters after lower secondary education: for those participants with the GESO certificate (ISCED 2) the programme is intended to promote their access to regular intermediate VET programmes (CFGM, equivalent to ISCED 3) and for those who finished compulsory education without any qualifications, the programme is structured in a way that can help them enrol in pending subjects and obtain the GESO certificate. The target group is basically unemployed early school leavers (16–25 years old) with a maximum education level of ISCED 2, registered in the Spanish EU Youth Guarantee Plan (PGJ). Amongst other training activities, as a compensatory measure to reduce ESL, this programme includes training with the aim of obtaining the GESO (ISCED 2) and/or preparation for access to intermediate VET programmes (ISCED 3 equivalent) via a specific entrance exam. It is important to highlight that this training is compulsory for all the participants that have not previously completed lower secondary education (ESO) by enrolling participants either in adult education centres or via an on-line public education platform that offers secondary education tracks (Open High School – *Institut Obert de Catalunya*).

The second measure is the Training and Labour Insertion Programmes (TLIP). Although officially, TLIP provides participants with the essential skills to access the labour market with better chances of getting a middle-skilled job, the main official goal of TLIP is to give the target group the opportunity of returning to the educational system, especially to continue vocational education. The TLIP are a set of different vocational training schemes apart from the official VET post-compulsory tracks. Three different categories are defined according to their management and the type of institution where they are offered: 1) school-to-work transition plans (the specific measure analysed in this chapter), organized by the Department of Education of the Catalan Government and the local councils; 2) Initial Vocational Plans, offered in public or private schools and approved training centres, and 3) Training Programmes and Professional Learning, only taught in public secondary schools. Until 2014–2015, these programmes were known as "initial professional qualification programmes" in Catalonia and formally granted direct access to intermediate post-compulsory VET tracks (ISCED 3). Since then, access to VET tracks is only possible through an exam, but these programmes still offer students the possibility of obtaining the GESO certificate (ISCED 2) by taking an extra core curricular module. The target group for this programme is unemployed youngsters between age 16 and 21 who have left or finished compulsory secondary education without the GESO certificate and who are not enrolled in any other educational or training programme. Since 2015, all participants must be registered in the Youth Guarantee Programme.

Access to the programmes has been increasingly restrictive and, although many young people are still unaware of their existence, the number of applicants exceeds available places. Only one youngster had applied after being informed "through a letter that arrived at our house, I think it was from the town council, calling for people from between 18 and 21", and a few other youngsters mentioned they had been informed in high school about the programmes. The guidelines for the selection process of both programmes are established by the Catalan government. Theoretically, these programmes target youngsters in vulnerable socioeconomic and educational situations, but these are not enough to be selected because the ultimate decision is based on the motivation shown by the applicant to participate in the programme as perceived by the staff. When asked about the selection processes, the youngsters tended to attribute their selection to luck.

Although this was not an official requirement, the language proficiency of the applicants in Catalan and in Spanish ended up operating as an informal, though widespread selection criterion that remained hidden for outsiders. Obviously, this language requirement can be detrimental for many young people with immigrant backgrounds. One staff member interviewed argued that, "Young people who may have arrived recently [through family reunification] have little chances of being selected for the programme, because they usually come in with lower levels of education ... although now this is not happening so often, most of the youth with immigrant backgrounds have been here for longer ... but ... yes, it's true we place a high value on knowing the language; there are kids whom we could barely teach."

Youth for Employment: a short-term, work-based programme officially aimed at tackling early school leaving

According to the opinions of both the youngsters and the teaching staff, all the reasons for participating in this measure were related to the difficulties that young people face in accessing the labour market rather than explicitly referring to re-engaging early school leavers in formal education. There was a lack of correspondence between the official goals of YfE and the actual goals youngsters expected to achieve from participating in it. Many of them desperately expected "to be able to add at least one line in the CV showing some kind of job experience, even if only corresponding to the in-job practices" of the programme, as one youngster interviewed literally said. Accordingly, the staff does not see YfE as primarily for tackling ESL but for improving the possibilities of labour market insertion for the participants. Therefore, the participants are identified only as young job seekers with low employability, not as early school leavers. Compulsory enrolment in ESO through Adult Education Centres or the Open High School was seen just as a prerequisite for those participants who did not have the GESO certificate, and not as a pathway to return to the educational system. Returning to the educational system – beyond the compulsory requirement to enrol for youngsters with no GESO certificate – is only promoted amongst those participants who specifically express this aim on an individual basis and if the youngster has a real motivation to do so in the opinion of the staff. Even for those participants who have the GESO certificate, there is no real guidance to re-engage in ISCED 3 tracks. One of the youngsters interviewed put it this way: "those who wanted to work, looked for work experience for themselves with a contract afterwards, so that they'd be hired, but they let us choose if we wanted to keep studying or not".

Youth for Employment is expected to work as a measure adapted to the social and educational realities of the area and to respond to a series of lacking skills and problems young early school leavers face on their way to accessing the labour market and the educational system. The existing training schemes are supposed to be designed in relation to the specific dynamics and labour demand of the local labour market, but participants very often felt that the training they got was far from what the labour market is demanding of them and found the training received in YfE to be very basic. In this sense, the training schemes and work sectors offered seemed to be conditioned by the existing facilities for carrying them out, rather than related to the real demands of the local market. In addition to this, YfE training schemes did not usually provide any official recognition or qualification with ISCED equivalencies. Participants only receive a certificate of attendance.

Finally, two essential shortcomings of this work-based programme are identified: the lack of a certificating system valid for modules or hours on any VET track, and the inexistence of a global assessment of the programme's outcomes, after running for five years. The staff carries out the monitoring of the youngsters' trajectories through phone interviews six months after the programme has ended, from which they hold positive views about its effectiveness: "It is clear that the programme works and indicators have proven it; for example, last year we were able to reach 50% employment.... Yes, there is a return both in jobs and in education". However, the outputs in terms of labour insertion identified may not directly stem from the programme, but from the participants' own job-searching strategies. In fact, although both in individual interviews and FGDs all participants expressed high levels of satisfaction with the staff, they also complained about them: "they said that 80% of the people who do this course get a job.... But if we are 20 and only two got a job ... [it is not true]". As for enrolment in ISCED 2 or ISCED 3 (depending on whether participants hold the GESO certificate on entry), it is often regarded simultaneously as a requirement for participation and as an indicator of success. However, information about those who re-engage and remain in education is unknown.

Training and Labour Insertion Programmes: a school-to-work transition plan aimed at re-engaging youth at risk of early school leaving in education

The Department of Education defines the general goals of Training and Labour Insertion Programmes (TLIP) as providing students with the necessary skills for their access to the labour market or for their continuation in education, especially in official VET. Participants initially enrol in TLIP also with the goal of getting into the labour market by the end of the programme. However, the staff argued that labour market insertion should not be the main goal of this measure, but rather to promote the students' return to the educational system. They believe the main challenge is the youngsters' complete disengagement from education and their lack of awareness of their actual situation with regard to the labour market. Students who enrol in TLIP soon after dropping out from lower secondary education usually have low self-esteem, lack motivation and are quite disoriented about plans and options. The focus on working to repair the participants' self-esteem was recurrent in the interviews with staff. On several occasions, the staff also mentioned problematic relationships between parents and youngsters, especially amongst immigrant families who had a shared feeling of failure, which they clearly intended to counteract as professionals: "We remove this label [school failure] from the very first moment ... because our kids come here really stigmatised, they have all this on their backs". Enrolling in TLIP was stigmatising in itself. According to the youngsters, the widespread belief in their peer groups was that these training schemes were good for nothing in the labour world compared with VET tracks and were associated with lazy students, unconcerned about their education.

They argued that participants are encouraged to analyse their situation with realism, to acknowledge their responsibilities and their potential, and to raise their awareness of the need to make a shift in attitude and *start acting like adults*. As one staff member put it: "We don't try to guide them to what they say they want to do but they make a mental shift; it's a turning point in their life". Consequently, they believe the key for TLIP to succeed lies in their task as educators, establishing with the youngsters an adult-like relationship based on trust and respect to promote their individual autonomy and generate a change in attitude and commitment. In their opinion, this change may have long-term consequences with regard to the youngsters' inclusion both in the labour market and in education. A staff member declared: "there is a moment in the group when you say, 'Now they've made the shift'. You get into the classroom and you realise ... maybe they cannot access the labour market right now, or maybe this or that student does not make it to get selected for formal VET programmes now, but he or she has already started to mature; you realise they now see things in a different way".

Even shortly after enrolling in the measure, all the youngsters interviewed highlighted that the most positive aspect of their participation in the measure is that they were treated with respect and consideration by both the staff and the institution and felt constantly encouraged by the staff to rely on their own potential. One of the youngsters expressed this feeling in precise words: "They treat us like adults here", a recurrent reflection of the youngsters in comparison to their experiences in high school. As for the consequences, another youngster put it this way: "What I learnt in ESO [lower secondary] in two years, I have learnt in TLIP in a month". In parallel, however, it was also common for them to explain their past negative experiences in self-blaming terms: "Well, it was partly my fault, I know now that it was my fault, it's clear to me now that it was my fault. ... I liked the street, I didn't like doing homework and that stuff. ... I never laid my hand on it", said another participant.

In short, both staff and participants have an overall positive assessment about the programme. Staff assessed the effectiveness of the measure based on the shift of perception of the youngsters about the usefulness and importance of their own learning processes, on their increased awareness of their own social vulnerability and their improved self-esteem and progressive adoption of responsibilities. After completing their training and in the second interviews, participants also had a positive view about the usefulness of the training they received and its capacity to generate their aspirations both in relation to the job market and further training or education. In contrast with most of the participants' initial expectations, they became motivated to return to education through VET studies and considered taking the entry exam. One youngster curtly summed it up: "Of course, I want to keep studying. I want training to be able to work and have a normal life".

Three factors for success in the view of the participants and staff can be clearly identified: 1) relevance of the processes of mentoring, guiding and individual support received during the training process; 2) increased empowerment and self-esteem resulting from the perception of being regarded as reliable and competent, and 3) teaching methodologies and pedagogical models that adapt instrumental contents to actual training needs in specific areas and build on different learning skills or previous knowledge. However, the TLIP programme lacks specific assessment indicators related to re-engagement and, as in the case of the YfE programme for young adults analysed previously, it provides no further support afterwards for this younger group. Despite this, programme staff members continued to offer informal support: "We work with them intensively for a year in a way that makes us become reference persons for the kids; there are young people who were with us years ago and they still come to visit today. They come and say, 'OK, I have a job offer; could you help me with the CV'. It also matters that we are still here; it gives them a sense of stability, too. They know they can come here anytime".

The limits of compensatory measures for transforming risk into opportunity

Our analysis reveals three significant findings. Firstly, the necessary perspective shift that brought ESL into the focus of out-of-school compensatory measures did not call for a thorough programme reform, but rather resulted in the reshaping of old programmes with additional "second-chance" goals, which has had important limitations. We found that recycling measures has had mixed effects on both teaching staff and beneficiaries. Secondly, while the scrutinised measures may not deliver innovative curriculum and pedagogical methods, broad, unspecific and unexpected success is perceived by both teachers and students, identified in both groups of youngsters' recurrent narratives of a change of attitude — namely, a *switch of gears* — towards the role of education in one's own life. Awareness about the wider opportunity structure accessible through education is essential to the empowerment process, which brings about new hopes. Nevertheless, our third finding reveals that students' reinterpretation of their former educational trajectory is often built on individual self-blaming, without recognising systemic and institutional forces that pushed them towards a progressive exclusion from the ordinary school system.

Despite its laudable aims, most school-to-work programmes, by focusing on generic skills, basic training and occupational socialisation, may serve to promote a precarious form of employability and may even reinforce the vulnerability of youngsters (Bynner & Parsons, 2002; Horcas López et al., 2015; Simmons, 2009; Thompson, Russell, & Simmons, 2014). Moreover, despite their success in increasing the youngsters' self-esteem, awareness and empowerment, these compensatory measures are failing to channel their positive attitudes towards re-engaging in education. There seem to be no further bridges to making re-engagement possible for these youngsters since systemic barriers persist and these measures can only work as limited alternative pathways or temporary lifebelts for them. For young early school leavers in YfE, the changes come too late in the current conditions of difficulty reconciling ISCED 3 options with the precarious jobs they can get; for the youngsters who drop out and enrol in TLIP, the ways back into formal education to complete ISCED 2 or access ISCED 3 are too narrow. In the long run, these interrupted education processes may have consequences similar to the *scarring effect* of early problems on later life chances associated with youth unemployment (Fondeville & Ward, 2014). These processes can be seen as part of the generational effects of current trends in contemporary education policies and labour market conditions in a global perspective, such as those described in France (Chauvel, 2010) and Australia (Cuervo & Wyn, 2016).

Educational engagement and disengagement have become central notions of an all-encompassing explanation of the risk of ESL, often ignoring its relation to social class and the experiences of students in different types of schools. Although youngsters' itineraries back to training or education can vary, it is much harder for those who come from disadvantaged backgrounds (García et al., 2013), since such youth are largely overrepresented in ESL figures. From this perspective, the process of re-engagement should not be understood as a recovery of normative motivation and identification with schooling and its routines, but rather as new possibilities for youngsters to develop aspirations and to work on plans for their lives. That is largely the responsibility of the educational system and its institutions, from which they were initially pushed out.

Notes

1 The average ESL rate in Spain was 19.4% in 2016 (23.2% among males and 15.4% among females) (EUROSTAT), and the unemployment rate for young people under the age of 24 was 41.5% in February 2017 (Encuesta de Población Activa).
2 At the other end, the issue of an "overqualified" young generation (more than 40% of young people are now graduates of higher education) has been discussed in terms of the distinction between vulnerable and not-vulnerable NEET youth to include highly educated youth with no working experience and low job opportunities as the target of

196 *Silvia Carrasco et al.*

specific measures within the Youth Guarantee Plan (Alegre, Casado, Sanz, & Todeschini, 2015; Serracant, 2012).

3 All regions in Spain have competencies to design and implement programmes to tackle youth unemployment and ESL by adapting general EU and nation-level guidelines and policies.

4 The impact of unemployment and significant reductions in social protections has been severe in most of the new neighbourhoods which grew in the 1960s out of intensive immigration flows from other Spanish regions as a result of the high demand for labour in the thriving industrial sectors of the time, mostly textiles and metal, in Catalonia.

References

Alegre, M. À., Casado, D., Sanz, J., & Todeschini, F. A. (2015). The impact of training-intensive labour market policies on labour and educational prospects of NEETS: Evidence from Catalonia (Spain). *Educational Research, 57*(2),151–167. doi:10.1080/00131881.2015.1030852

Blasco, J., & Casado, D. (Eds.) (2013). *Avaluació dels Programes de Qualificació Professional Inicial (PQPI)*. Barcelona: Ivàlua. Retrieved from www.ivalua.cat/generic/static.aspx?id=2544

Bloom, D., Levy Thompson, S., & Ivry, R. J. (2010, March). Building a learning agenda around disconnected youth. *MDRC*. Retrieved from www.mdrc.org/sites/default/files/building_learning_agenda_around_disconnected_fr.pdf

Bynner, J., & Parsons, S. (2002). Social exclusion and the transition from school to work: The case of young people Not in Education, Employment, or Training (NEET). *Journal of Vocational Behavior, 60*(2), 289–309. doi:10.1006/jvbe.2001.1868

Card, D., Jochen, K., & Weber, A. (2010, November). Active labour market policy: A meta-analysis. *Economic Journal, Royal Economic Society, 120*(548), 452–477. doi:10.3386/w16173

Carrasco, S., & Narciso, L. (2013). *ESL in Spain: Towards a policy analysis: RESL.eu country report*. Antwerp: RESL.eu Consortium.

Chauvel, L. (2010). The long-term destabilization of youth, scarring effects, and the future of the welfare regime in post-trente glorieuses France. *French Politics, Culture & Society, 28*(3), 74–96. doi:10.3167/fpcs.2010.280305

Clasen, J., Clegg, D., & Goerne, A. (2016). Comparative social policy analysis and active labour market policy: Putting quality before quantity. *Journal of Social Policy, 45*(1), 21–38. doi:10.1017/S0047279415000434

Cuervo, H., & Wyn, J. (2016). An unspoken crisis: The 'scarring effects' of the complex Nexus between education and work on two generations of young Australians. *International Journal of Lifelong Education, 35*(2), 122–135, doi:10.1080/02601370.2016.1164467

Cunningham, W., Sanchez-Puerta, M. L., & Wuermli, A. (2010). Active labour market pro-grams for youth: A framework to guide youth employment interventions. *World Bank Employment Policy Primer, 16*, 1–16. World Bank. Retrieved from https://openknowledge.worldbank.org/handle/10986/11690

De Graaf, W., & Van Zenderen, K. (2013). School-work transition: The interplay between institutional and individual processes. *Journal of Education and Work, 26*(2), 121–142. doi:10.1080/13639080.2011.638622

Fondeville, N., & Ward, T. (2014, October). *Scarring effects of the crisis: Research note 6/2014*. European Commission: Directorate-General for Employment, Social Affairs and Inclu-sion. Retrieved from http://ec.europa.eu/social/BlobServlet?docId=13626&langId=en

García, M. (2016). L'acompanyament a les transicions educatives com a política contra L'abandonament escolar prematur i millora de l'èxit. *Revista Catalana de Pedagogia, 10*, 33–45. Retrieved from http://ddd.uab.cat/record/167667

No bridges to re-engagement? 197

García, M., Casal, J., Merino, R., & Sánchez-Gelabert, A. (2013). Itinerarios de abandono escolar y transiciones tras la Enseñanza Secundaria Obligatoria. *Revista de educación, 361*, 65–94. doi:10.4438/1988–1592X-RE-2011-361-135

González-Menéndez, M. C., Mato, F. J., Gutiérrez, R., Guillén, A. M., Cueto, B., & Tejero, A. (2015). *Policy performance and evaluation: Spain. strategic transitions for youth labour in Europe.* STYLE Working Papers, WP3.3/ES. CROME, University of Brighton, Brighton. Retrieved from www.style-research.eu/publications/working-papers

Hadjivassiliou, K. P., Eichhorst, W., Tassinari, A., & Wozny, F. (2016). *Transition regimes in the EU assessing the performance of school-to-work transition regimes in the EU.* IZA Discussion Paper (10301). Bonn: IZA, Institute for the Study of Labor. Retrieved from http://ftp.iza.org/dp10301.pdf

Horcas López, V., Bernad i Garcia, J. C., & Martínez Morales, I. (2015). ¿Sueña la juventud vulnerable con trabajos precarios? La toma de decisiones en los itinerarios de (in/ex) clusión educativa. Profesorado. *Revista de currículum y formación del profesorado, 19*(3), 211–225. Retrieved from https://recyt.fecyt.es/index.php/profesorado/article/view/43644

Hutchinson, J., & Kettlewell, K. (2015). Education to employment: Complicated transitions in a changing world. *Educational Research, 57*(2), 113–120. doi:10.1080/00131881.2015.1030848

Jonker, E. F. (2006). School hurts: Refrains of hurt and hopelessness in stories about dropping out at a vocational school for care work. *Journal of Education and Work, 19*(2), 121–140. doi:10.1080/13639080600667988

Lindemann Nelson, H. (2001). *Damaged identities, narrative repair.* Ithaca, NY: Cornell University Press.

Martin, J. P., & Grubb, D. (2001). *What works and for whom: A review of OECD countries' experiences with active labour market policies.* Working Paper 2001:14. Uppsala: IFAU – Institute for Evaluation of Labour Market and Education Policy. Retrieved from www.ifau.se/globalassets/pdf/se/2001/wp01-14.pdf

Mattero, M. (2010). *Second chance education for out-of-school youth: A conceptual framework and review of programs.* Washington, DC: The World Bank.

Nelson, M. (2013). Making markets with active labour market policies: The influence of political parties, welfare state regimes and economic change on different types of policies. *European Political Science Review, 5*(2), 255–277. doi:10.1017/S1755773912000148

Olmos, P., & Mas, O. (2014). Jóvenes, fracaso escolar y programas de segunda oportunidad/ Youth: Academic failure and second chance training programmes'. *REOP, Revista Española de Orientación y Psicopedagogía, 24*(1), 78. doi:10.5944/reop.vol.24.num.1.2013.11272

Pérez Benavent, M. J. (2016). De liarla a rayarse: metáfora y coherencia en los relatos de cinco jóvenes que retornan a un CFGM. *Revista de Educacion, 373*, 33–56. doi:10.4438/1988-592X-RE-2016-373-320

Polidano, C., Tabasso, D., & Tseng, Y. (2012). *A second chance at education for early school leavers.* IZA Discussion Paper (6769). Bonn: IZA, Institute for the Study of Labor. Retrieved from http://ftp.iza.org/dp6769.pdf

Rambla, X., Tarabini, A., & Curran, M. (2013). *Policies to fight early school leaving in Catalonia and Spain: A realist analysis.* Congreso: Building Local Networking in Education? Decision-makers Discourses on School Achievement and Drop-out. ECER 2013 Porto.

Serracant, P. (2012). *"Generació Ni-Ni", estigmatització i exclusió social. Gènesi i evolució d'un concepte problemàtic i proposta d'un nou indicador. Col.lecció Aportacions, 48.* Barcelona. Retrieved from www.gencat.cat/joventut/aportacions/

Servei Comarcal de Joventut. (2015). *Treballar Amb Joves Inactius, Programes de Segona Oportunitat. Mataró: Consell Comarcal del Maresme.* Retrieved from www.ccmaresme.cat/ARXIUS/2015/Joventut/Treballar_amb_joves_inactius__programes_de_segona_oportunitat.pdf

Simmons, R. (2009). Entry to employment: Discourses of inclusion and employability in work-based learning for young people. *Journal of Education and Work, 22*(2), 137–151. doi:10.1080/13639080902854060

Simmons, R., & Thompson, R. (2011). Education and training for young people at risk of becoming NEET: Findings from an ethnographic study of work-based learning programmes. *Educational Studies, 37*(4), 447–450. doi:10.1080/03055698.2010.539783

Thompson, R., Russell, L., & Simmons, R. (2014). Space, place and social exclusion: An ethnographic study of young people outside education and employment. *Journal of Youth Studies, 17*(1), 63–78. doi:10.1080/13676261.2013.793793

Van Praag, L., Van Caudenberg, R., Nouwen, W., Clycq, N., & Timmerman, C. (2017). How to support and engage students in alternative forms of education and training? A qualitative study of school staff members in Flanders. *Journal of Education and Work, 30*(6), 599–611. doi:10.1080/13639080.2017.1319567

13 Alternative learning arenas in Portugal

Hope for young adults?

Eunice Macedo, Sofia A. Santos and Alexandra Oliveira Doroftei

This chapter focuses on the pathways and subjectivities of young people who left mainstream education at some point in their lives but found hope for their futures by reengaging in education. To analyse what makes young adults disengage and reengage in education, we look into the mechanisms and processes influencing their decisions both to leave mainstream school and to enrol in other educational institutions in light of the concept of *educational citizenship* (Macedo & Araújo, 2014). To describe the educational institutions outside mainstream education, we use *alternative learning arenas* (ALAs) (Van Praag et al., 2017) and not *alternative schools* (McGregor & Mills, 2012; McGregor, Mills, te Riele, & Hayes, 2014; Mills & McGregor, 2014; Wilson, Stemp, & McGinty, 2011) as we wish to emphasise the de-schooling of education (i.e. more practical) that seems to make it more attractive to some young adults.

In Portugal ALAs provide young people with professional qualifications at the intermediate level. Any student can subscribe as long as he or she has the required entrance qualifications. However, frequently, ALAs shelter students who faced school disengagement and early school leaving (ESL) and search for a second opportunity. ESL is a process influenced by micro (e.g. individual), meso (e.g. social institutions such as school, family, peers) and macro factors (e.g. educational system, labour market, broader society) (Clycq, Nouwen, & Timmerman, 2013). These are push factors that relate to the school environment and pull factors that include the causes outside of education that are not always inherent to the student. The latter relate to "financial worries, out-of-school employment, family needs, or even family changes, such as marriage or childbirth [and/or] illnesses" (Doll, Eslami, & Walters, 2013, p. 2). Whereas push factors are mostly situated at the meso level, such as the school context, this is not always the case. For example, student–teacher or student–student relations constitute push factors at the micro level. Pull factors may be at the micro or meso level. Macro-level factors may influence either one of the other levels as they reflect on the availability of resources that each previous level has to give education the statute of right (Bardsley, 2007).

The lack of meaningful curricula is amongst the factors for school disengagement for some young people. As McGregor et al. (2014) point out, children and young people are supposed to accept the learning that is offered by the school, but as they get older, they become more able to proclaim their opinions about learning, whether about knowledge itself or about how to learn and receive that knowledge and all other matters affecting their lives. Thus, some young people may leave mainstream education in search of a more *meaningful education* (McGregor et al., 2014). We use this concept as McGregor et al. (2014, p. 611) did "to describe programmes that resonate with the needs and aspirations of young people who find themselves on the outside of mainstream schooling pathways". ALAs offer vocational education and training (VET), which the young adults in our study consider meaningful education, as they point out the relevance of practical knowledge and preparation for the labour market. It is worth noticing that, in Portugal, VET was traditionally offered outside mainstream education (in ALAs) but, in trying to respond to the more direct needs of their diverse populations, mainstream schools enlarged their educational offerings by means of the introduction of VET courses in parallel with scientific humanistic courses.

The Portuguese educational system has been restructured with advances and setbacks, with periods of greater focus on social inclusion and others on making students more competitive in the labour market (Araújo, Magalhães, Rocha, & Macedo, 2014). Nevertheless, the diversification of educational offerings has been introduced and maintained as an educational policy to embrace all students. This diversification, mostly in the VET track, tries to encompass both the rationale of social inclusion and of the needs of the labour market as it aims to reduce the rates of school dropout (before the conclusion of grade 6 or 9) and early leaving from education and training (before the attainment of grade 12), and to qualify workers to the labour market.

With these concerns, we highlight the tensions between young adults' positioning in structures of power and their claim for citizenship. This may include the assertion of their voices by reengaging in education through ALAs. The work builds on the *democratic pedagogical rights* of *enhancement, inclusion* and *participation* (Bernstein, 1996) to be provided by institutions. *Enhancement* is the right to achieve "critical understanding and a sense of possibility" (ibid: 6); the second is the right to be included "socially, intellectually, culturally or personally as an individual and a member of a group"; and the third is "the right to participate in the procedures involved in construction, maintenance and transformation of order" (ibid: 7).

Two main concepts emerge from this theorisation: "citizenship construction authors" and "educational citizenship", which direct the focus to the subjects of pedagogy – the young adults. The assertion that young adults are *citizenship construction authors* means that they are citizens in the current period of their lives and not just citizens to become. Hence, in the use of – or claim for – their rights, they are able to reflect upon, report and act on their lives and educational pathways (Macedo, 2018). In this vein, *educational citizenship* (Macedo & Araújo, 2014) refers to young adults' use of the right to be heard and recognized (i.e. accepted and valued in their culture[s], interests, and life stories and conditions), and to reflect and act on their lives in and beyond school. That is, *educational citizenship* encompasses the development of a sense of belonging *to* and *within* the school culture, the broad participation as partners in the construction of school life as well as the achievement, and even surpassing, of the potential of each young person.

The concept of *educational citizenship* is a useful tool to understand disengagement and re-engagement in education through ALAs and was expressed in our former study in young adult voices as *educational citizenship of rights* and *educational citizenship of knowledge* (Macedo & Araújo, 2014). The first stream focuses on the rights mentioned above, which are to be exercised in the life contexts where young adult citizenship is constructed, including school, through the enactment of mechanisms of participation.

The second stream centres the possibility to access and have knowledge as well as to take part in its definition and construction by means of participatory methods that enable students to engage in decision making about what to learn, how to learn, and how to share learning with others. In our former study (Macedo, 2018), most of the time these two streams did not meet in students' claims. This right focuses on *participation* (Bernstein, 1996) on knowledge. *Educational citizenship* (Macedo & Araújo, 2014) can be achieved through *meaningful education* (McGregor et al., 2014) that ensures young adults' right to participate in the construction of the education and knowledge for their personal and professional lives. With this theoretical lens we analyse *if* and *how* mainstream education and the ALAs at focus provide space for *educational citizenship* on the basis of young adults' views and trajectories.

Methodological notes

As *citizenship construction authors*, young adults have the potential to be active members of the construction of their educational pathways and lives enacting their educational citizenship; however, the locations of power within which they inhabit do not always provide the conditions for this potential to be achieved (Macedo, 2018). The use of a qualitative method is the most adequate because it values and provides space for the emersion of their voices. Data were collected at four ALAs through four focus group discussions (FGD), one per institution, and 16 semi-structured interviews with eight young men and women, two from each FGD. The interviews took place one year apart and had a follow-up intention. Data were transcribed in Portuguese and translated into English; content analysis was performed using NVivo11®. Amongst other items, the consultation of young adults covered their previous educational trajectories in schools and their decisions to enrol in an ALA as well as their views on these measures. For this chapter, the reasons to leave and reengage in education were re-analysed through the lenses of *educational citizenship of rights* and *educational citizenship of knowledge* (Macedo, 2018).

Research setting

Three of the four ALAs were located in urban centres and one in a rural but highly industrialised setting. Table 13.1 summarises the features and educational offerings of the four ALAs in the study.

202 *Eunice Macedo et al.*

Table 13.1 The research settings: features and educational offerings

ALAs	Type of institution	Educational offering[1]	Certification	Young adult ages	Governance/ financing of educational offerings
A	Cooperative vocational school	Vocational courses[2] (VC)	Double level 4 NQF/ EQF[4] and ISCED 3	15–25	Ministries of Education and Labour; European funds
B	Training centre	Apprenticeship courses[3] (AC)	Double level 4 NQF/ EQF and ISCED 3	15–25	Institute for Employment and Vocational Training (IEFP); European funds
C	Second-chance school	Integrated education and training program (PIEF) and adult education and training courses (EFA)	Level 2 NQF and ISCED 2	15–28	Ministry of Education; local sponsors; European funds
D	Training centre	Apprenticeship courses	Level 4 NQF/ EQF and ISCED 3	15–25	IEFP; industrial association; European funds

Notes:

1 All the listed educational offerings may be considered school-based VET programs.

2 Introduced in Portugal in 1989 together with vocational schools to qualify "the human resources of the country" (Decree-Law 26/89, 21 January).

3 Introduced in Portugal in 1984 to tackle school dropout and youth unemployment (Law 102/84, 29 March).

4 NQF, National Qualifications Framework; EQF, European Qualifications Framework.

ALA.A invests in education and training based on cooperative principles. The trainees who participated in the RESL.eu project attended vocational courses (VC) directed at young people who concluded the ninth grade (15-year-olds). VC are integrated in the educational system and regulated by the Ministry of Education. Trainees get meal and transport subsidies as well as a scholarship during their traineeship. The courses last three school years, and the curricular plan includes sociocultural, scientific and technical components. The technical component includes a traineeship of about 420 hours, distributed throughout the three years of the course.

ALA.B offers apprenticeship courses (AC), considered at European level as "apprenticeship-type schemes" (European Comission & IKEI, 2012). The main characteristic of these courses is the alternation between on-the-job (+/– 40%) and off-the-job training (+/– 60%). The AC model was imported from the German Dual VET System, but there are vast differences such as the type of contract and the stipend. The courses are integrated in the labour market and not in the educational system. The curricula are based on pedagogical standards of the National Qualification Catalogue, regulated by the National Agency for

Qualification and Vocational Education (ANQEP). The courses are structured in four components: sociocultural, scientific, technological and work context training. The on-the-job training is about 1,500 hours.

ALA.C[1] is a second-chance school integrated in the European network of second-chance schools. This organisation provides a fully integrated vocational model to young adults from vulnerable contexts and who are at risk of social exclusion. Art education is a major part of the training programme, which is organised in flexible modules. Its distinctive feature is the support provided in various dimensions of young adult lives, and its expressed aims (per Ordinance 230/2008, March 7) are to reduce qualification deficits and improve trainees' employability and social and professional inclusion.

ALA.D is situated in a region with a tradition of wood and furniture industry, characterised by economic problems and low levels of educational achievement. As with ALA.B, it offers apprenticeship courses, in this case to supply the needs of the wood and furniture industry. There is a high rate of employment in the region for those who complete these courses.

The study participants at the four ALAs were ages 18 to 27 at the time of the FGD and first interview and had dropped out of school before concluding grades 6, 9 or 12. Most of them were born in Portugal, and four were from San Tomé and Mozambique, which are part of the African Countries of Portuguese Official Language, or PALOP.

All seemed to be challenged by the lack of financial resources, and they reported paths of truancy, school disengagement and grade retention. After leaving mainstream schools, some enrolled directly in ALAs while others tried to get into the labour market. Two stayed at home without studying for two or three years. Three had children. Table 13.2 describes the sociodemographic features of the participants.

As discussed previously, two participants from each FGD were invited to be interviewed individually. Their detailed characteristics are shown in Appendix 13.1 at the end of this chapter.

Table 13.2 Sociodemographic features of participants in focus group discussions

ALA	Sex		Age	Background	Educational situation	Number of students with work experience
	F	M				
A	4	4	19–21	4 PALOP, 4 PT	Vocational courses (grade 12)	1
B	5	5	18–23	10 PT	Apprenticeship courses (grades 10 and 12)	6
C	4	4	18–27	8 PT	Adult education and training courses (grade 9)	6
D	2	6	18–20	8 PT	Apprenticeship courses (grades 10 and 12)	2

204 *Eunice Macedo et al.*

Consultation with these young adults was the main research tool in line with the theoretical recognition of their voices as *citizenship construction authors* (Macedo, 2018). Following is an analysis regarding *if* and *how* the different educational institutions provide space for educational citizenship on the basis of young adult narratives about their past and present educational experiences.

Educational citizenship of rights and knowledge

This section discusses young adults' views on the specificities of different educational offers within the two streams of *educational citizenship – educational citizenship of rights* and *educational citizenship of knowledge* (Macedo & Araújo, 2014). If in the former study these streams did not combine, young adults' inputs in the current study suggest new possibilities of combinations between these political and cultural rights. The reformulation of the initial theory brings to the fore diverse aspects of the enactment of these rights: 1) sense of belonging and recognition; 2) partnership in the co-construction, co-maintenance and co-transformation of school life; and 3) achievement of the potential of each person. The discussion that follows draws on these aspects.

The matching of belonging and recognition

Reengaging in education in contexts where young adults are provided space for the use of the rights of inclusion and belonging constitutes an opportunity to support the educational paths. The young adults pointed out the lack of belonging and recognition as one of the reasons why they left mainstream education, where they felt somewhat anonymous, which they claimed negatively affected their grades. They also claimed that there is need to value their work on the labour market, where they envisage a relationship of interdependence between those workers with higher studies and those with vocational training. Moreover, the lack of recognition of VET may lead to the mitigation of *educational citizenship of knowledge* through a hierarchy amongst courses – the knowledge they provide – and the future division between highly recognised professions such as doctors and lawyers and less-valued occupations such as electricians and carpenters.

DAVID: A person that goes to university is the doctor.
MARIA: Maybe you tell a guy to connect a plug or sand a table; they don't know.
ANTÓNIO: Even so, you know that they will always be the intelligent, and we will be the dumb. That's stupid; why is a person who has a degree more intelligent than me?
DAVID: We'll conclude the course as technicians. It all can start by the architects. Architects leave something to be solved, for whom? For engineers. Engineers can't solve it, who's going to solve it? The technicians.
(ALA.C/FGD)

Alternative learning arenas in Portugal 205

I guess that everyone thinks that those who attend the VET course are dumb; they're unable to do anything in life and are there just because of that.

(Francisca/ALA.B/FGD)

There's a lot of stigma. Because people think that the grades are easily obtained in these courses. Okay, everything is much easier, that can't be denied. But it's easier if we just want to pass. But if we want to get 18 and 20, we've got to work.

(Alice/ALA.C/Interview)

The lack of recognition may occur outside ALAs' walls, where young adults face prejudice associated with the idea that VET courses are easy and less demanding. This seems to invalidate the construction of their *educational citizenship of rights*, in terms of the right of recognition and of respect for individual differences, and in terms of the diverse educational pathways that young adults may want to – or be pushed to – pursue.

As expressed by the interviewees, despite the expectancies for low-profile jobs in the labour market and of the stigma associated with ALAs, within these programs they felt closer to adults, including teachers, staff and the board of directors. Most teachers care about student educational performance, their personal problems and their needs. Teachers' care and concern within smaller educational institutions support young adults' sense of belonging, and these institutions become good vehicles for communication (About this matter, see also in this book, Chapter 12 by Carrasco et al.) This is especially important when stricter and unsupportive teachers in mainstream schools were identified as the main reason for school disengagement.

In apprenticeship courses, teachers fight for us more. They help a lot to improve the grade; they're always concerned about us, if we miss or don't miss.

(Camila/ALA.B/Interview)

People . . . are always with us, always available; from employees to teachers, everybody. . . . The school principal, if we want to talk to him, he's always available.

(Isabel/ALA.C/Interview)

When translated in encouragement and belief in young adults' abilities, recognition emerges as an important dimension for success.

We feel more motivated if people encourage us, if they believe that we have abilities and that we'll succeed. But if people are always telling us: "You won't make it", "Do as you please!", we lose heart.

(Alice/ALA.D/Interview)

The second-chance school (ALA.C) in particular was seen as a warmer environment – a "family" in which a holistic view on education is put into action. Hierarchies seemed to be blurred, and teachers and employees engaged in the same way with trainees so that they felt more affection, engagement and concern for their lives beyond their learning context. In this ALA, young adults felt visible, indispensable and valued, including in their styles (e.g. clothes, piercings, tattoos). This also highlights the pressure mainstream education puts on individuals who do not fit the traditional school model in various ways. This sense of belonging and recognition nurtures young adults' *educational citizenship of rights*.

> If we don't come they call us; they're more concerned about us. . . . Here it's like a family. We're always very comfortable. People interact much with each other.
>
> (Isabel/ALA.C/Interview)

According to most participants, when compared with the mainstream school where they did not fit in, the ALAs were a more adequate setting for developing a sense of belonging and recognition, mainly because of a closer relation with staff. This may be seen as a key circumstance for reengaging in education.

Partnership in the co-construction, co-maintenance and co-transformation of ALAs

Young adults' sense of partnership as co-constructors of their learning lives varied amongst the trainees at the different ALAs under focus. Followed by the cooperative school, the second-chance school was closer to the idea of partnership backed by *educational citizenship of rights*. This was expressed in inclusive teaching practices where workshops, lectures, worksheets and portfolios – developed as in most schools – were reconfigured to allow young adults' participation in the co-construction, maintenance and transformation of the syllabus. Special room was given to the visual arts and drama, which enabled participants to develop personal and social skills beyond the technical knowledge that was provided. Moreover, trainees' freedom to be or not in class and work at their own pace were seen as the most attractive features. They said they would appreciate if "all schools were like that".

> It's like the school's name. It's a second chance. . . . They let us follow more according to our will. . . . They give trainees more freedom. This school also helps us with our problems.
>
> (Artur/ALA.C/Interview)

> In a classroom we're sitting . . . facing the blackboard, the teacher explains. Here that doesn't happen. You choose where you want to sit; if you don't want to do something, you don't have to. I think we learn better. I always do performances, theatre plays, sing. I help with anything that's needed.
>
> (Isabel/ALA.C/Interview)

Alternative learning arenas in Portugal   207

Weekly assemblies in ALA.C enable young adults to debate their learning experiences, present proposals on everyday organisational matters, discuss the curriculum and identify personal and common needs. Their proposals often are welcomed by the school board, a circumstance that provides space for the enactment of their *educational citizenship of rights*.

JOANA: We discuss with each other.
CARLA: About school.
MARIA: A chaos.
JOANA: Proposals.
MARIA: About the bar, the radio . . .
CARLA: Field trips.
MARIA: I won't complain about that.
JOANA: What we can improve in school, materials.

(ALA.C/FGD)

In turn, in other ALAs, trainees seemed to deal with quite diverse experiences. In ALA.A, they complained about the lack of psychological support and encouragement to participate in school life, a situation exacerbated by a lack of consultation with trainees which pushes them away from decision making and reduces their citizenship in ALA. Trainees identified a lack of opportunity to express their own voices as a reason for estrangement and lack of engagement.

ANDREIA: The school should have a form, so we could say what we think should be applied in this school. What are the rules, what should be improved. . . . What are its negative and positive aspects. . . . We have talked, complained, we have done everything.
ROGÉRIO: But it is ignored.
JORGE: We do not participate in anything in this school. We are here only to stomach the schedule.
INÊS: They do not ask, "What is going on? What should we improve?" They do not speak. . . . Never, really [we are asked].
GUILHERME: Yes, we have [expressed interest in sharing our ideas] on several occasions.
SUSANA: The board of directors does not approve any project that we implement in the school. Because for them everything we do is wrong. We have tried to implement the student union and they did not want that.

(ALA.A/FGD)

Young adults assessed ALA.D positively but many felt they had no room to contribute more directly to the implementation of activities and to course design. The absence of participation was also referred to, for example, in their failed attempt to create the student union. Even if their ideas are not always considered, the young adults felt they were heard more than in mainstream education in certain circumstances:

If we say, "We like this better than that", they try to articulate things. They say, "Let's do it in terms of what they like better". Here our opinion is heard more; that's why people prefer to be here than elsewhere. With our coordinator, we had an hour a week just to . . . see if everything's okay with the disciplines, if there are any problems in the class, if we want to change anything. We may make a proposal but it may not be approved. Throughout all these years it has never been; I think it wouldn't be now.

(Alice/ALA.D/Interview)

The programs are already set. But if our class doesn't want, for example, to start that module now but only in a month's time, we anticipate next month's module and there's no problem. . . . We follow what maybe is better for our path. We schedule the tests. Teachers usually accept that.

(Filipe/ALA.D/Interview)

Participants from ALA.B did not add much to these debates and they did not express a sense of partnership in school life.

REGINA: No, nobody does [ask how to improve these courses].
FRANCISCO: They've already asked us; our class causes too much trouble.
BRUNO: To improve these courses. . . . Not that I can remember.

(ALA.B/FGD)

Regarding the definition of knowledge and its co-construction, maintenance and transformation, *educational citizenship of knowledge* seems to be lessened. The young adults criticised mainstream education as too theoretical, with a heavy burden of studying, excessive complexity and difficulty, leaving no room for self-expression and the construction of meaningful learning by each person. Despite this, some recognised the value of having access to a wider syllabus, where knowledge assumes a status in itself and shifts away from its usefulness for the labour market in the more utilitarian view of the ALAs.

In terms of knowledge I think that upper secondary school is better than the mainstream one because here [ALA] we have specific subjects and there you learn everything, from philosophy to French. There, regarding learning, one learns more, more contents of everything. Here, it's more specific to the course.

(Camila/ALA.B/Interview)

As the young adults saw it, conditions at the ALAs will improve their educational attainment. They felt more comfortable and encouraged, and they found other areas of study and knowledge which they believed would provide easier access to the labour market. They found space in the ALAs to enact some aspects of their *educational citizenship* in both its streams of knowledge and rights, even if the co-construction, co-maintenance and co-transformation of their education was mitigated.

Achievement of the potential of each person: meaningful knowledge in a holistic approach to rights

This dimension highlights the possibilities young adults have in an ALA to act towards the achievement of their potential as people, learners and future workers. We emphasise the articulation between the ALAs and the labour market as an opportunity of personal fulfilment for this specific group of young adults. It is worth noticing that many of them had some sort of disappointment with mainstream education that – as they see it – did not support them as a student nor as a person. For some, an ALA was not seen as a second opportunity but as a first choice. In these cases, in contrast with the mainstream school where the pressure of the curriculum left some of them behind, the more flexible nature of alternative education seems to have provided more space for the achievement of their potential. The key attractiveness of ALAs refers to the vocational track and its subsequent preparation for the labour market. Some felt that mainstream education is successful only for those who want to proceed to higher education, but they also believed that VET does not impede them from that pursuit either:

> Apprenticeship courses really help people . . . we have a specific area; we work more for what we will do. . . . The contents are fewer but with some final exams, we can always enrol in university.
>
> (Joel/ALA.B/Interview)

Concerning the "will" or need to find a job, ALA.D has higher rates of employment after training. The trainees saw the practical component as an advantage, as they better realised their potential and value the employability provided:

> We come here, go to an internship company and 98% of the times we stay working in the company with three years of work background.
>
> (Pedro/ALA.D/Interview)

> This was a good opportunity. All my colleagues who studied here got a job in large companies, right after they concluded their courses. That's what motivated me to come.
>
> (Filipe/ALA.D/Interview)

In ALAs, the usefulness of knowledge for labour insertion is due mainly to the on-the-job training. This motivates trainees to keep in the course, making it more feasible:

> They feel more motivated to come here and go to the labour market [traineeships] and get paid right away. It's a small amount, but you get paid anyway.
>
> (Alice/ALA.D/Interview)

In VET there is a very strong emphasis on skills anticipated to be important in the labour market but this may result in the possible loss of touch with more general/key competencies, skills and knowledge which limits citizenship for a small number of participants. Yet ALAs gave the trainees room to assert their *educational citizenship of knowledge*, and re-engagement in education brought them new hope and opportunity to achieve their potential by learning more and getting further:

> I like studying.... Every day you learn something new. I don't miss school.... People who don't have an education have a hard time finding a job. People who have an education get a job, go to other countries. . . . I don't know how to explain it but I know it's good.
>
> (Natália/ALA.A/Interview)

> If people make an effort, everybody can do it, at least the minimum. . . . In the country and the world we live in, if you don't have an education, you won't succeed.
>
> (Alice/ALA.D/Interview)

In other cases, it was the impact of not having the necessary skills and qualifications for the labour market that led young adults to reengage in education to achieve their potential as future workers. Returning to school became a requirement from the labour market and a way to have better chances to get a job:

> Today, grade 12 is a priority for almost all jobs. So, it's really necessary . . . even to clean the floor.
>
> (Eduardo/ALA.A/Interview)

> My working experience turned out to be useful because it made me grow . . . see the difficulties, see that I really had to get grade 12 or I wouldn't be anyone.
>
> (Camila/ALA.B/Interview)

More than the search for achievement, it was financial support for the basic needs (e.g. food, transport, accommodation) at ALAs that led some to opt for this track:

> Money. . . . Other schools didn't pay and this one does . . . although it's very little. . . . I heard about this scholarship, this school. I decided to seize the opportunity and came to study here because you have the food subsidy.
>
> (Natalia/ALA.A/Interview)

Participants value VET as a form of enhancing their potential. They denote the advantage of vocational preparation and labour market experience as ways to increase their chances to get a job. Together with other features, the

Alternative learning arenas in Portugal   211

flexibility and respect for their learning paces is more oriented towards *educational citizenship of rights*, giving them room to explore the achievement of their individual potential.

Final remarks

An important feature that needs to be taken into account in the views presented by these young adults is the specificity of their educational and life pathways before engaging and while in ALAs and how their experiences in mainstream education – in the matching up of micro, meso and macro factors – led to disengagement and/or failure and, in some cases, early school leaving. We also related young adults' decisions to leave mainstream school and reengage in education with the specifics of the new settings in what concerns the enactment of the *educational citizenship* in its streams *of rights and knowledge*.

As seen, some of the key reasons evoked for leaving mainstream education are the relationship with teachers and the lack of interest in the curriculum, seen as too theoretical and inadequate for the labour market, which is in the horizon for most participants. By engaging in an ALA, they found a closer relationship with teachers and a more practical syllabus comprising tools to provide knowledge for the labour market. Along with the financial support, the awareness that upper secondary education is crucial to get a job stood out as one of the main stimuli to enrol in an ALA.

In terms of *educational citizenship*, the construction by these young adults of a sense of belonging and recognition was not enacted in mainstream education but was reached in the ALAs, where the achievement of each person's potential was improved. The more practical and specialised knowledge provided by VET courses seemed to offer the young adults a greater sense of achievement, providing the first steps towards *educational citizenship of knowledge*. Regarding participation in educational life, only ALA.C got closer to this idea, whereas in the other ALAs, young adults had limited room for that partnership. This was shown by the fact that even when they were heard, they were distanced from decision-making processes.

Even if still limited in their *educational citizenship*, by reengaging in education young adults asserted their voices in the struggle for the rights of *inclusion, participation* and *enhancement* as pillars for the aspects explored in this chapter: construction of a sense of inclusion and belonging; participation in the co-construction, co-maintenance and co-transformation of educational life; and achievement of individual potential.

As *citizenship construction authors*, the young adults who participated in this part of the study seemed to be managing this endeavour, even if in a limited way, by facing the constraints and using the opportunities provided by their educational settings. The former include, for example, the social stigma of VET courses and the devaluation of the knowledge they provide, as well as the lack of voice in some of their educational settings. Even if the construction of knowledge in ALAs is instrumental to the labour market, enrolment in ALAs

212 *Eunice Macedo et al.*

has provided room for most participants to rehearse the achievement of their *educational citizenship* in terms of *rights* and *knowledge*.

In Portugal, ALAs have been part of the political effort to diversify the educational offerings in order to provide for the interests and needs of a wider number of groups and individuals in a perspective of democratisation of mass schooling. However, the concern remains that the investment in more practical aspects of education, as provided by VET courses in ALAs, may put at risk the possibility of developing other areas of the individual potential while mitigating *educational citizenship* as a holistic process of self-development with a view to reflection, participation and action. Hence, one may say there is need for more balanced educational practices which take into account both the individual, and the social and labour needs, while simultaneously providing space for the personal construction of knowledge and rights by means of participatory methodologies that listen to each person within education.

Appendix 13.1 Sociodemographic features of interviewees

ALA	Pseudonym	Sex	Age at first interview	Country of birth	Dropout grade	Grade repetition	Reasons to disengage from mainstream school	Reasons to enrol in ALA
A	Natalia	F	19	San Tomé	10	9 (twice)	Health problems, school demands, lack of resources	Scholarship and labour opportunities
A	Eduardo	M	21	Portugal	12	10 and 11	Lack of studying, difficulty understanding the syllabus, lack of teacher support, lack of resources	Work opportunities and attainment of grade 12
B	Camila	F	23	Portugal	11	7 and 9 (twice)	Did not like teachers' practices	Lack of qualifications for the labour market and attainment of grade 12
B	Joel	M	22	Portugal	7	5 and 7	Failure, lack of resources	Attainment of grade 12
C	Artur	M	21	Portugal	8	8 (twice)	Lost interest in school after failing grade 8 twice, lack of resources	Difficulty finding jobs and attainment of grade 9
C	Isabel	F	21	Portugal	8		Problems with peers, lack of resources, addiction	Mother's pressure to attain grade 9 and get vocational training
D	Alice	F	19	Portugal	12	12 (twice)	Problems with teachers and difficulty in concluding math, lack of resources	Work opportunities so that she could pay for her own studies because of parents' financial problems
D	Filipe	M	20	Portugal	12	10, 11 and 12 (twice)	Failing in concluding two school subjects	Attainment of grade 12

Note: F, female; M, male.

214   *Eunice Macedo et al.*

Note

1 Escola de Segunda Oportunidade de Matosinhos. The name is provided at the request of the director, Luís Mesquita.

References

ANQEP. (2017). *Cursos profissionais*. Retrieved 27 July, 2017, from www.anqep.gov.pt/default.aspx

Araújo, H. C., Magalhães, A. M., Rocha, C., & Macedo, E. (2014). *Policies on early school leaving in nine European countries: A comparative analysis*. Antwerp: University of Antwerp. Retrieved from http://ec.europa.eu/research/social-sciences/pdf/policies_early_school_leaving.pdf

Bardsley, D. K. (2007). Education for all in a global era? The social justice of Australian secondary school education in a risk society. *Journal of Education Policy, 22*(5), 493–508. doi:10.1080/02680930701541691

Bernstein, B. B. (1996). *Pedagogy, symbolic control, and identity: Theory, research, critique*. London, Washington, DC: Taylor & Francis.

Clycq, N., Nouwen, W., & Timmerman, C. (2013). *Theoretical and methodological framework in early school leaving* (RESL.eu Project Paper 2). Retrieved from www.uantwerp.be/images/uantwerpen/container23160/files/RESL%20PP2%20-%20final%20version%20-%2009%2005%202014.pdf

Doll, J. J., Eslami, Z., & Walters, L. (2013). Understanding Why Students Drop Out of High School, According to Their Own Reports. *SAGE Open, 3*(4).

European Commission, & IKEI. (2012). *Apprenticeship supply in the member states of the European Union: Final report*. Retrieved from http://ec.europa.eu/social/BlobServlet?docId=7717&langId=en

Macedo, E. (2018). *Vozes jovens entre experiência e desejo: Que lugares de cidadania?* Porto: Afrontamento.

Macedo, E., & Araújo, H. C. (2014). Young Portuguese construction of educational citizenship: Commitments and conflicts in semi-disadvantaged secondary schools. *Journal of Youth Studies, 17*(3), 343–359. doi:10.1080/13676261.2013.825707

McGregor, G., & Mills, M. (2012). Alternative education sites and marginalised young people: 'I wish there were more schools like this one'. *International Journal of Inclusive Education, 16*(8), 843–862. doi:10.1080/13603116.2010.529467

McGregor, G., Mills, M., te Riele, K., & Hayes, D. (2014). Excluded from school: Getting a second chance at a 'meaningful' education. *International Journal of Inclusive Education, 19*(6), 608–625. doi:10.1080/13603116.2014.961684

Mills, M., & McGregor, G. (2014). *Re-engaging young people in education: Learning from alternative schools*. New York: Routledge.

Van Praag, L., Van Caudenberg, R., Nouwen, W., Clycq, N., & Timmerman, C. (2017). How to support and engage students in alternative forms of education and training? A qualitative study of school staff members in Flanders. *Journal of Education and Work, 30*(6), 1–13. doi:10.1080/13639080.2017.1319567

Wilson, K., Stemp, K., & McGinty, S. (2011). Re-engaging young people with education and training: What are the alternatives? *Youth Studies Australia, 30*(4), 32–39.

14 The opportunities and challenges of apprenticeships in England

Alternative learning arenas or sites of exploitation?

Louise Ryan and Magdolna Lőrinc

In the UK, concern has been growing about the number of young people not in education, employment or training (NEET) and those "churning" (Furlong, 2006), that is, caught in a cycle of low-paid, insecure apprenticeships and jobs; unpaid voluntary work; periods of unemployment; and never-ending training courses without any clear employment opportunities in sight (MacDonald, 2011; Thompson, 2017). According to statistics, low academic qualifications are amongst the most important risk factors for unsuccessful labour market integration and becoming NEET (Brown, 2017).

A key aspect of the government strategy for reducing youth unemployment and NEET numbers has been the promotion of apprenticeships in order to keep young people in education and training, and equip them with in-demand skills (Brockmann & Laurie, 2016; Hogarth, Gambin, & Hasluck, 2012; Ryan & Lőrinc, 2018). Indeed, statistics show that apprenticeships have a high probability of leading to employment. According to the 2011 census results, 89.4% of 25- to 34-year-olds who completed apprenticeships were employed – the second highest employment rate after those qualified to degree level and above (90.5%; see Figure 14.1). Despite significant increase in take-up, nevertheless, in England, only a small proportion of young people opt for apprenticeships. Although the 2015/16 academic year saw the highest number on record for apprenticeship participation and an increase in apprenticeship starts (Department for Education, 2017a), still only 6.9% of 16- to 18-year-olds opt for apprenticeships (Department for Education, 2017b).

To increase uptake, the British government has taken measures to increase the number of apprenticeships in the coming years and improve the standards of training provision and assessment (Powell, 2017).

However, as is the case in many countries (see Jørgensen & Thunqvist, 2015 for a discussion of the Swedish context; Graf, 2016 and Lassnigg, 2016 regarding Austria, Germany and Switzerland), there are still many questions to be answered regarding this learning pathway (Brockmann, Clarke, & Winch, 2010; Green, 2015), including access to apprenticeships, quality of training provision and low pay, to name a few. In this chapter, we draw on our qualitative research with a range of stakeholders, trainers, employers and young apprentices, to explore these questions. We found a tension between government

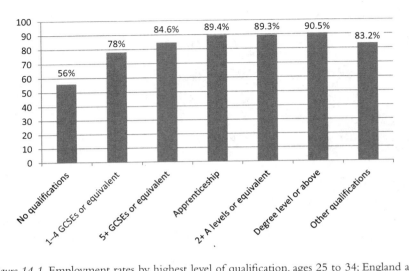

Figure 14.1 Employment rates by highest level of qualification, ages 25 to 34; England and Wales, 2011

Source: Census – Office for National Statistics.

policies which support the development of alternative learning arenas such as apprenticeships, and the overall perception amongst most of our participants that formal academic qualifications are still widely regarded in society as the "gold standard" to which all young people should aspire. On the one hand, the pressure on schools to raise attainment in secondary education – at GCSE (ISCED 3C, lower secondary) and A-level (ISCED 3A, upper secondary, academic route) – appears to reinforce the privileging of academic qualifications. On the other hand, decades of successive government reforms in vocational training have created a complex and fractured system with numerous courses and qualifications (Hogarth et al., 2012; Keep, 2015), which are of relatively low status and thus, function as a residual category for "low achievers" (Roberts & Atherton, 2011; Sloman, 2014). According to some participants, the country needs a cultural shift to value vocational qualifications, apprenticeships amongst them (Ryan & Lőrinc, 2015).

In this chapter, focusing on the opportunities and challenges presented by apprenticeship schemes, we investigate alternative learning arenas and pathways that lead to skilled employment. In doing so, we consider firstly the perceived advantages of undertaking these programmes despite the widespread concerns that still surround this type of training in the UK. Secondly, we examine some of the limitations and challenges of these programmes based on interviews with apprentices, their tutors, employers and several policy makers. These challenges include lack of information available to school leavers about apprenticeships, the low esteem of this learning pathway, financial limitations because of low pay for apprentices, low-quality or inconsistent training in some programmes, and a vocational education system that many find difficult to navigate.

Background on apprenticeships

Since the economic crisis, there has been growing international interest in apprenticeships, which are conceptualised as a response to high youth unemployment rates (Poulsen & Eberhardt, 2016). Because countries with high proportion of apprentices, such as Germany, Austria and Switzerland, have much lower youth unemployment rates, it is expected that apprenticeships will provide direct access to the labour market (Graf, 2016).

While national apprenticeship models can differ significantly, there are commonalities amongst contemporary European apprenticeships. Most importantly – as outlined in narrow definitions of this term – apprenticeships combine school-based education with company-based training. Other definitions include further characteristics, such as nationally recognised standards governing these programmes, often developed jointly between social partners: companies, the state, regional authorities, unions and so on. Apprentices and employers are bound by the training contract, and apprentices gain recognised formal qualifications upon successful completion of the course. Apprenticeships get dual funding, from the state and employers (Poulsen & Eberhardt, 2016).

However, major differences exist in the governance and degree of centralisation of apprenticeships in different countries, since apprenticeships are embedded into different types of vocational education and training (VET) systems. In Europe, three basic VET models have developed: the "liberal market model" in Britain; the French-type "state-regulated model"; and "the dual corporate model" characteristic to Germany, Austria, Switzerland and Denmark (ibid). Countries also differ based on the relative importance of apprenticeships and vocational training in their educational system. While in Austria, Belgium, the Netherlands and Germany, amongst others, a higher percentage of young people are enrolled in vocational upper secondary programmes than general ones, in the UK, enrolment rates in general programmes are more than double those at vocational courses (Poulsen & Eberhardt, 2016, p. 10).

In the UK, concerns have been expressed by government about the willingness of employers and young people to participate in apprenticeships (Hogarth et al., 2012, p. 41). Over the past 20 years, successive governments have sought to increase take-up of apprenticeships by young people through state-funded schemes involving "continuous waves of reform" and rebranding (Mazenod, 2016, p. 108). Brockmann et al. (2010), however, highlight the de-regulation of the labour market and its impact on insecure and flexible working which may make employers reluctant to invest in developing their staff. Rather than raising the status of apprenticeships, these trends in recent years have tended to further stigmatise vocational training (Mazenod, 2016). As a result, apprenticeships are still "not a mainstream pathway for young people in England" (Mazenod, 2016, p. 106).

Historically, apprenticeships were demand-driven as employers established the number of apprentices they wanted to take on (Fuller & Unwin, 2009). Although the notion of a "golden age" of apprenticeships has been much criticised (Vickerstaff, 2003), the ideal-type apprenticeships tend to be based on engineering and craft trades whereby young men served their time, mastered a trade and achieved good employment (Payne, 1987; Ryan, 2011). In the 1960s, decreasing manufacturing saw a fall in apprenticeships (Fuller & Unwin, 2009). By the 1980s, there had been a "dramatic decline in the number of apprenticeships available" (Payne, 1987, p. 443). As a result of rising youth unemployment, the government introduced the Youth Training Scheme (YTS) which subsumed apprenticeships. However, the YTS was poorly regarded by young people and their parents as a form of cheap labour with no guarantee of training (Hogarth et al., 2012).

In 1994 the government launched Modern Apprenticeships with the dual aim of improving the country's skills base and re-engaging low-qualified young people back into training (McIntosh, 2005). Since 2010/11, the apprenticeship programme has been further expanded as a result of increased government investment (Department for Education, 2017a). Consequently, more than three million apprenticeships were started since May 2010. By academic year 2015/16, apprenticeship participation increased to 899,400, the highest number on record. In 2015/16 alone, 509,400 young people started an apprenticeship course (Department for Education, 2017a).

Importantly, these new apprenticeships were designed to cover a wider range of sectors and occupations, beyond the traditional manufacturing industries, in order to become less ethnic and gender specific (Brockmann et al., 2010). As a result, the percentage of women starting apprenticeships in England has been higher than men for every year since 2010/11 (Mirza-Davies, 2016). In 2015/16, 51.1% of apprentices were female, 9.3% declared a learning difficulty and/or disability, and 10.6% were from an ethnic minority background (Department for Education, 2017a).

Indeed, as noted in other European countries also (see Fjellstrom & Kristmansson, 2016 on the Swedish context), efforts to expand provision beyond traditional manufacturing meant drawing in new sectors, such as retail and business administration, which had no history of apprenticeships and did not easily conform to the engineering ideal-type (McIntosh, 2005; Ryan, 2011). In the UK, these new sectors provide the majority of apprenticeship schemes nowadays. In 2015/16, just as in previous years, the majority of apprenticeship starts were in the service sectors. As illustrated by Table 14.1, almost three quarters (71%) of all starts were concentrated in three sectors: business, administration and law; health, public services and care; and retail and commercial enterprise (Mirza-Davies, 2016).

The shift in the apprenticeship model is also reflected in the "heavy involvement of private training organisations" (Brockmann et al., 2010, p. 116). McIntosh argues that the use of "training providers means that employers often have low commitment to the scheme, preferring to leave things to the trainers"

Opportunities, challenges of apprenticeships   219

Table 14.1 Apprenticeship starts in England by sector subject in 2015/16

Sector	Apprenticeship starts, thousands	Percentage
Business, administration and law	142	28
Health, public services and care	131	26
Retail and commercial enterprise	84	17
Engineering and manufacturing technology	77	15
Construction, planning and built environments	21	4
Leisure, travel and tourism	15	3
Information and communication technology	16	3
Education and training	8	2
Agriculture, horticulture and animal care	8	2
Arts, media and publishing	1	0.2
Other	6	1

Source: GOV.uk FE data library: apprenticeships.

(2005, p. 253). Fuller and Unwin describe Modern Apprenticeships as "divesting" employers of responsibility for training and "diluting" the concept to little more than work experience (2009, p. 411). Perhaps connected to this, only about 70% of young people enrolled in an apprenticeship complete their course and achieve their qualification (Mirza-Davies, 2016). In addition, while originally set at NQF Level 3 (upper secondary equivalent at ISCED 3A), over time, Level 2 programmes became the norm, which are equivalent to a lower secondary qualification at ISCED 3C (Brockmann et al., 2010).

Recent apprenticeship policies focused on raising standards and improving the quality of training schemes. As such, minimum durations of programmes have been introduced: for 16- to 19-year-olds, apprenticeships must last at least 12 months. In addition, apprentices must be employed for at least 30 hours per week and receive a minimum of 280 hours of guided learning in their first year, of which at least 100 hours must be off-the-job. Apprenticeships also have to offer training in English and math, if the apprentice has not yet achieved minimum qualifications in these subjects (Powell, 2017).

Nonetheless, on-going debates about the quality of apprenticeship learning continue in England. Concerns have been expressed that a narrow focus on meeting employers' current skills needs may mean that less general education is being provided than in comparable systems (Hogarth et al., 2012, p. 51). For example, the comprehensive nature of German apprenticeship programmes contrasts markedly with "minimalist apprenticeships" in England (Brockmann, 2013, p. 359). German apprenticeships enjoy "high social recognition" (Brockmann, 2013, p. 361), whereas in England, vocational education, including apprenticeships, hold a "relatively low status" (Brockmann, 2013, p. 361). Other research contrasts the English "restricted" work-based training model of apprenticeships with the more educational model in countries such as France, Finland (Mazenod, 2016) and Sweden (Fjellstrom & Kristmansson, 2016).

Hogarth et al. (2012) argue that apprenticeships in the UK now stand at a crossroad. There has been considerable growth in the range of apprenticeships on offer, especially at the lower levels (McIntosh, 2005). Hence, "apprenticeships are heterogeneous with respect to their duration, content and the returns they provide either to the employer or to the apprentice" (Hogarth et al., 2012 p. 42). In fact, there is so much heterogeneity that Ryan (2011) questions if what comes under the rubric of apprenticeships nowadays truly constitutes an actual apprenticeship.

Nonetheless, there is a broad consensus in academic and policy circles that apprenticeships can have enormous potential (Fuller & Unwin, 2009) and good schemes can be very rewarding (Hogarth et al., 2012). Research suggests that, at least for men who complete Level 3 apprenticeships, there are significant pay gains (McIntosh, 2005). However, to become a more attractive option, there is a need to develop high-quality learning so that apprenticeship "will be able to rid itself entirely of any stigma attached from it being considered a second-best alternative to the academic pathway by either young people or employers" (Hogarth et al., 2012, p. 53).

Our study explored these issues related to quality of training, access to apprenticeships and affordability of this provision through in-depth, longitudinal research with policy makers and stakeholders at both the local and national levels, as well as trainers, employers and young people on a range of diverse apprenticeships across London. It has been suggested that "the situation concerning apprenticeships is particularly critical in London in the context of high unemployment, child poverty and the media attention on youth crime" (Brockmann et al., 2010, p. 118) as London has one of the worst records in England on measures of youth unemployment (Brockmann et al., 2010, p. 119). Before presenting our findings we briefly describe our research study.

Methods

Data collection for this study on apprenticeship schemes in London was completed as part of the Reducing Early School Leaving in Europe (RESL.eu) project which aimed to provide insights into the mechanisms and processes that influence young people's decision to leave school or training early, before gaining adequate qualifications for today's demanding labour market. The project also sought to identify and analyse intervention and compensation measures that succeed in keeping or returning pupils in education or training, despite their high theoretical risk of early school leaving. Apprenticeships were included in the RESL.eu project in their capacity of "provider of last resort for those whom other forms of learning have failed" (Keep, 2015, p. 473), as they are frequently interpreted in England.

Our data collection on apprenticeships was undertaken in London, between November 2015 and July 2016. We identified apprenticeships in diverse sectors, including childcare, health and social care, information technology (IT), business administration, sport and clinical technology. We interviewed five staff members from these programmes: the vice principal of a South London

Opportunities, challenges of apprenticeships   221

further education (FE) college that runs some of these apprenticeship schemes, two apprenticeship teacher trainers from a North London FE college, and two employers – the director of a small South London company and a hospital manager.

The voice of young apprentices was collected through two focus groups and a number of in-depth, semi-structured interviews. The two focus groups were conducted at the childcare- and the IT-related apprenticeships. We also interviewed nine apprentices (some of whom also took part in the focus groups) from different programmes; six of them were re-interviewed approximately six months later. Altogether, 17 apprentices took part in this research. They were mainly female (11) and ranged in age from 16 to 24, but most were under 20 years, coming from varied ethnic backgrounds: three self-defined as white British, one white other (Romanian), one Middle Eastern, two Asian-British, three mixed (white/black) ethnicity and the remaining seven, black Caribbean.

All interviews and focus groups were conducted at the apprentices' training or learning sites. We invited participants to take part in the study through the apprenticeship programmes; hence they were largely self-selecting. Thus we make no claims to the representativeness of our participants.

This body of data was supplemented with nine semi-structured interviews and two focus groups carried out between July and October 2013 with the participation of 24 local and national stakeholders in education, training and youth services from two research areas, London and the North East of England. All interviews and focus groups were fully transcribed and analysed thematically, using both a priori and newly emerging themes, coded with NVivo 10 software. To protect participants' identities, all have been given pseudonyms.

Transforming vocational education/apprenticeships

The positive view: "it's such a good opportunity" (Pamela, former apprentice)

Amongst the practitioners working directly on apprenticeship programmes there was a good deal of positivity about the potential strengths of this training pathway. A tutor who delivered theoretical teaching for childcare apprentices in an FE college stated:

> So this route has been valuable to a lot of students in terms of their professional developments, giving them the skills and the recognised qualifications to get into the workforce. . . . So, it gives them an alternative.
>
> (Michelle, tutor)

In addressing skills and an alternative pathway into employment, she echoed points raised by several other practitioners. An employer who worked in the health sector expressed concern about the growing skills gap, especially in the more technical aspects of this sector. For her, as an employer, apprenticeships were a good way of training young people for the specific skills gaps in the

222 *Louise Ryan and Magdolna Lőrinc*

National Health Service (NHS). In this way, young people were being prepared for areas of the labour market where there is genuine demand for skilled technicians; hence they are guaranteed employment if they successfully complete their training. But this was not just about filling job vacancies – it was also about providing alternative pathways for young people who may have struggled in the formal educational system:

> We've had people who, for whatever reason, were disenfranchised by the school system, thought they had nowhere to go, no possible career prospects, and now they're halfway up the career ladder. . . . We have got evidence to show that we've changed people's lives.
>
> (Jane, employer, NHS)

Similarly, at the FE college, both staff members we interviewed agreed that the "the education system is failing those who need it most" (Paul) and many students who come on to college programmes had "negative school experiences" but now they are "flourishing" (Michelle). Michelle, a childcare tutor, suggested that schools are usually driven by "target measures" and meeting national target grades, rather than meeting the learning needs of individual students. Like Jane, the health sector employer, both of these tutors agreed that apprenticeships offer young people a second chance and an opportunity to succeed, "flourish" and change their lives:

> I've seen young people grow from people who had rather low GCSE grades, a lack of confidence, low self-esteem, into confident, academically strong learners and individuals applying for £30,000 jobs. . . . It wasn't one or two; almost all of them have done some truly amazing stuff.
>
> (Paul, tutor)

Overall, our participants were very positive about the potential of apprenticeships to raise the confidence of young people. An employer who had several apprentices working in his IT company also spoke about the changes he noticed in the young people:

> In terms of their skills, their confidence, their belief in themselves grows out of this . . . first shy to pick up the phone and talk to people; [now] they go out and talk with employers to recruit other apprentices; they are growing.
>
> (Angus, employer, IT)

This focus on skills, confidence and valuable work-based experience was repeated in the interviews and focus groups with the young apprentices. For example, Siobhan, who was attending the childcare apprenticeship, stated of the opportunity that it: "doesn't only give you a qualification, it gives you life skills; life skills of how to work and earn money and work in a setting with other professionals".

Pamela, a young woman who had completed school with very low grades, explained how the apprenticeship was a chance for her to turn her life around:

> I went to school, I attended every day, every lesson but I just didn't sit down and do the work. . . . I didn't have the attention span. . . . I remember I left my coursework to the last minute and then when it came to GCSEs . . . I went to the exams but I came out with like Ds, Es, Fs.
>
> (Pamela)

Even though Pamela went to a "good" school, she was "easily distracted" and did not achieve her full potential. On leaving school she got a low-skilled job but began to realise that she wanted more out of life: "I felt like when I did do my apprenticeship that was the only option at the moment. If I didn't succeed in it I don't know where I'd go or what I'd be doing". Upon completing both a Level 2 and then a Level 3 apprenticeship in health and social care she got a full-time job in a hospital.

Michelle, the childcare tutor, also highlighted that apprenticeships were useful for young people "who may need to be working and earning at the same time to get a qualification". She suggested that this may be particularly important for young people from socially disadvantaged backgrounds who made up the majority in her childcare apprenticeship programmes. The young apprentices also highlighted the appeal of earning while training. Reuben, who was on a clinical technologist apprenticeship programme, remarked: "I like to learn while I earn".

However, as discussed below, the payment earned by apprentices was often very low and risked reinforcing negative stereotypes of exploitative labour. Thus, despite this positivity, all our participants were also clearly aware of the many challenges and negativity that still surround apprenticeship programmes (see also Ryan & Lőrinc, 2018).

The challenges: "there have been ups and downs" (Cynthia, clinical technology apprentice)

Although one of the government's key selling points for apprenticeships is the slogan "earn while you learn", ironically, apprenticeships may not be a viable option for poorer families as the payment for young apprentices is well below the minimum wage and considerably below the London Living Wage. At the time of our fieldwork (2015/16), the minimum pay for apprentices aged 16 to 18 was £3.30 per hour, significantly lower than the London Living Wage, £9.40 at the time. Thus, for many young people these alternative options are still unaffordable:

> I've seen quite a lot of cases recently of people who've been given apprenticeships, hairdressing and some of the trades, and just being treated very badly. . . . People are being employed on that basis as cheap labour without

any consideration of supporting the training aspect and moving towards a qualification.

(Robert, council officer, North East England)

As suggested above, a major concern about apprenticeship schemes is that many are not well regulated and provide inadequate training for young people, which then leads to poor employment outcomes. Hence young people may be sceptical of undertaking such programmes: "So young people actually aren't putting any value onto apprenticeships because some unscrupulous employers actually use apprenticeships as cheap labour" (Keith, senior youth worker, North East England). Although new legislation was introduced in recent years to improve training and assessment in apprenticeship programmes, loopholes which can potentially be exploited still exist in the legislation. For example, the minimum 30 hours of employment per week can be reduced "if an apprentice's personal circumstances or if the nature of employment in a given sector make it impossible to work these hours" (Powell, 2017, p. 5). The minimum length of 12 months for an apprenticeship scheme can also be reduced for apprentices older than 19 "if they have relevant prior learning and achievement" (ibid).

Referring to the low rate of pay, and related to the above issues, Michelle, the childcare tutor, observed that "the apprenticeship, although it's good in its idealism, I believe it does lend itself to being abused by rogue employers". She noted that "I have seen people that have taken on apprentices only purely to use their skills at a really reduced rate. It happens".

Many of the young people we spoke to expressed concerns about low pay, especially given the high cost of living in London:

ELIZABETH: We need money to buy clothes, shelter, everything.
KIM: And to get around now as well. It's expensive to get around.
SIOBHAN: Yes, so if we have a job, you have to travel around London.
ELIZABETH: Yes, the bus ticket, oh my God, every week.

(Childcare apprenticeship FG)

For all the young people in our study, undertaking an apprenticeship was only viable if they lived at home with their parents. Phoenix, who was doing the clinical technologist apprenticeship, shared a flat with his brother: "I've had to move in with my brother because the wages that I'm earning here wouldn't have paid the rent of where I was living and I haven't got as much expendable resources".

Concerns about low pay and exploitation continue to reinforce the negative stereotypes of apprenticeships, especially in schools: "Schools are not keen on promoting apprenticeships. . . . Apprenticeships had a bad reputation. There were some people using it as slave labour" (Jane, employer, NHS). However, as she explained, there may be other motives for schools not to promote apprenticeships as a viable training pathway:

That was the reason schools gave for not promoting it. But actually, we know it's because they're funded to take A-level starters. . . . Until schools

Opportunities, challenges of apprenticeships 225

are really made to give proper informed information to young people, it's never going to change.

(Jane)

The young people we spoke to all agreed that apprenticeship schemes had not been advertised or promoted at their schools. Yazid, who was doing an IT apprenticeship, got little practical support or advice from his school:

There was one careers adviser; I told him I wanted to do an apprenticeship, but, yes, it wasn't really much help; he was just telling me, 'Oh, look, here's an apprenticeship; you should go home and look at it.' I wanted more guidance on it, like more depth into it, really.

(Yazid)

Amongst the young people, there was a shared view that schools were more interested in promoting traditional academic routes to university. Several participants observed that the drive towards universities was more in the interest of schools than students, schools being assessed on attainment at academic exams and number of students going to higher education: "so that they can say they've had this many people go to good universities" (Kim). Similarly, some families reacted negatively: "They were quite disappointed, and they kept pushing me and pushing me to go to university", Cynthia told us.

In common with researchers in some other European countries (see Jørgensen & Thunqvist, 2015 on Sweden and Denmark) our stakeholders identified a tension between official policies which support the development of alternative learning arenas such as apprenticeships, and the overall perception amongst wider society that formal academic qualifications are still widely regarded in society as the gold standard that all young people should aspire to achieve.

I think in this country . . . we never had a very high profile for vocational education and we haven't got a strong tradition of seeing it as a very positive route for young people.

(Eileen, Youth Service Council Officer, London)

There seems to be a genuine push to equip young people with in-demand skills through reform of the apprenticeship programme and other vocational offerings. However, the pressure on schools to raise attainment at GCSE and A-level appears to reinforce the privileging of academic qualifications. According to some participants, the country needs a cultural shift to value vocational qualifications, apprenticeships amongst them:

It sits on an unhelpful place somewhere between employment and training, so it's neither one thing, nor the other. Young people don't know about it sufficiently, and parents and teachers don't know about it sufficiently.

(Margaret, Senior Officer, London Councils)

Our practitioner interviewees also raised concerns about the level of training that young people received on some apprenticeship programmes. Paul, a tutor in health and social care, was particularly critical of the short, one-year Level 2 schemes: "I would get rid of all this 12-month nonsense because I don't know how much you can learn in 12 months". Instead, he would prefer courses of two to two and half years in length, with strong training components delivered by qualified tutors in colleges:

> So you would be at least three days in employment and working and earning money, but two days I would expect to really well develop the literacy and numeracy and have really, really good training and base it around developing not as a healthcare professional but also as a learner.
>
> (Paul, tutor)

This suggestion conforms more to apprenticeship models found elsewhere where young people receive a wide range of general education rather than being simply training 'on the job' for one specific set of tasks (see Brockmann, 2013 on Germany and Fjellstrom & Kristmansson, 2016 on Sweden). This tutor was also concerned about the level of partnership between the training providers and the employers. He believed that much closer partnership was needed so that staff from the college had more regular contact with the workplace setting:

> In my personal opinion, I should be spending a lot of time with my learners in their placements, working with them; not going to observe them for a couple of hours twice a year.
>
> (Paul, tutor)

Amongst the young people, we met one girl, Hope, who had changed her apprenticeship programme because she was not happy with the level of training provided. She explained that after a few months in her first apprenticeship she began to think that "something was wrong. . . . I wasn't getting training". She was effectively working full time without the required training element: "My employer wasn't meeting the contract rules appropriately", she explained. After much discussion with the employer and many promises of training which were not met, she decided to leave. In the academic literature there is concern about apprenticeships which do not provide adequate training opportunities (Ryan, 2011; Brockmann, 2013). Hope's experience was a clear example of an employer who seemed to regard apprentices as cheap labour and who did not provide the expected training.

Because we were conducting fieldwork with young people who were in the middle of doing their apprenticeships, we cannot say how successful they were in finding employment once they completed their courses. Further follow-up work is needed before we can assess how adequate their training proved to be.

Statistics, as mentioned earlier in the chapter, show that those who complete an apprenticeship have good employment outcomes (see Figure 14.1).

Nonetheless, it remains to be seen whether new policies will be able to address low-quality training provision and as a result, achievement rates on apprenticeship schemes.

Conclusion

In many European countries, the apprenticeship model is receiving increasing attention in policy discourses around academic underachievement in secondary education, skills shortages amongst young people and their difficult transitions into the labour market. As discussed earlier, apprenticeships are presented as a cure-all, a learning pathway that will provide an alternative option to young people at risk of early school leaving and becoming NEET, and help them stay in education and training longer in order to achieve qualifications valued by employers.

This chapter aimed to present a brief summary of the history of apprenticeships in the UK, and the academic and policy debates surrounding these. In addition, we explored some of the opportunities and challenges encountered along this pathway, as experienced and interpreted by policy makers, youth workers, tutors, employers and young apprentices.

Most participants were well aware of the limitations and challenges of apprenticeship schemes in England. According to our participants, the apprenticeship route is not adequately promoted in schools by teachers and career advisors. Many apprentices found their way to these schemes almost by accident, often against the advice of parents and teachers. The negative perceptions about apprenticeships, however, need to be interpreted in the context of decades of often low-quality apprenticeship provision. Some of our participants highlighted how vulnerable this scheme is to exploitation by unscrupulous employers who take advantage of young people without providing any meaningful training in return. Our participants also mentioned the low payment offered to young apprentices. It was apparent that apprenticeships are out of reach for young people from the poorest backgrounds who do not have family support and accommodation.

Nonetheless, we found that the majority of participants appreciated the potential of this scheme. The apprentices themselves narrated their experiences in mostly positive terms (Ryan & Lőrinc, 2018). They valued the opportunity to gain extensive work experience while still in education, and the policy mantra of "earning while learning" was echoed by many. Trainers and employers highlighted the positive impact of this scheme not only on young people's skill levels, but also on their self-esteem and confidence. It was generally acknowledged that, if executed appropriately, apprenticeships can engage young people who are less successful in mainstream education, and provide them an opportunity to gain valuable skills and qualifications, which in turn, can positively affect their later life outcomes.

In line with the wider literature, our findings suggest that the apprenticeship model offers tremendous potential as a valuable alternative learning and training pathway. To fulfil this potential, however, and combat negative perceptions, apprenticeship schemes in England need to address a number of significant challenges, as addressed here:

Policy recommendations: Crucially, the quality of training and monitoring of apprenticeship accreditation needs to improve to ensure that this provision meets the required standards to address the skills gap. In addition, stronger coordination is needed between employers and trainers so that skills training and work-place experience are more compatible.

We argue that serious consideration should be given to bringing training back into colleges. This would ensure that young apprentices have access to additional support services, such as welfare, safeguarding and career advice, and may help to improve progression to higher-level apprenticeship courses.

Finally, our findings strongly suggest that employers need to provide a proper living wage for all apprentices so that these training opportunities become viable for a broader range of young people.

References

Brockmann, M. (2013). Learning cultures in retail: Apprenticeship, identity and emotional work in England and Germany. *Journal of Education and Work, 26*(4), 357–375.

Brockmann, M., Clarke, L., & Winch, C. (2010). The apprenticeship framework in England: A new beginning or a continuing sham? *Journal of Education and Work, 23*(2), 111–127.

Brockmann, M., & Laurie, I. (2016). Apprenticeship in England – the continued role of the academic – vocational divide in shaping learner identities. *Journal of Vocational Education and Training, 68*(2), 229–244.

Brown, J. (2017). *NEET: Young people not in education, employment or training.* Briefing Paper Number SN 06705. 6 April 2017. House of Commons Library.

Department for Education. (2017a). *Further education and skills in England.* March 2017, SFR 13/2017, 23 March 2017 (revised 15 June 2017). Retrieved from www.gov.uk/government/uploads/system/uploads/attachment_data/file/618924/SFR13-2017-June-revision.pdf

Department for Education. (2017b). *Participation in education, training and employment by 16–18 year olds in England.* SFR 29/2017, 29 June 2017. Retrieved from www.gov.uk/government/uploads/system/uploads/attachment_data/file/623310/SFR29-2017_Main_text_.pdf

Fjellström, M., & Kristmansson, P. (2016). Learning as an apprentice in Sweden: A comparative study on affordances for vocational learning in school and work life apprentice education. *Education+ Training, 58*(6), 629–642.

Fuller, A., & Unwin, L. (2009). Change and continuity in apprenticeship: The resilience of a model of learning. *Journal of Education and Work, 22*(5), 405–416.

Furlong, A. (2006). "Not a very NEET solution": Representing problematic labour market transitions among early school-leavers. *Work Employment Society, 20*(3), 553–569.

Graf, L. (2016). The rise of work-based academic education in Austria, Germany and Switzerland. *Journal of Vocational Education and Training, 68*(1), 1–16.

Green, C. (2015). UK apprenticeships: Opportunity or exploitation? *Interdisciplinary Perspectives on Equality and Diversity, 1*(1).

Hogarth, T., Gambin, L., & Hasluck, C. (2012). Apprenticeships in England: What next? *Journal of Vocational Education and Training, 64*(1), 41–55.

Jørgensen, C. H., & Thunqvist, D. P. (2015). Inclusion and equal access at the same time: Comparing VET in Sweden and Denmark. In *ECER 2015 Conference*.

Keep, E. (2015). Governance in English VET: On the functioning of a fractured 'system'. *Research in Comparative and International Education, 10*(4), 464–475.

Lassnigg, L. (2016). *Apprenticeship policies in comparative perspective: ET-structures, employment, relationship, export.* Sociological Series. Working Paper No. 114. Institute for Advanced Studies, Vienna.

MacDonald, R. (2011). Youth transitions, unemployment and underemployment: Plus ça change, plus c'est la même chose? *Journal of Sociology, 47*(4), 427–444.

Mazenod, A. (2016). Education or training? A comparative perspective on apprenticeships in England. *Journal of Vocational Education and Training, 68*(1), 102–117.

McIntosh, S. (2005). The returns to apprenticeship training. *Journal of Education and Work, 18*(3), 251–282.

Mirza-Davies, J. (2016). *Apprenticeship statistics: England.* Briefing Paper Number 06113, 21 November 2016, House of Commons Library.

Payne, J. (1987). Unemployment, apprenticeships and training: Does it pay to stay on at school? *British Journal of Sociology of Education, 8*(4), 425–445.

Poulsen, S. B., & Eberhardt, C. (2016). *Approaching apprenticeship systems from a European perspective.* Discussion Papers B. 171. Federal Institute for Vocational Education and Training, Bonn.

Powell, A. (2017). *Apprenticeship policy in England: 2017.* Briefing Paper Number CBP 03052, 29 June 2017. House of Commons Library.

Roberts, K., & Atherton, G. (2011). Career development among young people in Britain today: Poverty of aspiration or poverty of opportunity? *International Journal of Education Administration and Policy Studies, 3*(5), 59–67.

Ryan, L., & Lőrinc, M. (2015). Interrogating early school leaving, youth unemployment and NEETs: Understanding local contexts in two English regions. *Educação, Sociedade and Culturas, 45.*

Ryan, L., & Lőrinc, M. (2018). Perceptions, Prejudices and Possibilities: young people narrating apprenticeship experiences. *British Journal of Sociology of Education.* Retrieved from https://doi.org/10.1080/01425692.2017.1417821

Ryan, P. (2011). *Apprenticeship: Between theory and practice, school and workplace.* Economics of Education Working Paper Series, 64.

Sloman, M. (2014). A long journey to a cul-de-sac: A reflection on UK skills policy, *Human Resource Development International, 17*(2), 222–230.

Thompson, R. (2017). Opportunity structures and educational marginality: the post-16 transitions of young people outside education and employment. *Oxford Review of Education, 43*(6), 749–766.

Vickerstaff, S. A. (2003). Apprenticeship in the 'golden age': Were youth transitions really smooth and unproblematic back then? *Work, Employment and Society, 12*(2), 269–287.

Conclusion: lessons learned from the RESL.eu project
Main findings and policy advice

Elif Keskiner and Maurice Crul

Introduction

This concluding chapter presents policy advice synthesised from the five-year findings and publications of the Reducing Early School Leaving in Europe (RESL.eu) project. The first section offers insights gleaned from extensive qualitative research on mainstream secondary education and alternative learning pathways in the project's data collection countries: Belgium, the Netherlands, Poland, Portugal, Spain, Sweden and the United Kingdom. We present an evaluation of intervention, prevention and compensatory measures for all seven countries, pinpointing effective measures as well as challenges in implementing them. Drawing on RESL.eu survey data, the second section discusses the significant protective factors for school engagement. We provide an overview of patterns in early school leaving (ESL) and main protective factors identified per country. The chapter closes with national comparisons and recommendations, relevant for school stakeholders, school-level policy makers and other interested parties.

School-level findings: intervention, prevention and compensatory measures

This section draws on RESL.eu data collected from 28 secondary schools in seven countries, using in-depth qualitative research methods with school leaders, teachers, students and parents. (Besides examining ESL intervention and prevention measures in mainstream educational contexts, we studied 28 measures in alternative learning pathways that offer ways to obtain educational qualifications other than the traditional means of gaining access to, or completing, set curricula (Nouwen, Clycq, Braspenningx, & Timmerman, 2015; Van Praag, Nouwen, Van Caudenberg, Clycq, & Timmerman, 2016). Our analysis presents a unique opportunity for countries with both relatively high and low ESL rates to learn from one another's experiences and practices.

An evaluation of school-based measures' efficacy in combating ESL within mainstream education revealed which measures were most commonly applied and what struggles various stakeholders regularly encountered. The measures we examined included early warning systems, socio-emotional and behavioural support, career guidance and academic support – for each, we identified major challenges and successful strategies. We also identified the set of contextual factors needed for measures' efficacy as well as prevention measures against ESL. Professional training for teachers, for example, proved vital because it enabled school staff's systematic detection of at-risk factors, which include cognitive as well as behavioural and psychological indicators. Such training is not intended only to facilitate early warning systems, but also applies to other intervention measures and can be integral to ESL prevention (Araújo et al., 2013). Another important contextual factor was a student-centred ethos, noticeably achieved when students were given a voice of their own and a sense of ownership. This kind of approach positively influenced student-teacher relations, which our quantitative analysis also found were pivotal. Interviews with staff revealed how teachers perceived ESL as rooted in students' family problems, notably lack of parental involvement. 'Blaming the parents' was common across country settings. Yet, our evaluation showed that schools fostering a more positive, inclusive attitude towards parents, especially those from socially disadvantaged and/or ethnic minority backgrounds, yielded more parental involvement at school and greater family-institution cooperation. For any and all measures to succeed, individualised and flexible learning was seen to be highly effective. Both students and staff believed a holistic approach, accounting for cognitive and behavioural risk factors as well as emotional disengagement, was vital. The view of ESL thus shifted from being an individual decision to a process embedded in a broader context encompassing neighbourhoods and the educational system at large. This more nuanced outlook was complicated for schools requiring close coordination between various stakeholders, though some had success in adopting this stance. Strikingly, the compensatory measures we singled out proved more effective in individualised learning pathways and a holistic approach.

As for compensatory measures to reduce ESL, we mostly examined alternative learning pathways for reintegrating into education and the labour market. These arenas not only benefitted the young people they targeted, but also could serve as exemplary models for mainstream secondary education. Often more flexible in terms of programmes offered, individual attention and assessing students' challenges in a more inter-relational light, many successful anti-ESL measures outside mainstream secondary education used a holistic approach to help students re-engage. Adaptability, personalisation and a caring environment that transcends academic support were all deemed essential for mainstream secondary education institutions, though these elements were more common in alternative arenas. Work-based learning was another successful alternative learning pathway. Unfortunately, these alternative arenas were susceptible to being marginalised and students who benefitted from them were negatively stereotyped. Closer cooperation between in-school and out-of-school measures in terms of guidance and direction could therefore benefit both institutions and students at risk of ESL.

School-based intervention and prevention measures

The RESL.eu project noted inspiring examples of actions taken to combat ESL within mainstream secondary education and subsequently enacted policies. It also documented the difficulties encountered by teachers, support staff, students and parents. This section addresses school-based measures encountered in most of our targeted countries across different types of educational systems.

Early warning systems

Early warning systems (EWS) were popular measures for reducing ESL in all the countries. They were usually activated in the process leading up to ESL, when only some risk factors were already visible. School staff expressed a strongly held belief in the necessity of using at-risk indicators in a detection and monitoring system. Most EWS focus on behavioural indicators, such as truancy and involvement in disruptive classroom behaviour. However, this is a rather narrow focus; EWS perceived to be more effective also evaluated dips in students' academic progress and/or displays of emotional disengagement. In recognising early signs, the role of teachers proved to be crucial. It became clear that a major challenge to reduce ESL is to train teachers, mentors and support staff to interpret risk indicators correctly and apply EWS at an early stage in the school careers of all students.

Socio-emotional and behavioural support

INCLUSIVE INCENTIVES TO COUNTERACT TRUANCY

The RESL.eu survey data showed a strong correlation between truancy and ESL. Tackling truancy could therefore be seen as tackling ESL. Our study illustrated how truancy was frequently met with mostly punitive interventions. Yet, interviews with a wide range of stakeholders demonstrated that disciplinary punishment (notably student exclusion from school) can raise the risk of ESL. In our research, correlative escalations in punitive measures with truancy and misconduct regularly turned up, to the point where it seemed neither staff nor students were motivated to realign relations. In most cases, schools invested more in isolating at-risk students than endeavouring to keep them enrolled. This pattern was difficult to break, suggesting that a more inclusive approach, which also considers the views of the students themselves – whether in the form of disciplinary action and/or other remedies for misconduct – can improve students' sense of accountability.

COUNSELLING, COACHING AND MENTORING

School staff and other stakeholders cited one-on-one emotional and behavioural support as key to preventing motivational and behavioural problems.

Such personally tailored guidance might help with prevention, though most schools predominantly practise intervention. They are more likely to apply punitive measures to visible symptoms (e.g., absenteeism), whereas proactive emotional and behavioural support usually are applied too late. Individualised care provided by schools varied greatly, from highly structured weekly care team meetings, including cross-sectorial partnerships, to ad hoc reactions to student needs. The disparity in professionalisation levels across support staff posed a major challenge. We included staff ranging from regular teachers without specific training, to care professionals such as student counsellors, social workers and school psychologists. Designers and implementers of professional support considered access and availability of funding for such support essential. Nevertheless, our study revealed that students often preferred support from someone they recognised and trusted rather than some visiting professional they did not know.

SOCIAL SKILLS TRAINING AND EXTRACURRICULAR ACTIVITIES

Previous studies have shown how social skills and extracurricular activities have a major intervention function. They help young people build self-confidence and hone a sense of identity, which can encourage them to stay in school (EC, 2013). Our study found few schools that explicitly focused on developing social skills, and measures that did tended to segregate students showing high levels of emotional and behavioural risk. While a more intensified student-focused approach can benefit at-risk youth, placing them in special education groups makes them vulnerable to stigmatisation, as was confirmed in interviews with students and staff. The availability and scope of extracurricular activities also differed across schools.

Career guidance

Teachers and students agreed that having career guidance and support throughout educational and professional trajectories was a decisive preventive measure. However, more personalised career guidance that could help students in a direct, personally relevant manner was hard to find. An integrated, more long-term approach has so far proven effective because its success is less contingent on the commitment and/or availability of specific staff members.

Academic support

TUTORING

A prominent form of academic support in almost all the schools was tutoring. This measure signalled awareness of the need for committed schools and staff to support disadvantaged children. A stumbling block here, however, was that getting tutoring was usually voluntary, so the remedial students who were likeliest to profit from such support rarely received it. Moreover, this spirit of self-volunteerism is often precisely what makes these measures successful. Meanwhile, schools have learned that the manner in which students are approached makes all the difference in securing participation. Budgetary constraints also hampered progress here; teachers frequently took up tutoring on a voluntary basis, on top of regular teaching loads. These restrictions made tutoring too dependent on the willingness of the stakeholders involved.

FLEXIBLE LEARNING PATHWAYS

'Individualised learning' has become a buzzword in education, with a growing awareness that standardised learning methods and requirements leave too many students poorly served. This proved painfully obvious for schools with many at-risk students from disadvantaged families. Many institutions we studied, worked with flexible programmes and adaptive teaching styles, tailoring their curricula according to students' specific learning needs and ability levels. Usually, the staff decided which students should be so accommodated. We often saw how programmes that allowed for students' voices to be heard in decision making had positive results. Flexible learning paths also gelled with peer tutoring.

SPECIAL EDUCATION NEEDS SUPPORT

We saw how more and more children with special educational needs (SEN) were being integrated into mainstream secondary schools across European educational systems. This integration only worked when the student-teacher ratio was kept in check, a flexible SEN-sensitive curriculum was offered and staff was well trained and supported while working with such students. A major setback was the lack of funding; government cuts usually led to SEN students' neglect and was mentioned as playing a role in processes leading to teacher burnout.

Contextual factors

Certain contextual factors were deemed essential for school-based intervention measures to counteract ESL. These factors could also be seen as important prevention measures, fostering a school environment that facilities trust and cooperation amongst different stakeholders. Policy makers are advised to take these contextual preconditions as inspiration in their own efforts to improve school-based measures. Furthermore, most of these factors lay the groundwork for compensatory alternative pathways for students at risk of ESL.

Professional development and support of staff

Previous studies have noted the utility of teacher training in tackling ESL (Downes, Nairz-Wirth, & Rusinaitė., 2017) and the need for school staff to develop awareness of ESL and trigger factors (Nairz-Wirth & Feldmann, 2016). Our survey results emphasised that preventing ESL requires detecting

Conclusion 235

and monitoring signs early on, though many staff members indicated feeling insufficiently equipped to take on this role. Further professionalisation and in-service training are clearly needed, though were seldom feasible because of financial constraints.

Student voice and ownership

Research has shown that students' active participation in school improves their engagement and motivation and, in turn, cultivates a sense of school connect-edness for all the students (Smyth, 2006; EC, 2013). Our findings indicate that students are rarely involved in such measures' design or implementation. This is a lost opportunity because understanding how students see a programme's scope and aims is valuable; the measures' efficacy improves when students are motivated and participate.

Supportive student-teacher relations

As recent studies have established, teachers' attitudes, behaviours and the qual-ity of their relationships with students significantly affect school achievement (Van Uden, Ritzen, & Pieters, 2014), school disengagement and ESL (De Witte et al., 2013). Teachers remain the most important actors in students' educa-tional trajectories. Schools investing in their relations tended to facilitate regular one-on-one meetings for students in the form of feedback exchanges and talks with teachers, mentors, youth coaches and student counsellors.

Parental involvement incentives

The RESL.eu project surveyed nearly 2000 teachers across seven countries. Asked to choose a measure from a given list, the majority of teachers in all countries agreed on 'parental involvement being the most crucial policy to tackle ESL' (Kaye, D'Angelo, Ryan, & Lőrinc, 2016). This is consistent with previous research noting how teachers regularly blamed parents for children's lack of academic engagement which, in turn, leads to ESL (Downes et al., 2017). In the context of promoting parental involvement in school, school staff may sometimes perpetuate negative stereotypes about lower-class and/or immigrant parents being unengaged or uncaring. Our project, however, illustrated how adopting a more positive, less stigmatising approach allowed some schools to engage parents more successfully, which subsequently led to children's greater involvement.

A holistic, multi-professional approach

Previous studies have advocated an inclusive school system that endeavours to address emotional, physical, cognitive and social needs (Downes et al., 2017). This can be implemented not only by responding to cognitive and behavioural risk factors, but also by preventing potential emotional disengagement from school while still addressing students' most basic needs. Moreover, holistic policies do not see ESL as a rational decision by an individual, but rather as a process embedded in a broader, more complex context. Our findings underscored the utility of acknowledging which institutional and structural dimensions are at play. The most fundamental precondition for schools to keep students on track to attain educational qualifications was ensuring that basic human needs, such as food and shelter, were met. These measures thus implied the involvement of parents (ibid.). While mainstream educational institutions should also pursue such holistic approaches, we detected their practice above all in alternative learning pathways conducive to individualised, flexible learning environments.

Compensatory measures: alternative learning pathways

Arenas providing compensatory measures for reintegration into education and the labour market were usually implemented by alternative learning pathways, not mainstream schools. The two alternative learning pathways discussed here provided effective measures, though were stigmatised for allegedly offering less prestigious education and suffering from a lack of communication with mainstream education.

Work-based learning

Dual learning pathways – which may take the form of going to school part time and doing part-time work-based learning (WBL) through apprenticeships or internships – help combat early leaving from education and training. In this way, they are important preventive and compensatory measures. A recent report by Cedefop (2017) revealed that 'a combination of vocational education and training (VET) with social and employment measures helps to tailor responses to the different profiles of young people at risk of early leaving' (p. 14). WBL usually has a dual aim: to create opportunities for gaining professional skills and to work towards an education qualification. However, most WBL pathways are perceived as 'second best' or 'last resort' options since they frequently follow negative experiences in mainstream education. They tend to compensate for the lack of practical training and individualised support in mainstream systems. Students and project staff repeatedly gave feedback that mainstream programmes provided insufficient and incorrect information regarding dual-learning options and labour market opportunities. Our study showed that WBL was a viable alternative for students more interested in gaining work experience. Greater communication across, and permeability between, mainstream and WBL are thus highly necessary.

Innovative pedagogy

Innovative pedagogical approaches mainly stemmed from experiences in which approaches used in mainstream secondary education failed to meet the needs of students from disadvantaged backgrounds or those at risk of ESL. While more students could benefit from innovative pedagogy, particular groups seemed to encounter difficulty fitting into rigid conventional structures. Much of the innovation in alternative learning pathways promotes flexibility, takes lessons from prior successes, applies more practical learning methods and helps students access transferable skills, such as communication, presentation, leadership and networking – all of which are perceived as mandatory for pursuing an education and surviving in the labour market. The goal is to encourage students' motivation and sense of ownership by giving them space to voice their thoughts about the learning process. Such measures have been relatively successful at reaching vulnerable youth, yet are frequently associated with negative stereotypes and get branded with lower status in society.

National and regional findings of the RESL.eu survey

This section presents the protective factors we singled out for school engagement using the RESL.eu survey, which sampled more than 19,631 respondents across the seven countries (for detailed information about the RESL.eu survey, see Kaye, D'Angelo, Ryan, & Lőrinc, 2017).

Previous research shows that ESL is the result of an extended process of disengagement. ESL is preceded by indicators of withdrawal (e.g., truancy) or unsuccessful school engagement (e.g., academic or behavioural difficulties) that can be present in earlier stages (De Witte & Csillag, 2014; Frederiks, Blumenfeld, & Paris, 2004; Nouwen, 2015). Accordingly, our focus on school disengagement indicators used cross-sectional data from the first wave of the RESL. eu survey (Kaye et al., 2017). This data better represents socioeconomic status (SES) and ethnic diversity in school composition. It includes detailed information on students' prior achievements and school careers; perceived support from school staff, family and peers; sense of belonging; value of education; academic self-concept – the extent to which they feel they are 'a good student' – and disposition towards self-regulated learning; along with behavioural engagement traits proven to be strong predictors for ESL. In the following sections, we present the protective factors we have singled out based on our analysis for predicting school disengagement variables of truancy, school compliance, attentiveness and study behaviour.

One of the RESL.eu project's central aims is to move beyond the usual risk status indicators of socio-demographic characteristics, which are more difficult to alter by educational policy makers and widely known amongst policy makers and researchers. The survey design builds heavily on school engagement and motivational development theory, explaining educational engagement and outcomes by a reciprocal process of identification with, and participation in, school. This process can be facilitated by the support students perceive in their social context (Nouwen, 2015). We therefore sought to identify protective individual, contextual and structural factors that can be modified through educational system reforms by local policy makers and educational professionals.

238 *Elif Keskiner and Maurice Crul*

Seeking to deepen our understanding on these factors, we give qualitative research examples per setting (Van Caudenberg, Van Praag, Nouwen, Clycq, & Timmerman, 2017).

Common protective factors in high-risk educational contexts

Our analysis of RESL.eu survey data identified three main protective factors for school engagement. These factors overlap with the aforementioned school-based measures, showing how our quantitative analysis supports our qualitative findings from the school-level study.

Positive student–teacher relations and teacher aspirations

In line with school-level findings, positive student–teacher relations and the role of teachers emerged as significant protective factors for engagement. In Poland, teachers' social support and aspirations were also significant factors protecting against truancy and encouraging school compliance. In Spain, aspirations proved to be a significant factor protecting against all school disengagement variables, including truancy, and encouraging school compliance, attentiveness and study behaviour. In all seven countries, teachers' social support was a significant protective factor for study behaviour and classroom attentiveness. In high-risk educational contexts, positive student–teacher relations were vital for students' sense of belonging and behavioural engagement in education.

These quantitative results were largely consistent with our qualitative data and study of schools, showing how all settings with strong positive student–teacher relations reported substantial support for students.

A positive school environment

Fostering a positive academic environment and tackling bullying emerged as main policy points for improving compliance in all countries. The data showed that low discipline and high victimisation contexts tend to increase non-compliance, especially amongst students in VET and socially disadvantaged groups. In Belgium, Portugal and the UK, incorporating parental control in the approach contributed to a positive school environment. Teacher aspirations contributed to classroom cohesion, which proved to be a significant factor in Poland, Spain and the UK. Sustaining class cohesion and tackling bullying also helped to stimulate positive peer relations, and peer aspirations were significant protective factors for increased school compliance in Poland, Spain, the UK and Sweden.

Increased parental involvement

Parental involvement, support and control emerged as protective factors for increasing study behaviour in all countries. Parental social support was a

Conclusion 239

significant protective factor for improving classroom attentiveness in Belgium, the Netherlands, Spain, the United Kingdom and Sweden. These findings were largely supported by the qualitative data. Schools often interpreted parents' being less active communicators or participants in formal school activities as lack of interest. Our qualitative findings, however, showed that it is parents' perceived distance between themselves and school staff that largely determines their involvement. This finding points to the potential resource provided when schools cultivate students' and parents' positive attitudes towards education, yielding a positive effect on education engagement and outcomes.

Protective factors in high-risk educational contexts per country

Belgium

Youth at risk for ESL in Flanders were highly concentrated in urban vocational schools. In this Dutch-speaking educational system, most students were commonly perceived as having 'downward' track mobility because they repeated grade levels and transferred from more academically oriented institutions. The vocational track is generally characterised by higher numbers of less-engaged students, greater classroom misbehaviour and disciplinary problems, such as peer victimisation. Despite these structural features, a number of protective factors could be identified. Schools that invested in discipline and addressed peer victimisation seemed most successful in supporting student engagement within the given school. In these vulnerable educational contexts, students' relationships with teachers were crucial for their sense of belonging and behavioural engagement in education. Negative peer pressure – linked to a high concentration of socially disadvantaged students who have experienced educational failure – was, at least in part, countered by positive student-teacher relations, which helped increase feelings of school belonging and overall engagement. The qualitative interviews revealed that most students and parents saw education as a way to improve their life prospects. When schools draw into such positive attitudes towards education, we saw a positive effect on student school engagement and outcomes.

The Netherlands

The Netherlands is one of the EU countries that is reducing ESL most quickly. Dutch policies have focused on combating truancy and reintegrating dropouts. The Dutch school system placed students with learning and behavioural problems on the two lowest of four vocational tracks in secondary school. These students, many with severe learning or behavioural problems, were already being pushed to decide on their career at age 14 and transition to senior vocational education (SVE) at age 16. Care structures seemed to function better in lower-secondary education than SVE, where students with various issues could fall between the cracks. Furthermore, the compulsory age of leaving school is

18, unless one receives a minimum qualification. Under these circumstances, we saw groups of students who were unwilling to be in education but were forced back into school repeatedly. ESL thus became a moving target, with people in this age group popping in and out of school and switching between programmes. Investing in a positive environment and tackling bullying were successful protective factors for school compliance. The data showed that positive student-teacher relations and teacher aspirations played a crucial role in enhancing school engagement. Teachers, therefore, were key to tackling ESL. Schools that welcomed and promoted parental involvement were successful in counteracting truancy and increasing school engagement.

Poland

Of the surveyed countries, Poland had the lowest ESL rates yet the highest percentages of truancy and lowest student engagement levels. This is partly due to Poland's comprehensive school system and compulsory education ending at age 18, leading to most students passing the ESL age threshold. A low ESL rate therefore does not necessarily eliminate the potential youth at risk. Poland's schools displayed great variation when it came to truancy and other school engagement indicators. This could be attributed to upper-secondary-level school segregation, mainly between vocational and general (academically oriented) tracks, which is strongly linked to students' socioeconomic characteristics. Our analysis showed that schools invested in strengthening a positive, supportive environment and tackling bullying were more successful at stimulating school engagement. The findings also pointed to the role of teachers, offering the least perceived social support in Poland than any of the other countries. Mainly focused on knowledge transfer, teachers in Poland seemed less equipped to provide support, especially for students at risk. Qualitative interviews also revealed that career guidance opportunities need improvement and more cooperation should be fostered between schools and family, social care and labour market institutions to help at-risk youth.

Portugal

Portugal, being amongst countries with the highest ESL rates, managed to substantially decrease ESL through comprehensive long-term educational reforms. These reforms include extension of compulsory education until age 18 or grade 12; the addition of alternative learning pathways (ISCED 3); implementation of teacher-tutors at schools to address individual students' needs; and curricular flexibility allowing schools to define 25% of their own curricula. The analysis shows that current ESL rates are linked to repeating grade levels and academic failure, as well as the need for better organisational measures (including EWS and teacher awareness of intervention measures). Vulnerable students are frequently found on the vocational track, where they feel socially stigmatised. Social support from teachers, experienced largely by alternative learning students, was found to be a significant protective factor. Parental involvement in academic behaviour was a significant protective factor in all educational settings, highlighting how poorly educated parents can nonetheless support their children's learning trajectories.

Spain

Spain still has the highest percentage of early school leavers of all the countries in our study although it has declined from 25% to 20% in the past four years. In Spain, compulsory schooling ends at age 16 (ISCED 2) and there are no specific measures to keep students in education beyond this level. Problems relating to ESL seemed to cluster in the transition to upper secondary school and the first years of academic and VET tracks. Students from low-income and migrant families were overrepresented amongst those who do not pass compulsory education, thus being left to follow out-of-school training programmes – from which it can be difficult to return to official tracks. Whether existing vocational programmes adequately address the needs of at-risk youth in Spain remains uncertain. Austerity measures and resource reduction compelled cuts in public services, often forcing schools to award extra support to students who are most likely to succeed over those who are most in need. Public schools serving the most at-risk students suffered from the most severe budget cuts. RESL.eu findings highlight the importance of teachers as protective factors. Paradoxically, Spain's elevated ESL rates go hand in hand with a high level of perceived teacher support and highly aspiring students. Our qualitative study shows that teachers were unaware they were key agents in tackling ESL. Raising their awareness and giving them professional training could thus help build positive student–teacher relations.

Sweden

ESL percentages in Sweden were relatively low, yet our findings showed that many students demonstrated low levels of school engagement and thus were at risk of ESL. These students were mostly concentrated in highly segregated schools lacking the appropriate environment and resources to serve already vulnerable students. School segregation therefore emerged as a major problem in Sweden. In these highly segregated schools, teacher support and student involvement in school organisations and/or associations proved crucial for developing positive attitudes towards school and increasing engagement. In the qualitative study, many Swedish participants reported that teacher support made them re-evaluate their aspirations and motivated them to complete upper-secondary school qualifications. Another protective factor was parental involvement; schools with active parent associations and those forging effective ties with neighbourhood civil society organisations increased student engagement. We saw, too, how the Swedish educational system provided ample opportunities for second-chance learning in adult education.

The United Kingdom

The UK has emphasised early identification of people at risk of becoming NEETs: youth who are not in education, employment or training. Studies on dropouts, disruptive transitions and NEETs find these decisions are the end result of a gradual process of academic disengagement. The RESL.eu study highlighted how, despite persistent structural inequalities in the UK, schools, families and communities can influence education engagement and outcomes – a key way to generate opportunities for student engagement. Encouraging academic self-concept is a major factor in students' performance and wide engagement in school. Positive student-teacher relations are vital, with teacher support proving vital for students' sense of belonging and behavioural engagement in education. Schools that invest in tackling negative classroom environments and assist teachers in support provision could help increase compliance and foster engagement.

Concluding remarks

In the RESL.eu study we have pursued a multi-level approach where we aimed to understand the ESL phenomenon on the micro level, the meso level and the macro level (see the Introduction). Here, we present our final remarks following this multi-level structure.

At the micro level, our analysis of RESL.eu data has shown that investing in students' academic self-concept as well as self-confidence could help improve their school engagement. Hence, policy advice concerning the micro level should focus on measures that would help students develop academic self-concept and self-confidence to improve their school engagement. Yet, our study underlined that explanations for ESL should not be sought only on the individual level but that the processes leading to ESL and school disengagement are embedded both on the family and school level as well as on the macro level of education systems.

At the meso level, we underline first the role of teachers as a significant protective factor for school engagement in all the countries. This quantitative evidence confirmed findings of our qualitative ethnographic studies of schools that teacher awareness must be championed; teacher knowledge, specifically concerning the role they play in tackling ESL, should be deepened through professional training at the programmes' onset and throughout. Schools should invest in improving student-teacher relations to create a safe and cohesive academic environment. Next, the role of parents also emerged as a protective factor in our quantitative and qualitative analyses of school disengagement. Hence, more inclusive measures can be taken to welcome parents, especially those from disadvantaged backgrounds, at school. Peer aspirations are another important protective factor for school engagement in all countries; therefore, investing in safe school environments and cohesion in classrooms can help to support relations amongst pupils. Last but not least, school segregation was a critical issue in all seven countries in the RESL.eu study. Ethnic and social school segregation increased vulnerability mostly for students from disadvantaged backgrounds in urban areas. Although segregation seems to appear as a problem on the school level, it is in fact embedded in larger macro-level inequalities in the neighbourhoods that end up affecting schools and processes that occur within schools. Desegregation policies should thus be promoted to foster equal educational opportunities for all. Another solution foresees better guidance during educational transitions to ensure admission processes be informed by the principle of equity.

At the macro level, the following conclusions are listed from the RESL.eu study. Tracking and especially vocationally tracked programs emerged as an institutional setting where we studied and found the group most vulnerable to school disengagement and ESL. In Europe's larger urban areas, many students from low-educated and/or migrant families were redirected to vocational tracks in stratified school systems or to vocational programmes or tracks in upper secondary schools within comprehensive school systems. We observed this in countries with intensive tracking such as Flanders in Belgium and the Netherlands, but also in Spain and Poland, where the educational systems were often considered 'medium comprehensive' since the vocational track was not well developed. Our policy advice, therefore, is for educational systems to ensure access to high-quality VET. This would mitigate the stigmatisation of such tracks and raise their prestige. Cooperation between employers and schools should be improved to provide students better internship opportunities, which have proven crucial for the successful completion of such training and an effectively functioning VET, overall. Furthermore, we also observed how certain educational transition periods were especially critical in academic trajectories, such as the transition to upper secondary education in the Netherlands, Poland and Belgium, and the post-16 transition in the UK. Policy measures should ensure that improved educational and career guidance support be provided during these transition processes.

We also have uncovered alternative learning pathways, which proved successful in accommodating institutional flexibility and offering individual solutions and a caring environment in the majority of the countries we studied. They were effective at reintegrating youth into education and work, and also facilitated the combination of work and school – a reality for students dealing with financial hardship. Even though alternative learning arenas function at the meso level, their establishment and support requires macro-level initiatives. In this spirit, we recommend that alternative learning pathways be reinforced through increased availability and improved access. Their prestige should be magnified by ensuring access to high-quality second-chance education. Furthermore, mainstream education and alternative learning arenas should cooperate in providing compensatory measures via better and more informed guidance.

The final macro-level recommendation we underline concerns the school-leaving age. Encouragingly, we observed an ESL decrease in countries where the compulsory school-leaving age had risen to 18, such as in Poland, the

Netherlands and Portugal. However, this did not resolve school disengagement, nor did it wipe out the phenomenon of at-risk youth. We noted that setting the age as low as 15 or 16 pushed students with learning and/or behavioural problems out of school before they passed the age threshold. Portugal was once a case in point; nowadays this is mainly a problem in Spain. Still, systems that forbid pre-threshold leaving were left with unmotivated students, causing problems not only for the individuals themselves, but also for their classmates. To illustrate, in the Netherlands, ESL has become a moving target: young people constantly move in and out of education, or switch between studies and programs, until they reach the compulsory age. A sustainable national strategy must therefore be adopted in all countries. It should prioritise close monitoring of youth beyond the compulsory school-leaving age in education and after the attainment of a minimum educational qualification, thereby ensuring they have reached their maximum educational potential and successfully transitioned to the labour market.

References

Araújo, H. C., Magalhães, A., Rocha, C., Macedo, E., Ryan, L., Lőrinc, M., D'Angelo, A., & Kaye, N. (2013). *Policies on early school leaving in nine European countries: A comparative analysis.* Middlesex University. Retrieved from www.uantwerpen.be/images/uantwerpen/container23160/files/RESL%20Publication%201.pdf

Cedefob (2017). *Annual Report 2016.* Luxembourg: Publications Office. Cedefop information series. Retrieved from http://dx.doi.org/10.2801/474919

De Witte, K., & Csillag, M. (2014). Does anybody notice? On the impact of improved truancy reporting on school dropout. *Education Economics, 22*(6), 549–568.

De Witte, K., Nicaise, I., Lavrijsen, J., Van Landeghem, G., Lamote, C., & Van Damme, J. (2013). The impact of institutional context, education and labour market policies on early school leaving: A comparative analysis of EU countries. *European Journal of Education, 48*(3), 331–345.

Downes, P., Nairz-Wirth, E., & Rusinaitė, V. (2017). *Structural indicators for inclusive systems in and around Schools.* Analytical Report. Luxembourg: Publications Office of the European Union. Retrieved from http://nesetweb.eu/wp-content/uploads/2015/08/Structural-Indicators-.pdf

European Commission. (2013). Reducing early school leaving: Key messages and policy support. *Final Report of the Thematic Working Group on Early School Leaving.* Retrieved from http://ec.europa.eu/dgs/education_culture/repository/education/policy/strategic-framework/doc/esl-group-report_en.pdf

Fredricks, J. A., Blumenfeld, P. C., & Paris, A. H. (2004). School engagement: Potential of the concept, state of the evidence. *Review of Educational Research, 74*(1), 59–109.

Kaye, N., D'Angelo, A., Ryan, L., & Lőrinc, M. (2016). *Attitudes of school personnel to early school leaving.* Middlesex University. Retrieved from www.uantwerpen.be/images/uantwerpen/container23160/files/Publication%202_revisedfinal.pdf

Kaye, N., D'Angelo, A., Ryan, L., & Lőrinc, M. (2017). *Risk and protective factors: Findings from the RESL.eu international survey.* Middlesex University, University of Sheffield. Retrieved from www.uantwerpen.be/images/uantwerpen/container23160/files/Publication%204%20final%20version.pdf

Nairz-Wirth, E., & Feldmann, K. (2016). Teachers' views on the impact of teacher-student relationships on school dropout: A Bourdieusian analysis of misrecognition, *Pedagogy, Culture & Society, 25*(1), 1–16.

Nouwen, W. (2015). *School engagement and early school leaving in vocational education.* Paper presented at the Doctoral Seminar, Antwerp.

Nouwen, W., Clycq, N., Braspenningx, M., & Timmerman, C. (2015). *Cross-case analyses of school-based prevention and intervention measures.* CeMIS, University of Antwerp, Retrieved from www.uantwerpen.be/images/uantwerpen/container23160/files/RESL%20eu%20 Project%20Paper%206%20-%20Final%20version.pdf

Nouwen, W., Van Praag, L., Van Caudenberg, R., Clycq, N., & Timmermann, C. (2016). *School-based prevention and intervention measures and alternative learning approaches to reduce early school leaving,* RESL.eu Publication 3, University of Antwerp.

Smyth, J. (2006). 'When students have power': Student engagement, student voice, and the possibilities for school reform around 'dropping out' of school. *International Journal of Leadership in Education, 9*(4), 285–298.

Van Caudenberg, R., Van Praag, L., Nouwen, W., Clycq, N., & Timmerman, C. (2017). *A longitudinal study of educational trajectories of youth at risk of early school leaving.* CeMIS, University of Antwerp. Retrieved from www.uantwerpen.be/images/uantwerpen/container23160/ files/RESL%20eu%20Publication%205%20FINAL%202.pdf

Van Praag, L., Nouwen, W., Van Caudenberg, R., Clycq, N., & Timmerman, C. (2016). *Cross-case analysis of measures in alternative learning pathways.* CeMIS, University of Antwerp. Retrieved from www.uantwerpen.be/images/uantwerpen/container23160/files/ RESL%20eu%20Project%20Paper%207%20FINAL%2026-09-2016.pdf

Van Uden, J., Ritzen, H., & Pieters, J. (2014). Engaging students: The role of teacher beliefs and interpersonal teacher behavior in fostering student engagement in vocational education. *Teaching and Teacher Education, 37,* 21–32.

Index

Note: Page numbers in *italic* indicate a figure and page numbers in **bold** indicate a table on the corresponding page.

absenteeism: progressive absenteeism and disengagement 172; among Roma students 40; sudden 172
academic qualifications, employment rates by highest level *216*
academic self-concept 27–28
access to training programmes 190–191
achievement, SES as determinant for 2–3
"adapted aspirations" 181n3
adolescents: ESL among 33; Youth for Employment 189–190
agenda of equality of condition 150–151
ALAs (alternative learning arenas) 187–188, 199, 201; alternative learning pathways in Sweden 53; development of 225–226; training centres 202
ALMP (active labour market practices) 185
apprenticeships 215–217, *216*, **219**, 227–228; background on 217–220, **219**; in England by sector **219**; German programmes 219; ideal-type 218; minimum pay for 223–224; Modern Apprenticeships 218–219, **219**; policy on 219–220; quality of apprenticeship learning in England 219–220; transforming 221–227
Araújo, Helena C. 9, 10, 47–60, 149–163
aspirations 124–128; "adapted aspirations" 181n3; attending university as 170–171; characteristics of schools in study on **120–121**; educational aspirations of minorities 165; and expectations 103; obtaining a diploma as way to find work 168–169; teacher and family support for 176–179; university, attending 170–171

assessment: of early childhood education 68–69; IVÀLUA 188; PISA 50
'at-risk' students 5, 179–180; identifying 17–18; school failure as trajectory in 172–174, **173**; in Spain 166; unexpected low performance in post-compulsory education 174–176, **175**
attitudes toward school 22
austerity policies 164
Austria, ESL rates in 61

behavioural engagement 18
Behtoui, Alireza 9, 10, 47–60, 102–116
Belgium: C-certificate 77; comparison of Dutch and Flemish educational systems 136–138; protective factors for school engagement 239; social and ethnic stratification in 79–80; *see also* switching practices
Bereményi, Bálint-Ábel 11, 185–198
Bertran-Tarrés, Marta 11, 164–182
Björklöf, Marie 10, 102–116
"blocked opportunities" 106
Bourdieu, Pierre 105–106; *habitus* 149–151

care provided by teachers 179
Carrasco, Silvia 11, 164–182, 185–198
Chicago Child-Parent Center 68
"churning" 215
"CITO" test 137
City Connects programme 69
class, measuring 22
Clycq, Noel 1–13, 77–89, 135–148
coaching 232–233
cognitive engagement 19

comparison: of Dutch and Flemish educational systems 136–138; of ESL in Sweden, Portugal and Poland 57–58; of international survey country datasets 25–27, **26**

conceptual framework for ESL 2–4, *4*

conditions of inequality 154–158; inequality of love, care and solidarity 156–158; inequality of power 158–159; inequality of resources 155–156; inequality of work opportunities 160–161

contextual factors for school-based interventions 234–236

cooperative vocational schools 202

cost-benefit analysis of ESL 68–69

costs of ESL: for employment and income 63–64; for healthcare 66–67; for the justice system 64–66; for public transfer systems 64; research in 62–63, **63**

counselling 232–233

creative responses 149–151

Crul, Maurice 10, 11, 117–131, 135–148, 230–245

curricula: as factor for school disengagement 199–200; 'hidden curriculum' 118

D'Angelo, Alessio 9, 17–32

decentralisation 52

decision-making, agenda of equality of condition 151

differentiated secondary school systems: in England 127; in the Netherlands 124–125

diploma, obtaining as way to find work 168–169, 180n2

disadvantaged students 2; inequality 3

disengagement (school) 3–4, *4*, 90–91, 195; negative impact of 18; re-engagement 204–206

Doroftei, Alexandra Oliveira 11, 199–214

dual learning pathways 236

early childhood education, assessment of 68–69

early school leavers, defining 1

economic costs of ESL 67–68

education: inequality in 34, 79–80; in the Netherlands 125–126; in Poland 54–57; in Portugal 200; in Sweden 51–52

educational citizenship 199, 200–201, 204–206, 208, 211–212; of rights and knowledge 204–208

educational systems: Dutch and Flemish 137; free choice in Hungary's school system 35–36; 'freedom of choice' in Swedish schools 52; in the Netherlands 117

educational trajectories *see* trajectories

emotional/affective engagement 18–19

engagement (school) 3–4, *4*, 10, 17, 18, 195; affective 18–19; behavioural 18; cognitive 19; context, importance of 20; descriptive statistics for school engagement scale **22**; dimensions of 17, 18–19; gender as predictor of 19; implications of statistical model for 28–29; measuring 18–19; multidimensional aspect of 19; operationalisation of 19; positive impact of 18; predictors of 29n3; protective factors for 27–28, 238–242; SES as determinant for 19; statistical model of 24–25, **24**, 28–29; *see also* disengagement (school)

England: apprenticeships 215–217, *216*; apprenticeships by sector **219**; education system 127–128; Modern Apprenticeships 218–219, **219**; Ofsted 129n1; protective factors for school engagement 242; quality of apprenticeship learning in 219–220; secondary education 127

EQF (European Qualification Framework) 47

equality of condition 150–151, 160–161; conditions of inequality surrounding ESL 154–158; *see also* conditions of inequality

ESF (European Social Fund) 55

ESL (early school leaving) 1; advances and setbacks of early school leavers in Portugal 151–154; in Austria 61; conditions of inequality surrounding 154–158; cost-benefit analysis of 68–69; departing educational experiences among Roma students 36–38; fiscal costs of **63**; in the Flemish education system 79–80; governmental responsibility for reducing 33; institutional context for 10; lack of awareness on 185; metaphors of turbulent trajectories 91–92; narratives of Simon and Karim 81–86; in Poland 54–57; in Portugal 50–51; preventing 69–70; private costs of **63**; pull factors 199; push factors 199; research in costs of 62–63, **63**; social costs of **63**; in Spain

248 *Index*

195n1; stigmatization of 61; in Sweden 51–54, 61; tendencies between countries 57–58; theoretical and conceptual framework for 2–4, *4*; vague knowledge about in Hungary 33–34; vulnerable groups 2; 'white flight' 36; *see also* disengagement (school); engagement (school)

EU (European Union): defining early school leavers 1; ESL as policy target 61–62

Europe 2020 Strategy 48, 58

European Commission, educational policy recommendations 48–49

Europeanisation, dynamics of 48–49

European Toolkit for Schools 69

EWS (early warning systems) 232

"Excellent education for all of America's children, An" (Levin et al.) 62

expectations 106; and aspirations 103; theoretical framework for aspirations research study 118

extra-familial social capital 113–114

families: extra-familial social capital 113–114; support for student aspirations 176–179; within-family social capital 110–111

FGDs (focus group discussions) 201; sociodemographic characteristics of participants **203**

financial assistance, costs of ESL for public transfer systems 64

fiscal costs of ESL **63**

Flanders *see* Belgium

flexible learning pathways 234

frameworks: EQF 47; for ESL 2–4, *4*; theoretical framework for aspirations research study 118–119; theoretical framework for social capital study 104–106

freedom of choice: in Hungary's school system 35–36; in Swedish schools 52

gender, as predictor of school engagement 19

ghetto schools 45n3

Gitschthaler, Marie 10, 61–74

governance: educational 47; multiple-scale 47, 48; networking 47; by opinion formation 48

governmental responsibility for reducing ESL 33

grade retention, C-certificate 77

group culture, *habitus* 149–151

groups vulnerable to ESL 2

GSCE (General Certificate of Secondary Education) 127–128

gymnasium 39, 51–52

habitus 162; deterministic view of 150; and genesis of creative responses 149–151

health and link to education 67

healthcare costs of ESL for 66–67

'hidden curriculum' 118

High Cost of Low Educational Performance, The (OECD study) 67–68

High/Scope Perry Preschool Program 68

holistic approach to rights 209–211

Human Capital Development Strategy 2020 54

Hungary: church/religious schools 36; comprehensive education in 35–36; National Public Education Act of 2011 38; National Strategy for Preventing School Leaving without a Qualification 38; personal conditions of Roma students 40–42; public education, Roma students in 36; Roma students, ESL among 33–34; secondary-level departures in light of policy changes 38–40; secondary-level school tracking system 39; selective nature of school system 34; Strategy for Lifelong Learning 2014 38; structural and regional inequalities among Roma students 35–36; Study Hall programme 45n7; types of secondary-level schools 39; vague knowledge about ESL 33–34; vocational schools 42, 44

identifying 'at-risk' students 17–18

immigrants: aspiration paradox of 165; 'at-risk' students 166–167; children of foreign-born parents in Spain, prevalence of 164; and school engagement 19–20; trajectories of 171–172; *see also* minority groups

income, costs of ESL for 63–64

'individualised learning' 234

inequality 3, 154–158; agenda of equality of condition 150–151; of care 156–158; dimensions of equality 150–151; in education 34, 79–80; among immigrants 19; of love, care and solidarity 156–158;

of power 158–159; of resources 155–156; of work opportunities 160–161; *see also* switching practices
Initial Vocational Plans 190
innovative pedagogy 236–237
institutional context for ESL 10
institutional racism 35, 43–44
integration versus segregation 43
intersectional approach to educational differences 2–3
interventions: contextual factors for school-based interventions 234–236; early warning systems 232; socio-emotional and behavioural support 232–233
ISCED (International Standard Classification of Education) 23
ISCO-08 (International Standard Classification of Occupations) 22
IVÀLUA 188

Joves per l'Ocupació see Yf E (Youth for Employment Programme)

Kaye, Neil 9, 17–32
Kende, Ágnes 9, 33–46
Keskiner, Elif 10, 11, 135–148, 230–245

labour market theory 61; ALMP 185
Lifelong Learning Perspective 54
Lisbon Agenda 48, 58
Lisbon Strategy 2000 61–62
Lőrinc, Magdolna 11, 215–229

Macedo, Eunice 9, 10, 47–60, 149–163, 199–214
macro-level structural conditions 43–44, 103, 199
Marchlik, Paulina 9, 10, 47–60, 90–101
meaningful education 200–201
measuring: educational aspirations 23; engagement 18–19; peer aspirations 23; self-perception 23; SES 22; students' support from teachers 23
mentoring 232–233
meritocracy 79
meso-level institutional racialisation 43–44, 103
methodological individualism 104–105
methodology of turbulent trajectory analysis 92–93
micro-level racialisation 43–44, 103

minority groups: 'at-risk' students 166–167; educational aspirations of 165; inclusion 200; trajectories of 171–172; *see also* immigrants; Roma students
model-building procedure for statistical model of school engagement 24–25, **24**
Modern Apprenticeships 218
multidimensional aspect of engagement 19
multi-disciplinary approach to educational differences 2–3
multiple-scale governance 47, 48

Nairz-Wirth, Erna 10, 61–74
Narciso, Laia 11, 164–182
National Agency for Education 53
National Dropout Prevention Center 69
National Public Education Act of 2011 38
National Social Inclusion Strategy 38
National Strategy for Preventing School Leaving without a Qualification 38
NEET (not in education, employment or training) 96, 107, 215
Netherlands, the: aspirations 120, **120–121**; comparison of Dutch and Flemish educational systems 136–138; differentiated secondary school systems 124–125; education system 125–126; protective factors for school engagement 239–240; Randstad 129n2; secondary education 117; vocational schools 125; *see also* switching practices
New Opportunities Programme 50
New Public Management agenda 52
Nouwen, Ward 1–13, 135–148

occupations: ALMP 185; "churning" 215; diploma, obtaining as way to find work 168–169, 180n2; employment and income costs of ESL 63–64; inequality of work opportunities 160–161; TLIP 186, 190, 192–194; Youth for Employment 185–186, 189–192
Ofsted 129n1
Open Method of Coordination 47
operationalisation of school engagement 19
opinion formation, governance by 48
opportunity, equality of 150–151
Orozco, Mariana 10, 135–148
"overqualified" youth 195n2

parents: measuring survey respondents' support from 23; within-family social capital 110–111

250 *Index*

partnership in construction of ALAs 206–209
peer aspirations 27; measuring 23
'perceived' support 29
PISA (Programme for International Student Assessment) 50, 56, 67
Plan of Implementation of Youth Guarantee 56
Poland: ESL in 54–57; Plan of Implementation of Youth Guarantee 56; protective factors for school engagement 240; tendencies in ESL with other countries 57–58
policy: on apprenticeships 219–220; austerity policies 164; ESF 55; ESL as EU policy target 61–62; European Commission, educational policy recommendations 48–49; IVÀLUA 188; New Public Management agenda 52; Plan of Implementation of Youth Guarantee 56; prevention of ESL in Poland 54–55; recommendations for apprenticeship schemes 228; on reducing ESL 33; re-nationalisation policies 47
political grammar 48
Portugal: advances and setbacks of early school leavers 151–154; ALAs 199, 201, 206–212; characteristics of early school leavers **152**; compulsory education in 50; education system 200; ESL in 50–51; protective factors for school engagement 240–241; tendencies in ESL with other countries 57–58; trajectories of early school leavers **152**; transitions of early school leavers in 151–154; VET in 200
positive impact of engagement 18
power, inequality of 158–159
power relations 151
predictors of school engagement 29n3; SES 19; sociodemographic characteristics 25
prejudice: against minority students 81–86; against Roma students 41
prevention of ESL 69–70; in Poland 54–55
private costs of ESL **63**
progressive absenteeism and disengagement 172
protective factors for school engagement 27–28, 238–242
'Prussian-style teaching' 45n4
public transfer systems, costs of ESL for 64

pull factors 199
pupils *see* students
push factors 199

qualifications, employment rates by highest level of *216*
Qualtrics 5

racism, institutional 35, 43–44
Randstad 129n2
Reading Partners 69
recommendations: apprenticeships, policy recommendations 228; European Commission, educational policy recommendations 48–49
Reducing Early School Leaving in Europe *see* RESL.eu project
re-engagement 3–4, *4*, 204–206
reforms: in Polish education 55–56; in Swedish education 52–53
re-nationalisation policies 47
RESL.eu project 1, 165; data collection 20–21; data collection for apprenticeship schemes study 220–221; data collection for compensatory measures study 188–189; descriptive statistics for school engagement scale **22**; implications of statistical model for school engagement 28–29; international survey 17, 20–24, **21**, **22**; longitudinal data collection for 8–9, **8**; operationalisation of school engagement 19; qualitative data collection 6–9, **8**; quantitative data collection 4–6; questionnaires 5; surveys 5–6
RESL.eu survey 17, 20–24, **21**, **22**; comparison between country datasets 25–27, **26**; measuring educational aspirations 23; measuring peer aspirations 23; national and regional findings 237–238; personal characteristics of respondents 21–22; school-level findings of 230–237; selection criteria for international survey respondents 29n1
RESL.eu website 2
resources, inequality of 155–156
rhythmising of human action 105
rights of enhancement, inclusion, and participation 200
Rocha, Cristina 9, 47–60

Index 251

Roma students 33–34, 44–45, 179–180; aspiration paradox of 165; aspirations 166–168, **167**; attending university 170–171; departing educational experiences 36–38; ESL among 33–34; living conditions of 40–42; obtaining a diploma as way to find work 168–169; 'otherness' of 42; personal conditions of 40–42; poverty among 40–42; prejudice against 41; prevalence of ESL in 164; in public education 36; regional inequalities among 35–36; school failure as trajectory in 172–174, **173**; secondary-level departures in light of policy changes 38–40; structural and regional inequalities among 35–36; Study Hall programme 45n7; sudden absenteeism 172; trajectories of 171–172; unexpected low performance in post-compulsory education 174–176, **175**
Ruiz-Haro, Isidoro 11, 185–198
Ryan, Louise 11, 215–229

Santos, Sofia A. 10–11, 149–163, 199–214
school-based social capital 111–113
school-level findings of RESL.eu project 230–237
school-to-work transition plans 190, 195; TLIP 192–194
school types: church schools in Hungary 36; Dutch and Flemish educational systems 137; in England 127–128; ghetto schools 45n3; *gymnasium* 39, 51–52; secondary-level school tracking system in Hungary 39; second-chance schools 202–203; VET 44
second-chance schools 202–203
"second-chance trajectories" 188, 194–195
second wave of international RESL.eu survey 20–21
segregation: consequences of 37–38; departing educational experiences among Roma students 36–38; ghetto schools 45n3; in Hungary's school system 36; versus integration 43
self-blaming narrative 179, 195
self-concept 27–28
self-esteem 28
self-perception of survey respondents, measuring 23, 27

SES (socioeconomic status): as determinant of educational attainment 2–3, 19; measurement 22
significant others 105, 115
social capital 103, 114–115; context of Swedish study 104; extra-familial 113–114; individual characteristics of respondents 107, **108–109**; school-based 111–113; within-family 110–111
social costs of ESL 63
socialisation 150
sociodemographic characteristics, as predictor of school engagement 25
socio-emotional and behavioural support 232–233
soft law 47
solidarity, inequality of 156–158
sophisticated thinkers 162
Spain: 'at-risk' students in 166; ESL rates in 195n1; prevalence of ESL in 164; protective factors for school engagement 241; school failure as trajectory in 172–174, **173**; sudden absenteeism in 172; tackling youth unemployment 186–188, 196n3; TLIP 190, 192–194; trajectories of Roma and minority students 171–172; unexpected low performance in post-compulsory education 174–176, **175**; Youth for Employment 189–190, 191–192; *see also* Roma students
Stam, Talitha 10, 117–131, 135–148
status attainment theories 105
stigmatization of ESL 61
Strategy for Lifelong Learning 2014 38
Strömberg, Isabella 10, 102–116
structure of this book 9–11
students: aspiration paradox of immigrant students 165; attitudes toward school 22; care provided by teachers 179; disengagement 3; engagement 18; expectations versus aspirations 103; identification of 'at-risk' students 17–18; micro-level racialisation 103; selection criteria for international RESL.eu survey 29n1; support from teachers, measuring 23; *see also* Roma students
Study Hall programme 45n7
substance abuse 97–98
sudden absenteeism 172
support from teachers, perceived 29

252   *Index*

surveys: international RESL.eu survey 17, 20–24, **21**, **22**; recruited respondents **8**; for RESL.eu project 5–6
SVE (senior vocational education) 138
Sweden: alternative learning pathways in 53; ESL in 51–54, 61; individual characteristics of social capital study respondents 107, **108–109**; National Agency for Education 53; protective factors for school engagement 241; results of social capital study 106–107; social capital study 104; tendencies in ESL with other countries 57–58; Youth Centre 53–54; "Youth In" (*Unga In*) project 54
switching practices 135–146; in the Dutch and Flemish educational systems 136–138
Szalai, Júlia 9, 33–46

Taylor, Charles 105
teachers: ascribing quality to 179; care provided by 179; measurement of teacher support in survey 23; support for student aspirations 176–179
TEIP (Programme Educational Territories of Priority Intervention) 51
thematic narrative analysis 80
theoretical and conceptual framework for ESL *4*
theoretical approaches to school disengagement 91
theoretical framework: for aspirations research study 118–119; for ESL 2–4; for social capital study 104–106
Timmerman, Christiane 1–13, 77–89, 135–148
TLIP (Training and Labour Insertion Programmes) 186, 192–194; access to 190–191; limits of compensatory measures 194–195
Tomaszewska-Pekala, Hanna 9, 10, 47–60, 90–101
tracking system, of Dutch secondary education 117
training centres 202
Training Programmes and Professional Learning 190
trajectories: attending university 170–171; conditions of inequality surrounding 154–158; *habitus* 149–151; of immigrant and minority students 171–172;

obtaining a diploma as way to find work 168–169; in Portugal **152**; progressive absenteeism and disengagement 172; school failure 172–174, **173**; "second-chance trajectories" 188, 194–195; sudden absenteeism 172; switching practices 135–136; transforming apprenticeships 221–227; turbulent 92–93; unexpected low performance in post-compulsory education 174–176, **175**
turbulence 92
turbulent trajectories 92–93; Marcin 96–97; Marek 95–96; Maria 94–95; Mariola 93–94; Mariusz 97–98; metaphors of 91–92; methodology of analysis 92–93
tutoring 233–234

UK (United Kingdom) *see* England
unemployment, "churning" 215; *see also* youth unemployment, tackling
unexpected low performance in post-compulsory education 174–176, **175**
Unga In ("Youth In") project 54
university, attending 170–171

Van Caudenberg, Rut 1–13, 77–89, 135–148
Van Praag, Lore 1–13, 135–148
VET (vocational education and training) 39, 44, 45n4, 200; enrolling in 169–170; lack of recognition in 204–206; in Portugal 200; TLIP 190, 192–194; training centres 202; transforming 221–227; Youth for Employment 189–190, 191–192
vocational schools 39, 45n4; cooperative 202; in Hungary 42, 44; lack of recognition in 204–206; in the Netherlands 125; in Portugal 50–51; SVE 138; TLIP 190, 192–194; training centres 202; transforming 221–227; work-based learning 236; Youth for Employment 189–190, 191–192
VO-raad 117

WBL (work-based learning) 236
welfare, costs of ESL for public transfer systems 64
"white collar crime" 66
'white flight' 36
within-family social capital 110–111

work-first-oriented compensatory measures: TLIP 186; Youth for Employment 185–186
work opportunities 160–161
Wrona, Anna 10, 47–60, 90–101

Yf E (Youth for Employment Programme) 185–186, 189–192; access to 190–191; limits of compensatory measures 194–195
young adults, ESL among 33

Youth Centre 53–54
Youth Guarantee Plan 185, 189; "overqualified" youth 195n2
"Youth In" (*Unga In*) project 54
youth unemployment, tackling 186–188, 196n3; "overqualified" youth 195n2
YRCs (youth recreation centres) 114

ZEP (*Zone d'Éducation Prioritaires*) 51